Entrepreneurs
in the Faith Community

Entrepreneurs
in the Faith Community

PROFILES
OF MENNONITES
IN BUSINESS

Edited by
Calvin W. Redekop & Benjamin W. Redekop

HERALD PRESS
Scottdale, Pennsylvania
Waterloo, Ontario

Library of Congress Cataloging-in-Publication Data
Entrepreneurs in the faith community : profiles of Mennonites in business /
    edited by Calvin W. Redekop and Benjamin W. Redekop.
        p. cm.
    Includes bibliographical references.
    ISBN 0-8361-9034-3 (alk. paper)
        1. Mennonites—United States—Biography. 2. Businessmen—United
States—Biography. 3. Business—Religious aspects—Mennonites.
4. Mennonites—Membership. I. Redekop, Calvin Wall, 1925- .
II. Redekop, Benjamin W., 1961- .
BX8141.E54 1996
289.7'092'273—dc20
    [B]   95-52887
                                                                                  CIP

The paper used in this publication is recycled and meets the minimum requirements of American National Standard for Information Sciences—
Permanence of Paper for Printed Library Materials, ANSI Z39.48-1984.

Grateful acknowledgment is made to persons profiled and others who
provided photos; and to Mennonite Library and Archives, Bethel College,
North Newton, Kansas, for photos in chapter 7.

ENTREPRENEURS IN THE FAITH COMMUNITY
Copyright © 1996 by Herald Press, Scottdale, Pa. 15683
    Published simultaneously in Canada by Herald Press,
    Waterloo, Ont. N2L 6H7. All rights reserved
Library of Congress Catalog Number: 95-52887
International Standard Book Number: 0-8361-9034-3
Printed in the United States of America
Book design by Gwen M. Stamm

06 05 04 03 02 01 00 99 98 97 96 10 9 8 7 6 5 4 3 2 1

*To all entrepreneurs
and businesspeople
who seek to remain
in creative relationship
with their faith community.*

Contents

Acknowledgments

THE EDITORS express thanks and gratitude to the authors who contributed the narratives presented in this volume. As will become obvious, only dedicated and extensive research could have provided the range and depth of analysis necessary for this kind of study. And as authors, we in turn thank the entrepreneurs who allowed themselves to be interviewed and to have their personal lives examined and analyzed in considerable detail. We hope their generosity will be rewarded by greater public understanding of the challenges and realities faced by entrepreneurs who attempt to remain true to their religious convictions and their faith community.

Thanks also to Michael A. King, Herald Press book editor, and Gwen M. Stamm, Mennonite Publishing House designer, for the gracious help they and other publishing staff provided in bringing the book to fruition.

Introduction

THE ENTREPRENEURS profiled in this book are, for the most part, rather special individuals. Yet many of their experiences could also be those of your neighbor, of an aunt or an uncle, or even your own parents. They might even reflect your own experience, or perhaps your dreams of what might have been. But whether or not one feels a personal connection to any of these people, their stories are certain to entertain, instruct, and enlighten. What better way to think about the complex relationship between religious belief and aggressive economic activity—entrepreneurship[1]—than through real-life experiences?

The entrepreneurs presented here have faced more difficulties than members of most religious traditions. As the title suggests, they belong to a specially restrictive religious tradition—that of the Anabaptist-Mennonites. Anabaptist-Mennonites are among the more radical offshoots of the Protestant Reformation. They were persecuted for generations for their radical Christian beliefs about, among other things, the nature of church and society. Their concerns about mutual aid and Christian discipleship were so strong that some branches of the movement shared most possessions, while other segments strongly rejected personal acquisition at the expense of neighbors.

Like the English Puritans, the Mennonites—named after Menno Simons, an early Anabaptist leader—were called to follow a strict moral code. This set of principles made a distinction between the "kingdom of this world" and the kingdom of God. Business and commerce, with some exceptions, had even less legitimacy than in the Calvinistic and Puritan traditions. This was because such activity could not be a "calling." Rather, it was something that could tempt one away from serving the kingdom of God and the sanctified church community. One could not after all serve the kingdom of God and the faith community by pursuing wealth and power in the "world."

Over time the majority of Anabaptist-Mennonite communities took on a solidly rural character, with farming the main occupation. This pattern allowed for a good degree of self-interested, acquisitive activity while containing it within the norms of the Mennonite community.

This book tells the story of eleven individuals who grew up in the Anabaptist-Mennonite tradition, and how they have reconciled their religious commitment and conviction with their urge to be involved in entrepreneurial activities, or business. In a few cases these activities were more in the realm of institution-building than business proper. However, all of the figures can be located on a continuum that stretches between purely acquisitive economic behavior, on the one hand, and the desire creatively to transform one's environment in the service of one's faith and community, on the other.

Being religious and being in business or institution-building has often been difficult enough in other religious traditions. But these stories are perhaps more poignant because being religious in the Mennonite community has traditionally included strict adherence to values and ethical behaviors which could stifle almost all creativity and individual interest, or at least challenge the pursuit of economic gain within the larger economic framework of the business world.

Some aspects of the tradition have aided entrepreneurial talents and success and will become obvious in the stories contained in this collection. Nevertheless, in most cases there are clear moral concerns or dilemmas present. Some are large, some smaller, but all indicate an ongoing struggle to harmonize a particular set of Christian beliefs and values, informed by a strong sense of church and faith community, with entrepreneurial activity. How to be both a good businessperson and a good Christian: that is the question.

We chose the subjects we did because we wanted to present the widest possible array of historical and sociological dimensions of Mennonite entrepreneurs. We considered time period, region, gender, Mennonite conferences (reflecting the variety of theological and social traditions), and type of business.

These carefully selected "profiles" still do not reflect the complete spectrum of religious entrepreneurs, not even Mennonite entrepreneurs. More work needs to be done, for example, on women in business.[2] But we maintain that a fairly wide-ranging description and analysis of Mennonite entrepreneurial experience has been captured, and that this provides a good place to begin for understanding the issues at stake among all entrepreneurs with religious affiliations.[3]

It must be added that the businesspeople profiled in this collection can be separated into two broad ethnic and religious groupings —Mennonites of predominantly Swiss-South German origin who migrated to eastern North America from central Europe starting in the eighteenth century, and Mennonites of primarily Dutch-North German origin who migrated to Prussia and on into Russia before settling in the North American Midwest and West starting in the later nineteenth century.[4] The distinctive emphases and personality types of these two groups make it tempting to divide the book into two parts corresponding to the groups. However, we feel there is more to be gained from alternating stories of individuals from the Swiss-German with those from the Dutch-Russian tradition. This allows fruitful and interesting parallels and contrasts to emerge. Despite a number of differences, the two groups do share a common religious heritage. Thus the chapters have been arranged more or less in pairs which highlight either similarities, differences, different approaches to the same goal, or some other relationship between the entrepreneurs.

Although there is much biographical material included in these accounts, they are not biographies in the traditional sense. They are, rather, focused accounts of how individuals' entrepreneurial and religious lives have interacted with each other. Reading these stories, one learns not only about the individual entrepreneurs but also about the "ins and outs" of the world of business in which they have operated. Also, an attempt has been made to make each profile as interesting and entertaining as possible, each with its own theme and particular character. To that end, a lively, readable, and uniform style was an important goal of the project. We have tried to cast a critical eye upon our subjects; weaknesses, tensions, and failures have not been glossed over. The point of these stories is not to glorify the individuals profiled, although in many cases there is much to admire.

There are broad similarities running through these accounts of individual lives. There is a dogged commitment to be true to the religious community and its expectations. Few if any have easily or willingly given up their membership in the faith community. The entrepreneurs have struggled, often mightily, to harmonize the demands of the business world with the faith and norms of the Mennonite church. One can see again and again the attempt to bring two "worlds" together. How this is done varies, but the striving is almost always apparent. All of the businesspeople profiled see their work as in some way contributing to the work of the church—but their ways of achieving this are many. Some work from the margins of the faith community, while others are comfortable working more from the center.

Many of the figures are noteworthy for their ability to weave together potentially conflicting "worlds" into a satisfying synthesis; others are more content to allow their worlds to remain separate, if related. There is much variety among the entrepreneurs in relation to the ease with which they have been able to reconcile their religious heritage with their business careers. This of course depends on a number of factors, including the degree of commitment and submission to the Anabaptist-Mennonite faith community and its demands. This variety, we are confident, reflects faithfully the great amount of difference in attitudes and relations in the church community, not only among entrepreneurs, because the church itself is becoming rapidly more diverse.[5]

Most if not all of the entrepreneurs profiled have possessed much energy and drive, creativity, willingness to take risk, "will to succeed," and ability to recover from setbacks. All of these figures have been innovators. In many cases that ability is clearly present in all aspects of their lives, whether in the world of business or the church, or in bringing the two together in fruitful and creative ways. But these characteristics can be seen as part and parcel of the larger phenomenon of modern individualism, with its emphasis on individual success and achievement.

The norms of success and achievement are the heartbeat of America. In a classic text on American society, Robin Williams states,

> American culture is marked by a central stress upon personal
> achievement, especially secular occupational achievement. The
> "success story" and the respect accorded to the self-made man

are distinctly American if anything is. . . . It has endorsed Horatio Alger and has glorified the rail splitter who became president.[6]

To the degree this describes Mennonites in business, it might be possible to assume that North American Mennonite entrepreneurs have simply accommodated themselves to the prevailing achievement norm. There is undoubtedly some truth to this conclusion. Early in the twentieth century, Max Weber proposed that Mennonites were among the outstanding entrepreneurs who contributed to the development of capitalism. He maintained that Mennonites were the leaders in the development of the "Protestant ethic and the spirit of capitalism" based on individual submission to God's rule.[7]

But careful analysis of the material presented in these profiles gives rise to an interesting counter-proposition that raises questions about Weber's assumptions. The tensions between entrepreneurial activity and religious life suggest that Mennonite entrepreneurs have always faced an inherent contradiction between Mennonite and capitalistic economic values, and that the basic incompatibility between these two sets of values has caused Mennonites to move either in the direction of submission to Mennonite religious communalism and/or its values—or toward acceptance of the achievement values noted above and resulting alienation from the Mennonite community.

That a number of individuals profiled achieved some kind of creative synthesis of these poles only points to the presence of potentially contradictory elements. The fascination in many of these stories lies in how individuals have been able to overcome the contradiction between communal/religious and capitalist values. Nevertheless, in all cases one can discern at least the potential outlines of the problem. In our conclusion we analyze further the contours of this conflict, and in an appendix we provide some questions on each chapter for those interested in further probing the issues at stake in these stories. For now, we bid you to enjoy the stories, in whatever order you like, and draw your own conclusions.

Calvin W. Redekop, Harrisonburg, Virginia, and
Benjamin W. Redekop, Vancouver, British Columbia

Entrepreneurs
in the Faith Community

1

Jacob A. Shenk:
Business Was Servant to the Church

BY CALVIN W. REDEKOP

Jacob A. Shenk (1900-1950) was born into a conservative eastern Men-nonite community. Jacob, who always felt that Christian service was the highest good, took over a business even before he graduated from high school. He displayed sound business judgment, impeccable ethics, and a keen desire to innovate in the chicken hatching and breeding business.

At the same time he became a leading institution-builder in his faith community, donating a large percentage of profits to the church. Al-though Jacob's business activities were thus devoted to the church, his submission to its norms was tempered by his flaunting some of its lifestyle restrictions.

THE NEWS that Jacob A. Shenk had been killed in a plane crash stunned the Harrisonburg, Virginia, community and left his family, the church community, and others who had known him in a state of shock and disbelief. The news reverberated through the larger Mennonite community, and spread to Mennonite workers in Europe, where I was stationed at the time as a Mennonite Central Committee (MCC) worker. One reason Jacob was well known in the Mennonite community and even beyond was that it was widely reported that he had dedicated 90 percent of his business profits to the church.[1]

On March 24, 1950, Jacob was returning with Melvin Weaver from a church planting trip for Virginia Mennonite Conference. Near Mountain City, Tennessee, the plane apparently "encountered violent air disturbances and was thrown out of control. The maneuvering plane broke up in midair, throwing both men to their deaths."[2] An official investigation was never conducted, so no authoritative cause has ever been established. A co-worker noted that "as increasing duties in connection with his business and church interests required more and more of his time away from home, Brother Shenk became interested in the advantages of air travel." He thus took training as a pilot, and purchased his first airplane in the mid-1930s.[3]

Jacob was born on February 17, 1900, in Warwick County, Virginia, into a modest and pious Mennonite family. He grew up helping to convert a native forest into productive farmland[4] and began working his way through Eastern Mennonite (High) School in 1920, graduating in 1927. He married Lucy Wenger in 1926. He developed an entrepreneurial track in the chicken hatchery industry which included building the first electric hatchery in the region, initiating profit-sharing with his egg producing clients, contributing to upgrading the quality of chicken production, and boldly speaking out for high ethical standards in business.

Early Years

Little in Jacob's early life forecast the direction he took. He did not show unusual entrepreneurial talents nor interest in becoming wealthy, powerful, or successful. His parents were known in the community as average farmers. His mother and father were faithful members of the Mennonite church at Denbigh, Virginia, where his father was deacon.

Relatives may have influenced his later development. His older brother Coffman was reputed to be one of the best Fuller Brush salesmen the company ever had. "He was selling Fuller Brushes from his hospital bed on the last days of his life." Another brother was an "average farmer who was not 'overly obsessed' with the achievement ethic" though still considered "quite successful, having developed a substantial peach orchard." A friend of Jacob's was a creative inventor but did not have great managerial skills, so he worked mainly for other Mennonite businessmen in the Harrisonburg community. Family members believe the maternal side of Jacob's ancestry may have been equally important.[5]

At Eastern Mennonite (High) School, Jacob was remembered as "a person that took his work seriously and seemed to be a good student."[6] Another friend remembered him as a "quiet type who had a part-time job to pay his way through school at the hatchery close by. And in that sense he was not as much involved in the social activities of the campus as most of us. I was never quite sure whether it was of financial necessity that he did this or whether he found satisfaction in it rather than to get involved in student activities. . . . But it wasn't that he was negative in his attitudes."[7] He was hall manager at the school for a year, sang the solo part of Jesse in the school's production of *David the Shepherd Boy* in 1921, participated in other musical events, and sang with many groups which served in mission outposts.

While Jacob was attending high school he found summer employment at various jobs, including helping to build houses in Washington, D.C. (1926), and working part-time at a local hatchery and chicken farm (1927). After his marriage to Lucy Wenger in 1926 he began building a house on a lot which he had bought from the hatchery owner.[8] During this time he and his wife helped in Sunday school work at a local mission church where Jacob served as Sunday school teacher as well as superintendent.

Entrepreneurial Beginnings

There were many small hatcheries in the area. Through his experiences at the hatchery, Jacob learned about the industry. When a local hatchery became available, Jacob, age thirty-two, immediately decided to buy it. Despite the fact that the incubators and buildings were in bad shape, Jacob did not question the advisability of purchasing the hatchery.[9] He felt he could make it succeed, and never expressed any

Shenk Hatchery staff. Jacob at right.

doubts or regrets about his ability to run it. Jacob bought the company on a shoestring. The local bank later loaned him considerable amounts based on his integrity. "I remember the bank president saying that if Jacob A. Shenk hadn't had the integrity he had, they wouldn't have loaned him the money without him taking out a life insurance policy, which Shenk would not have done."[10]

Jacob launched the business as a family partnership with himself as president and Lucy as secretary. The two worked long hours to get the business started. According to Lucy, "Initially the operation was small so we did most of the work ourselves. Often on Monday morning while I did my washing I also watched the hatchery, taking in eggs brought by flock owners. . . . While I was watching the hatchery, Father would be gathering eggs from farms over the countryside."[11] Son Paul says that "Father had incredible energy; I seldom saw him go up a flight of stairs one at a time."

Lucy still remembers clearly when Jacob told her that the company had cleared $2,000 for the year. "What a great responsibility," he said. "I grew up with so little so I feel a great responsibility to the Lord. . . . He must have something special for me to do." Lucy recalled that "mission work was his first desire, but it never worked out."[12] Lucy did not participate in the daily management of the company but was always fully informed and was consulted regarding all major company decisions. But one major proposal, giving 90 percent of net profits to charity, gave Lucy some unease for a time.

Operating Style

Jacob's business philosophy and business operations developed in a methodical and pragmatic way. Having learned basic operating principles of the hatching industry, he complemented those with his own business philosophy and orientation. Jacob's style had been one of developing a broad base of expertise, doing the work to perfection, and expecting the same of others.

For example, since he had learned carpentering he could do some of his own work on his home and business. He took a drafting course by correspondence during his high school years, which allowed him to become a leader in many building projects, both in the business and in the church.

His son Paul remembers an incident that illustrates Jacob's philosophy. Paul was pitching manure in a rather uninspired way, so Jacob began "instructing me on the finer points of throwing cow manure out of the stable. I foolishly remarked that I had higher ambitions than being expert in pitching manure. His reply was perfect. He said 'My ambition is to be expert in whatever I do.' "[13]

Jacob did not have a very explicitly stated personnel policy and business philosophy. Nevertheless aspects of his style can be identified. He hired some of the best people available and placed them in responsible positions, giving them the freedom to exercise the authority of their position. He expected the best from his employees and rewarded them for their efforts. Consequently he dealt with each person individually, arranging wages and benefits on a confidential basis.

One employee remembers the following episode soon after he was hired (1940). "Brother Shenk called the employees together and said, 'I've tried to start you off on a fair wage. After that, it is up to you. I want to pay you what you deserve.' And that's the way he treated me. Not everybody was satisfied with the wages they received, but I was."

Jacob conducted biweekly meetings to communicate his concerns with his employees. These meetings were always opened by prayer, either by Shenk or an employee. He gave bonuses to some salaried employees, but no one knew what salaries or bonuses other colleagues were receiving. In meeting minutes for July 15, 1943, Jacob penned, "Bonuses—year or longer, divide with you. Amount is my business and yours, no one else's business." No one seemed too concerned about the fairness of this kind of policy because, as several ex-employees said, "We trusted Mr. Shenk; he was fair and generous."

In one of the few statements Jacob made regarding his business philosophy, entitled "Creating Wholesome Industrial Relations," the subheadings are instructive: "An Atmosphere of Understanding; Determine Christian Policies; The Payment of Fair Wages; Working with His Men; Keeping Cool and Confident; Concern for Spiritual Well-Being; An Obligation to the Community."[14]

Hanging in Jacob's office was a plaque which most employees, visitors, and clients would have noticed—"Trust in the Lord with all thine heart, and lean not unto thine own understanding" (Prov. 3:5). This was probably the most explicit and public statement of Jacob's philosophy of life.[15] While attesting to his integrity it also might indicate authoritarianism. However, the policies that guided Jacob's business dealings with clients, suppliers, and customers soon became widely known as enlightened, fair, and generous. Jacob assumed that integrity and quality were the principles essential to the success of any business.

Innovations

After having been in business only a short time, Jacob set up an innovative "field man" position which provided for a direct contact with all the egg producers on at least a monthly basis. The field man visited each producer, discussed the particular problems or concerns the producer had, and informed him or her of any company changes or activities of relevance. The field man also provided the producer with all the latest information, insights, hints, and ideas related to becoming a more profitable egg producer. Needless to say, the field man role was soon imitated by other hatcheries.

Jacob's philosophy of payment for services was the ultimate reason for the widespread loyalty to him and contributed to his ability to produce high quality chicks. He told his producers that the hatchery could only make money if they also made money, so he paid the highest price for high quality eggs.[16] But what cemented the loyalty was the profit sharing Jacob introduced. He gave his producers bonuses on their egg supplies according to how profitable the business had been that year.

On receiving a substantial check, one large producer returned it to Jacob with the note, "We do not think we deserve this bonus, since you have already paid us more than we could get at any other place." Jacob told his field man to return the check with the comment that "This is company policy, period." According to the testimony of the field man, the loyalty of the egg producers was so great that there was a long waiting-list for getting on board with Shenk Hatchery. This loyalty was also useful later when hatcheries, including Shenk Hatchery, were invaded and threatened with infectious diseases.

To assure a stable supply of eggs for hatching, contracts for egg supplies had to be made months in advance. Thus Jacob introduced a guaranteed purchase of stipulated numbers of eggs from egg producers, a practically unique innovation quickly copied by others. And his concern for fairness in business relations prompted him to pay above-market prices.

In a March 9, 1949, letter Jacob writes,

> Dear Flock Owner: There are three things I want to discuss briefly in this letter. First I find that some of you do not know that we are paying above market price for your eggs. Some weeks ago when the price of eggs dropped rather definitely we decided to maintain a floor of seventy-two cents per dozen for the eggs that are brought into the hatchery and seventy-one cents per dozen where we gather them up. That has been ten to twelve cents above the market price for several weeks. In addition we, of course, will continue the regular hatchability premium. We did that because we felt that the flock owners had not quite had a fair break last year. You are entitled to get a little more out of your laying flock this year if possible.

Shenk chick customers were also treated with integrity and care. The stability and prosperity of the hatchery business required a dependable balance between the supply of eggs and customers for the chicks. In one biweekly meeting (Oct. 1, 1942), Jacob reports on a personal trip to flock owners, then suggests ways the health of chicks can be enhanced. Jacob occasionally visited customers himself to keep in touch. He eventually hired a sales representative to make contacts with potential customers, arrange contracts with them, and make regular calls to make sure everything was in order.

Jacob was the first in the valley to replace free of charge, no questions asked, any chicks lost up to two weeks after delivery.[17] Jacob's reputation resulted in chick customers in all of Virginia, West Virginia, and into neighboring states as far north as Massachusetts and south to Georgia. Hence he could advertise in the *Virginia Poultryman* in 1947, "Total capacity of Hatchery, 1,212,000 eggs."[18]

A Growing Industry

The success of Shenk Hatchery cannot, however, be attributed solely to the leadership, business practices, innovations, and personal integrity of Jacob A. Shenk. The hatchery industry in the Shenandoah Valley and in the nation has to be seen in the context of the evolution of the chicken industry. When Jacob bought the hatchery, there were literally hundreds of little hatcheries geared to local demands distributed almost at random through the eastern United States.

The commercial poultry growing industry began to take off around 1925, but the advent of World War II, with its demand for a larger labor force including women, dramatically increased the need for commercially produced food. The chicken growing industry responded to this need, indicated by the fact that broiler production grew from 34 million chickens in 1934 to 6,312 million in 1950. The year Shenk died.

This war demand provided Jacob with the opportunity he needed—hatcheries run efficiently were able to take advantage of the new market and were more prone to succeed.

With the increase in commercially produced food, competition for profits began to play a larger role in the development and upgrading of the hatchery industry. Better quality hatching eggs (meaning a higher percentage of hatches per hundred eggs) and healthier chicks contributed to profitability. Along with others in the business, Jacob had developed a close relationship with egg producers. He expanded services by helping them to achieve more hygienic conditions and healthier laying hens as well as healthier chicks.

So Jacob benefited from the general economic boom, but he also introduced many innovations. He began sponsoring annual "flock-owners meetings," where he presented special speakers on the latest methods and discoveries. He also provided producers with disease control information and advice, especially after he hired Dr. A. B. Godfrey, a nationally known geneticist, as the company's laboratory scientist.[19]

These actions served Shenk Hatchery well. When in the 1940s a number of poultry diseases, especially pneumonia and pullorum, had begun to make their appearance and threatened poultry production, Jacob was ready. His practices not only helped his egg clients produce healthy eggs and have an edge on the competition, they also provided him with the resources to begin developing his own strain of disease-resistant chickens. This was a very advanced development but also expensive—and some fifteen years later contributed to the closing of the company.[20]

During the period the hatchery was struggling with infected chickens, Jacob made a number of trips to customers, including several to New England states, to try to keep several customers who were losing many chicks through disease. He tried to make sure there was no misunderstanding and full satisfaction or at least amicability. In one case, Jacob replaced a large order of chicks with a competitor's chicks since his were badly diseased and did not survive satisfactorily, whereas the competitor's seemed relatively free of disease.[21]

Jacob had instituted a breeding farm to develop a breed of efficient chickens that would resist disease and mature with the least amount of feed. At the time of his death he was making arrangements with major feed companies to provide nutritious and efficient feeds for the egg producers and the chick raisers. His management staff believes that if he had survived, vertical integration would have been a reality. That is, the hatchery would have become a poultry-producing organization which would have contracted with individual egg producers and chicken growers to provide an integrated system of scientific and feed services as well as marketing of products.

The company grew remarkably for a number of years, as Jacob controlled a number of the factors influencing the hatchery business. Shenk's Hatchery revenues grew from $134,425 in 1939 to $1,050,404 in 1949.

A Major Loss

Jacob had become a leading force in the poultry business in Virginia and beyond. On receiving news of his death, the board of directors of the Virginia State Poultry Federation sent a message to Lucy stating, "The enclosed resolutions (6) convey to you an earnest and sincere message from our board of directors." Resolution 2 said that "his friends in the poultry industry in Virginia will sorely miss his unfailing kindness, his generous assistance and counsel, and his strong Christian business principles which have so often steered us in the right direction and kept us from many errors."[22]

The local civic community had also noted Jacob's stature. Jacob had been elected member of the local hospital board in 1947 and served as a member of the fundraising committee. In February 1950, a month before his death, he was elected vice-president. In March 1952 an article entitled "Jacob A. Shenk: Biography of a Man Who Was a Steward of the Lord" appeared in *Virginia and the Virginia County*. The author begins, "This is the story of a man who achieved a tremendous personal and business success through application of the principles of Christianity which Christ gave to all of us in his Sermon on the Mount." Continuing her tribute, the author says, "The Shenk Hatchery affects a large number of people . . . employees, flock owners who supply eggs, and customers who have learned through experience that they not only get fine products, but a fair deal . . . always."[23]

When Jacob died, the company was losing considerable money in the breeding program. Attempts to stem the costly inroads of the poultry diseases seemed futile. Thoughts of selling the company had already been entertained by some management staff, and Jacob's death only strengthened such thinking. But Lucy Shenk ran an announcement that "the Shenk Hatchery will continue to operate as formerly and provide quality chicks."[24]

However, many large obstacles confronted the company. First Lucy had to convince the banks that the company would be able to function and that a substantial loan Jacob had received from a Richmond bank would be paid off. After considerable negotiation, the bank decided not to call the loan.[25]

The financial situation was not the only problem confronting Lucy. As long as Jacob was present, potential disagreements between staff members and disagreements about management philosophy were dissipated and controlled. But on his death they began to surface. The field representative submitted his resignation within a year of Jacob's death, and others began to look for alternate employment. Some of the unrest stemmed from the increasing difficulties connected with the disease problem, the expensive breeding program, and increased competition. But a considerable amount derived from the loss of strong personal leadership.

Jacob had earlier drawn up a will which stipulated that Lucy would be president in his absence or death and be assisted by a consulting or advisory group composed of John Alger and P. G. Wenger. The employees supported Lucy's leadership of the company, but because of the greater pressures on her to nurture the surviving members of the family,[26] she polled the management team on whether P. G. Wenger (Lucy's brother) would be acceptable as manager. The response was not enthusiastic. Observers believed that because such a strong loyalty to Jacob had developed, only management staff who were around while Jacob was alive were acceptable. Robert J. Messner was thus appointed general manager and was in charge until the company closed some eight years later.[27]

The sons of Jacob and Lucy were not in a position to join in managing the business. Paul, nineteen when his father died, had not developed great interest in the business, and the younger son James, who subsequently did carry on part of the business, was too young (age sixteen at his father's death) to become part of the business at the time.

Finally in 1958, the decision was reached to close the business. Much of the equipment and machinery was sold, although James later used some of the hatchery equipment. Most of the buildings and real estate were retained and subsequently adapted to other uses. All outstanding debts were paid off.

Profits to the Church

During the early years of prosperity the Shenks did not develop a plan for contributions to the church. Lucy says that

> For a good many years our giving was rather unplanned. We gave
> as a need arose, but nothing in a systematic way. Then Jacob felt

that as our business grew we should be giving more and in a planned way. About this time he read a book entitled *God Runs My Business*, about R. G. LeTourneau written by Albert W. Larimer. This told of a system worked out by the government for individuals who gave 90 percent of their profits to charities for ten years; after that all money given to charities would be tax free. I couldn't see how we could raise the family on 10 percent. Nor did I think the business would be able to survive, and pay its debts. But Father didn't push me and finally I was ready to go on that program. I'm happy to say that it wasn't long before I could tell him, "I'm back of the program a hundred percent."[28]

After checking with his bankers, tax consultants, and finally the Internal Revenue Service, Jacob determined that he would give 90 percent of net profits to the church. Lucy states that after three years, "With much thinking and praying, I finally agreed, trusting Jacob to do what he thought was best." Shenk Hatchery was placed on a special IRS arrangement for an experimental ten-year trial period. The 90 percent of the net profits were to be turned over to the church tax-free.[29] Beginning in 1943 the company books indicate termination of income tax payments and payment of massive charitable donations (with a curious substantial IRS payment in 1949).[30]

Jacob's generosity through the years made him a natural target for solicitation; he was constantly besieged by solicitors. One widely circulated story concerns a fundraising project for a worthy church cause. Jacob was solicited by a man whom some people considered a bit of a boaster. Jacob asked if the solicitor would match what Jacob gave.

The man said, "It's a deal."

Jacob replied, "Okay, I'll give $10,000."

A witness reported that the color drained from the man's face. He quietly backed out of the office and left, no doubt wondering how he would get out of this fix.[31]

The company was in its seventh year of the probationary period stipulated by the IRS when Jacob was killed. The IRS was suspicious of Jacob's motives and many times had sent an auditor to check on Jacob's huge charitable contributions. On one occasion, an IRS agent asked Jacob for documentation of donations. Jacob turned to his desk, pulled out a drawer, and handed the agent the sheaf of receipts documenting all the donations for that year. The agent told the company accountant sometime afterward, "I was never so embarrassed in all my life, but the IRS would not believe that Jacob would give this kind of money away."

The magnitude of Jacob and Lucy Shenk's charitable giving through Shenk Hatchery was widely and informally known through-out the local Mennonite community and in Virginia Conference. But little overt documentation is available because the Shenks wanted to keep the donations as anonymous as possible. Substantial amounts went to local congregations, Eastern Mennonite College (EMC), the Virginia Mission board, and causes in the local community.

Commented one local Mennonite leader, "I have often said that some building on the EMC campus should have been named for Jacob A. Shenk because it was his contributions (financially and personally) that largely contributed to building a number of them."[32] By age fifty Jacob had established himself as "one of God's stewards, and God's interests were always first with this Christian man whose life stands as a symbol of what can be accomplished by one who is in partnership with God."[33]

Many who were not privy to the details of the Shenk business and giving policies deduced that he was "flush" and assumed Jacob was simply someone who could make money at whatever he did. But that was not nearly as easy as people assumed. Due to the expansion of his business, Jacob was always in need of extra capital and had con-tinuing loans at the banks.

Though he did his banking with a local bank in Harrisonburg, he soon had to get loans at a larger corresponding bank in Richmond. A close relative came to Jacob in 1948 and requested that Jacob help him with a house he hoped to build. Jacob said, "I would like to help you, but let me tell you something, I am borrowed to the hilt in every bank in town." The informant was "really impressed." Then Jacob told him that because of his practice of giving 90 percent of net profits to the church, the only way he could keep his commitments and stay in busi-ness was to borrow as heavily as possible.

Jacob's commitment to the church and community went beyond finances. He drafted the plans for North Lawn, a women's dormitory at EMC and helped lead its construction. He also drew plans for many other buildings at the college. He was elected to the board of directors of the college in 1942, served as chairperson of the building committee in 1949, and drew the plans for the EMC chapel, which he heavily subsidized.

In 1940 he was ordained deacon and served in a local mission church which later became Chicago Avenue Mennonite Church. He served as deacon at the Lindale church for many years and gave major leadership and financial help during its membership growth and building program. In 1942, at age forty-two, he was elected to the board of the Virginia Mission Board. He was president of the Mission Board from 1943 until his death.

During those years he continued to work for the mission program of planting and nurturing mission churches in outlying areas.[34] Linden Wenger testifies that "Brother Shenk's interest in the active affairs of his church may be thought of as being lifelong. During all his mature years he was engaged as a teacher or superintendent in Sun-

Jacob being greeted by J. D. Graber, missions executive.

day school work of his home district, serving sometimes in the mountain churches."

Tensions

Jacob's relationship with the church included tensions, however. Virginia Conference felt that rapidly changing and burgeoning innovations were bringing "worldliness" into the church. Jacob on the other hand was a progressive, innovative person. A lover of music, he owned a guitar, record player, and many classical records. After his marriage he ritualistically listened to classical music in "his" corner of the living room after work.

Even though there was no clear decision on banning music in the home, Virginia Conference slowly moved toward the position that "the pastors and deacons were not to have instruments in their homes," including radios and record players, and were not to listen to music.[35] Jacob felt strongly about the issue and in a letter stated that "I wish it were so that some of the things our church stands for would be easier to explain to [the children, so] that there would never be occasion for them to begin to question the things we stand for. I think it would be easier to make strong Mennonites of them then.[36]

But Jacob's loyalty to the church transcended his interest in music. When the bishop had informed him that his name was going to be "in the lot" (entered in a draw) for the position of deacon, Jacob and Lucy had already decided what they would do. "Before the lot took place, Jacob and I discussed it. We knew what the conference had decided regarding musical instruments, and agreed that if [Jacob] were chosen, we would dispose of our musical instruments." Hence when the lot fell on Jacob, he "disposed of his player with alacrity, but with regret," until the ban was lifted.[37] One person recalls that "the day the ban was lifted, Jacob bought a new record player."[38]

Another area of conflict in the conference concerned use of the airplane. In 1929, Virginia Conference minutes decreed that for various reasons the ownership and use of the airplane was not appropriate.[39] Jacob had taken flying lessons in the mid-1930s, and in about 1936 bought an airplane. Jacob anticipated the changing attitudes toward planes, however, for by 1950, when he was killed, airplanes were used extensively and perhaps four to six Mennonite businessmen/farmers in the area owned planes.

Jacob apparently managed to avoid potential conflict and alienation from the church by his congenial temperament, his submission and commitment to the church, and the Shenks' financial contributions. "He didn't always agree with the church [on specific issues], but he was diplomatic enough that it did not come to the surface. He was very generous with his money. The conference couldn't have tried very hard to antagonize him. It didn't hurt that he was a good supporter. This helped people to 'look the other way' on certain issues."[40]

Jacob did have some conflicts and disagreements with others, but he always tried to work through the conflicts with fairness and grace. One of his employees had aspired to a church position but was denied ordination because several church officials, including Jacob, felt the person was not qualified for the role. This employee later expressed his desire to become a partner in the company by buying shares. Jacob replied, "With your boys and mine coming into the company later, we might run into difficulty. So instead, I am going to turn over part of the business to you for you to manage. You will be in charge. Just be prepared to give me any information when I want it." There seemed to be no lingering unresolved tensions between Jacob and the employee.[41]

A Faith Lived with Integrity

People who knew Jacob describe him as having been honest, hard-working, full of integrity, faithful, wealthy, successful, generous, thankful, and humble. As one interviewee put it, "One cousin said, 'The Lord knew whom he could trust with wealth.' Another person asked, 'Did you give so much to the Lord so he could bless you more?' This never entered Jacob's head. Jacob simply responded to these questions by saying, 'I got into the right business at the right time.' " A close relative states, "He was a humble man. He said on many occasions, 'I don't think that I am smart enough to have done this by myself. The Lord did this, and it is the Lord's business. Here it is, and I have to do something with it.' "[42]

This awareness of mutual obligation was expressed in his speech to the second annual Southeastern Poultry and Egg Association. "In our very highly developed and organized industry we are much more dependent one upon another than formerly. To the extent that we are dependent one upon the other . . . we are responsible to help each other." This mutuality expressed itself in Jacob's belief that each person should receive an appropriate benefit from being in the business of supplying human need. As an example, Jacob had ordered a hatchery table from a local craftsman. During delivery, the businessman mentioned what the table had cost him, intending to assure Jacob that he was not being cheated. "Mr. Shenk looked at the man and said, 'Mr.—, you cannot stay in business with that small profit,' and proceeded to pay him a more profitable amount."

Jacob believed faith had to be expressed in one's vocation. "I firmly believe that one can be a good Christian and also a good businessman."[43] The editorial in the April 1950 issue of *The Virginia Poultryman* noted that

> The sudden death of Jacob A. Shenk . . . takes from the Virginia poultry industry and from the poultry industry of the Southeast, one of the most progressive poultrymen of the area. With his interest in the progress and well-being of the poultry industry as a whole, Mr. Shenk combined deep loyalty and devoted service to his church and community. His well balanced life of service gave him a broad viewpoint, and his considered opinion was highly valued by all who knew him.

In an essay on his father, Paul Shenk wrote, "Intellectually he was a master of detail and technique. He felt he was somewhat lacking in ability to grasp and to evaluate broad perspectives. In discussion of political, theological, and philosophical issues he was sometimes drawn beyond his depth. . . . Father was not a great communicator: his words did not flow with rapidity and eloquence; but what he said was reliable. He did not talk unless he knew what he was talking about, and I have never known anyone with higher standards of veracity. He spoke in the soft accents of the Shenandoah valley."[44]

Jacob possessed many of the traits assigned to entrepreneurs. He was innovative, took risks, initiated business activities and structures, and managed people well (four traits usually mentioned as those most nearly describing the entrepreneurial personality.)

Jacob was also somewhat traditional, individualistic, and paternalistic, at least when looked at from our present perspective. He was perhaps simplistic in his understandings of power in social institutions and thus did not "rock the boat" when he might have exerted some leadership for change in the religious context.[45] But Jacob also was different from most entrepreneurs. His modest material and social lifestyle hardly changed during his lifetime. He resisted using his economic and social power to exploit or benefit from others under his control. Paradoxically, though somewhat individualistic and independent, he submitted himself to the authority of the church community in which he gained his sense of belonging and purpose. He had a modest and realistic self-understanding.

One personal characteristic mentioned by several persons who had lived in his home was his sense of humor. His niece, who lived in the home and helped care for the children for a time, said that "Uncle Jacob was forever teasing people, and enjoyed it immensely. After my fiancé left for Europe to serve in a church assignment, Uncle Jacob said time and again, 'I will be happy to pay for your telephone call, and you can talk as long as you want to, if you will just let me listen in.' " Lucy recalls that "Jacob's delight in teasing and having fun was well known." Jacob's sense of humor was likely key to his success in dealing with people.

Jacob was known as a frugal and watchful owner of his business. One knowledgeable informant said, "I don't remember any serious shortcoming associated with Mr. Shenk. Criticism of him, if there was any, was that he was too far ahead of us, that he was a big-time businessman, ahead of us farmers and workers, and made too much money. People felt he was in a class by himself. It seems to me people did not quite know what to do with this man."[46]

Jacob was flawed like anyone else. When asked whether Jacob had shortcomings, respondents usually offered a reluctant, "Yes, but his strengths overshadowed them."

The influences of family, church, and the larger community contributed to the substance of Jacob's life and work. His piety and personal devotion to his Mennonite church is due at least in part to the piety of his parents and of the Warwick congregation. But how did Jacob avoid the alienation from church typical of many successful entrepreneurs? What explains his humble submission to the rather restrictive church order?

Jacob allowed no insurmountable barriers to develop between his family and the church community. Jacob's children recall that little consciousness existed among themselves that they were wealthy. "There was nothing said about our situation. We didn't know what Father and Mother were giving. The only way we found out that we had money was from the neighbor kids, who said, 'You are rich!' We lived simply. The house we lived in and the car we drove showed it."[47]

Jacob did leave clues to his motivation in his few writings. "God gave the best that heaven had because of his love for the world. Jesus gave his life which was the greatest gift that the world ever received. . . . When we consider the need . . . in the world today . . . , can we allow ourselves to lay up personal fortunes at the expense of starving and hungry people? If we keep before us the idea that we are stewards and not owners I believe that the matter of giving will take on an entirely new meaning for us."[48] There is perhaps no better summation of Jacob's philosophy of giving.

Jacob's operating principle seemed to be thinking, belief, and action must be mutually and consistently integrated. As the above quote illustrates, Jacob took ideas and beliefs seriously as the proper ground for action and character. As he put it in an article entitled "Right Thinking," "Our thinking has an influence upon our lives which perhaps few of us are aware. . . . He who thinks great thoughts, who tackles difficult problems with open and honest and balanced thinking, who follows these problems through to logical and right conclusions will in time bear an imprint that speaks of ability, of rightness and of soundness in judgment. . . . Very definitely our actions are the results of our thinking, our characters are molded by our actions, and our destinies determined by our characters. . . . THINK ON THESE THINGS."

Jacob's concern with personal and religious integrity may be viewed as an expression of the Anabaptist/Mennonite environment in which he had been nurtured. His relations with family, church, and the wider community, his consumption styles and levels, and his treatment of people, including those under his authority, were those of a servant. Jacob A. Shenk simply and even naively tried to live the Sermon on the Mount, which Jesus summarized as "doing unto others as you would have them do unto you." Hence business, wealth, and power were placed in proper subordination. He no doubt struggled with temptations to live selfishly—but a simple faith lived with integrity can achieve remarkable results.

2

Abe Kroeker:
Whole-Life Entrepreneur

By Wally Kroeker

Born into a family that had emigrated from Russia eighteen years earlier, Abe Kroeker operated on a multiple track all his life. He developed an innovative farming operation into a corporation which later involved most of his offspring. At the same time he became a leader in educational as well as other church institutions. Like Jacob Shenk, Kroeker's business activities were infused with a sense of purpose that went beyond profit. His service and leadership in the church helped him to remain sensitive to the values of his faith community.

When the eighty or so owners of Kroeker Farms get together for their annual business meeting, it is like an extended family reunion. The shareholders are all children, grandchildren, or great-grandchildren of Abram and Elizabeth Kroeker. Every year they come to southern Manitoba from all over—from the prairies, the Maritimes, New England. Sometimes they meet in a city hotel, or at a lake shore camp, or perhaps at a Bible institute near the corporate headquarters in Winkler. It's a three-day event, part business, part family, part church, and it's not always clear where one part ends and the others begin. The late patriarch of this business/clan would no doubt approve. To him, business, church, and family were all part of a common fabric.

Abe Kroeker, now gone for more than a decade, still has an imposing presence in the various worlds he inhabited. Manitoba's agriculture industry remembers him for pioneering new crops and methods that transformed the region's farming base. The Mennonite Brethren Conference remembers him as "Mr. Sunday School," a man whose entrepreneurial vision bolstered religious education in his church community. A common theme in both worlds is that he was an innovator with a unique ability to "see around the corner" and an eagerness to improve the lot of others.

If entrepreneurship is defined by risk-taking and innovation, Abe Kroeker gets top marks. But business was perhaps not even his primary interest. Some say he was a farmer and businessman only to achieve other ends, such as on behalf of the church.[1] To all his pursuits he brought foresight, energy, and determination. In whatever he did, he was an entrepreneur.

Abe Kroeker's story is one of "firsts." He may have been the first Mennonite in Manitoba to own a motorcycle. He and his brothers were among the first to succeed in business. He was the first in the province to grow corn as a commercial grain, the first to grow onions as a storage crop. He loved new gadgets and was often first to try the latest piece of technology. He had movie cameras and tape recorders long before they became widely accessible. He liked new things, new ideas, new methods. Like most entrepreneurs, he was never content with the status quo.

How did this innovator survive amid the traditional Mennonite conservatism of turn-of-the-century Manitoba? What made him different from other young men in the Old Colony Mennonite settlements? In later years Abe would often tell his students that three factors determine what a person will become—heredity, environment, and individual will.[2] Abe was never one to let the first two factors inhibit the third. He came to terms early with the boundaries of his tradition and learned to overcome whatever constraints they imposed on his innovative and independent spirit. That he managed to remain and work in his church culture, rather than leave it behind, is a tribute to his personal charm as well as his eagerness to share widely the material and intellectual fruits of his success.

Old Colony Roots

Abe Kroeker's family came from Old Colony Mennonite stock, the same group of Russian immigrants who later fled from Manitoba to Mexico to escape what they perceived as the encroachment of "modernism." His parents, Abram and Helena Kroeker, were part of the first wave of Mennonite settlers to move into Manitoba in the 1870s. Shortly after their arrival in 1876, they homesteaded on a quarter section of land which later became the west end of the town of Winkler. When Mennonite Brethren missionaries from Minnesota visited Manitoba in 1885, Abram and Helena were among the earliest Old Colony Mennonites to convert to this new brand of Anabaptism. They became part of the first Mennonite Brethren church in Canada, established at nearby Burwalde in 1888.

Abe was born into this family on December 6, 1892. He learned early the habit of hard work and began working in his brother-in-law's print shop at the age of nine. He recalled, "I had to pedal the press with my feet and I could really make it go! My brother-in-law was very proud of how fast I could operate that machine. He always showed me off when visitors came. Before I went to school in the morning I came in and started a fire in the shop. Then I went from business to business asking, 'What do you want printed?' I took the orders. By noon the printery would be warm and I would print the orders and in the evening I'd deliver the goods. Oh, did I ever work!"[3]

He was also introduced early to the marvels of technology. Few people in those days, particularly Mennonites in Winkler, had much to do with photography. When Abe was 12 his mother bought him a camera (the kind with plates and a big black hood) from a Sears catalogue. Abe was soon much in demand as the community photographer. "It was customary then to have pictures taken at a funeral," he recalled. "A nice clear picture of the person in the coffin, that's what they generally wanted, and then, of course, the relatives standing around the coffin. I was invited to quite a few funerals and weddings to take pictures; I took some pretty good ones."[4]

The camera also became the occasion for a brush with Old Colony leaders. While passing through the village of Reinland, Abe stopped to photograph some young people gathered on the porch of a farmhouse. He printed the photographs in postcard size and took them to his brother-in-law's drugstore in Winkler, where he placed a display rack and put the pictures up for sale.

"When I came back a week later they were all gone. So I made some more. When I came back another week later they were all gone again. My brother-in- law said, 'Yes, they're all gone but it's on the definite instructions that you won't make any more.' The ministers had bought them all. Photography was definitely against the rules of the churches. Vanity. The ministers couldn't figure out how I kept making more after they'd bought them up."[5] Abe's early fascination with this new medium of expression never waned. Throughout his life he enjoyed recording and preserving images of his community, work, church, and family. New technology intrigued him. He was always an early consumer of new devices—movie cameras, three-dimensional photography, dictating equipment, tapes, records, and the like.

At age thirteen Abe lost his father. His mother remarried a widower with several children. Abe's mother, a woman of keen insight and high spiritual values, provided as well as she could for the children she had brought to this expanded family. But Abe couldn't help but feel shortchanged when his step-siblings received favored treatment from the new man in the household. This likely strengthened Abe's resolve to enter on his own the world he saw beyond Winkler.

Abe worked on the family farm for several years but wanted an education. He described the situation this way. "In general, when I was a boy and a young man, we boys got two horses, a set of harness, and a wagon, and that would start us off. The girls got a cow. And then you were ready to set up your own house. And that's probably what I would have got. I went to my stepfather and I said, 'I don't want the horses and I don't want the wagon and I don't want the harness. I only want permission to leave, that's all!' And I borrowed money from my older brother to go to school. Teaching was a stepping stone in general for a lot of working-class boys so I went into teaching."[6]

Teachers didn't need much education in those days. Abe completed grade nine at the Mennonite Collegiate Institute in Gretna, thirty miles away, then attended the provincial Normal School (teachers college) in Manitou. His first teaching placement was at Edward School, a mile north of Winkler.

Abe was married in the summer of 1914 to Elizabeth Nickel from Hepburn, Saskatchewan, whom he fondly described as "a hundred pounds of joy, laughter, and love." The young couple moved into the Edward School assignment for a happy first year.

A Writer Named Grove

A pivotal influence during this time was Frederick Philip Grove, the mysterious immigrant writer who would later emerge as a prominent figure on the prairie literary landscape. Born in Germany, Grove was a widely traveled "renaissance man" who, it was discovered many years later, had left a shadowy past behind when he emigrated from Germany in 1909. He showed up in Manitoba in late 1912 and was immediately engaged by provincial educators to teach in the German-English bilingual schools of the Mennonite Reserve west of the Red River.

In January 1913, he was sent to teach in the one-room school in the village of Haskett, about ten miles south of Winkler. In September he became principal of the Winkler Intermediate School and moved onto the second floor of a harness shop owned by Abe's older brother. He was not yet established as a serious writer but in time (as his works came to include *Over Prairie Trails*, *Settlers of the Marsh*, and *A Search for America*) he would be described by critics as "Canada's first important novelist."[7]

At this time Abe was a young teacher, about twenty-one. He and another Mennonite teacher, John Enns, arranged to receive special tutoring from the elder specialist Grove. Steeped in the German educational philosophy of the nineteenth century, Grove had an "eagerness for new methods, new devices, new texts, and new educational theories."[8] The Mennonite communities gave his progressive spirit a mixed reception. It was said that he was "simply too far ahead of the mentality not only of the rural public but of the teachers of the time."[9] There were raised eyebrows over his perceived worldliness. Some thought he was overbearing and arrogant. In her biography of Grove, Margaret Stobie suggests that the friendship of Abe and John helped Grove weather administrative storms during this period. Abe recalled, "He was older than John and me, a lot older; at the same time we were friends—not just students and instructor—we were friends."[10]

Grove took Abe and John with him to the annual teachers' convention in Winnipeg and introduced them to a larger urban world. Abe remembered being taken to dinner at the Canadian National Railway hotel, then one of the grandest hotels on the prairies. Abe and John found their mentor fascinating, as did the younger students who, half a century later, still spoke fondly of Grove's classes in nature study. Abe's oldest son, Walter, believes his father's many sermon illustrations drawn from the natural world can be traced to Grove's influence. Moreover, Grove nurtured in Abe the openness to new ideas that would serve him so well in agribusiness. Grove might be horrified to have any capitalist instincts traced to him, yet nourishing Abe's taste for new methods, even new worlds, was certainly no handicap to the young man's emerging entrepreneurial spirit.

Born for Business

While Abe enjoyed teaching and would be involved in some form of education for many years to come, he was also drawn to the world of business. "I was born a businessman," he told an interviewer in the early 1970s.[11] He gave up teaching and went into business with his older brother Jake, who had been operating a general store and harness shop. Abe enjoyed business and especially what he considered to be the playful jousting with rival Jewish merchants who until then had dominated Winkler's retail trade. A legendary prankster, he loved telling his grandchildren stories about his days as a merchant.

One story concerned a farm woman who came to his store with a package of freshly churned butter. She had an odd request. She wanted to exchange her butter for a different batch. "You see, Mr. Kroeker," she said, "I had just finished churning this butter but I turned my back on it for just a few minutes. When I came back to it, I saw a little mouse climbing out of the churn. I shooed the mouse away and cleaned up the butter, but I couldn't possibly use it myself because I know what's been in there. Couldn't you exchange it for different butter? Whoever buys this will never know. What people don't know won't hurt them."

Abe looked into the woman's pleading eyes for a moment, then without a word took the butter to the back of the store and wrapped it in new paper. When he handed the woman the "new" package she breathed a great sigh of relief and left, full of gratitude. Abe's grandchildren were never completely sure whether the story was fact or fable. But his enthusiastic telling of it suggested there was at the very least an object lesson for them.

The Kroeker store was a rarity, as running a business was not really proper for a Mennonite, and "a lot of the Old Colony Mennonites would rather deal with a [Jewish merchant] than with a Mennonite who had fallen by the way. So we had to get our customers through [bargain pricing]. You know, it wasn't *that* wrong if you could get something at half price."[12]

Abe and his brothers brought the first sale to Winkler. They publicized their buying trips to Montreal with reports of the new merchandise they would be bringing home. They papered the local villages with circulars. "We announced that on such and such a day we would not sell anything. We only wanted people to come and see what we had bought. We filled the whole store full of counters and displayed goods. It looked as though we had bought out Montreal! We announced that there'd be door prizes. That was something unbelievable to ordinary people, the idea that we'd give something away! We displayed the prizes in the windows. That day at noon, from our store to the hotel, the people were standing just as thick as they could stand. We gave a lot of door prizes away, mostly hardware like aluminum kettles. It was a big success."[13]

The competitors thought the secret of Kroekers' success lay in the writing of the circulars. When a competitor later bought the store from the Kroeker brothers, it was on condition that Abe continue to write the advertising. Abe knew better. His secret of consumer psychology was that you not only have to give people a bargain, they have to *know* it's a bargain.

Abe's business acumen extended into the dubious territory of taking advantage of religious differences between Mennonites and Jews. "We timed our sales for the Jewish holidays. And that really got under their skin! Oh, it was mean, yes! Because I had been a 'printer's devil' I could do a job fast. We just printed the circulars to go out into the villages two days ahead of time. The Jews wouldn't know about it. Then I would go out with packages of candy for every village and the first boys that I met I said, 'Boys, will you take a circular to every home? Here are thirty circulars and here's a bag of candy for taking them out.' Then on to the next village and I covered the whole of southern Manitoba in one day. Of course the next day the Jews would know about the sale but what could they do? They *had* to close up.'[14]

Heather Robertson suggests that Abe Kroeker's early success was due to his ability to take advantage of the turn-of-the-century cultural shifts among conservative Manitoba Mennonites. "Most Mennonites who dared dabble in trade were dealt with swiftly and harshly; one of Winkler's first Mennonite merchants was excommunicated and boy-cotted by members of his church because he moved to town and sent his children to a public school . . . Abe Kroeker was [one of the first Mennonites] to succeed in business in the Winkler area, and his leg-endary achievement is a direct product of Mennonite values and the unique opportunities presented by a disintegrating society to a man of unusual imagination."[15]

Studies in California

Abe's Old Colony Mennonite background was not one to inspire a thirst for education. Education was often dismissed with a popular Low German expression—*De jeleehda, de vekeehda* ("the more learned, the more misguided"). Abe felt differently. His early yearning for more schooling had not diminished. Even while he enjoyed being in-volved in business, he also felt stirrings for formal Bible training so he could more visibly and effectively serve God in the church and the Mennonite Brethren Conference. His consuming interest in Christian education became the defining passion of his life.

The immediate options boiled down to two—Moody Bible Insti-tute in Chicago, and the Bible Institute of Los Angeles (later known by its acronym, Biola). The schools were similar in their fundamentalist orientation; in fact, the founder of Biola, Reuben Torrey, had pre-viously been at Moody. Abe Kroeker had been a great admirer of Tor-rey, who was to the fundamentalist world of 1920 what Billy Graham is to evangelicals today. Biola was a leading Christian school of the time. Torrey had visited southern Manitoba on a speaking tour; perhaps it was then that Abe heard and was favorably impressed by the inspirational speaker. Other Mennonites had gone to Biola and apparently brought back good reports.

So in 1920 Abe took a two-year leave of absence from the Kroeker business. The family of five (including children Walter, Mary, and Alfred) enthusiastically prepared to head for the land of palm trees and citrus groves. But they hadn't counted on an irascible American consul in Winnipeg. He did not like Reuben Torrey and refused to authorize Abe's trip. "If you wanted to go to any other place, I would let you go, but there is no sense in going to that grafter, Torrey," the consul told Abe.

Typically, Abe did not give up. He took the matter to his friend Valentine Winkler, after whom the town of Winkler was named and who was then Manitoba's minister of agriculture. The issue climbed up the bureaucratic ladder. After several months, Abe received permission to cross the border to attend Biola. Meanwhile the troublesome American consul in Winnipeg was replaced.

In California Abe worked hard to support his family and complete his studies after his untimely delay. He got a job as a "storeman" in a large restaurant, working from five in the morning until noon. In the fall he got a job driving truck. The family lived frugally, buying only the necessary items of furniture. For daughter Mary they made a makeshift bed by nailing four legs to a wooden box. They bought stale bread and cheap oranges. Abe liked telling the story of standing around the sink with Walter and Alfred eating small oranges which were available at next to nothing. When they counted the peels they found they had consumed fifty-two oranges.

A transcript of Abe's six terms at Biola shows he took a full load of courses including Christian doctrine, Bible content, apologetics, homiletics, pastoral theology, evangelism, church history, missions, teacher training, and practical work. His grades were exceptional, considering he had a family to tend to. He received forty A's, twelve B's and one C.

After graduation he returned to Manitoba to participate again in the Winkler business. He brought back not only enthusiasm but also new ideas and new songs that sounded strange in the old wooden sanctuary. He had new techniques, such as "chalk talks," for making

Scripture lessons come alive for young people. Southern Manitoba Mennonites had never before experienced lessons illustrated with colored chalk.

Though still immersed in business, Abe maintained his passion for Christian education, especially for the young. He loved children—his own as well as others'—and devoted much energy to their spiritual nurture. "Our first and greatest attention should be centered on work for and with children," he once wrote. "Not only because God has entrusted them to us and thus it is our first and holy duty, but also because they are our most fruitful field of mission. Furthermore, it's the most enjoyable."[16] This vision would be manifested in his extensive work in Bible school, Sunday school, and camping ministries.

Winkler Bible School

In 1925 Abe, with two other Winkler businessmen, was a prime mover in founding Winkler Bible School (WBS) and hiring the newly immigrated Abram H. Unruh as its leader. In 1929 Abe became a part-time instructor and continued with the school for the next fifteen years.

He taught a variety of courses connected with Sunday school and other ministries for children, son Peter recalls. He brought the school into membership of the Evangelical Teacher Training Association so graduates from the Sunday school courses received certificates from this organization. His goal was for WBS graduates to become leaders in their home churches. For many years, this was the case. Until the formation of the Mennonite Brethren Bible College in Winnipeg in 1944, in which Abe also had a hand, Winkler Bible School was the leading institute of advanced learning for Canadian Mennonite Brethren.

Vacation Bible schools grew out of the Bible school activity. "Dad saw the empty schools during the summer holidays as tools for an outreach for Christian education for children," says Peter. "He was a prime mover in initiating vacation Bible schools in many school districts. I remember the trips he made in bringing teachers to their schools, visiting them, and encouraging the teachers. In retrospect I can well appreciate that there was a great deal of organizational work which I was not aware of as a young boy."

Retreat to the Farm

By all appearances in the late 1920s, Abe Kroeker seemed to "have it made." The business was thriving, the family was expanding, and Abe's growing involvement in the Bible school gave him an outlet for creative ministry. There had been no hint that the land had any attraction for him. He had grown up on a farm, but at the first opportunity had left it for pursuits in education and business.

Thus, recalls son Walter, the 1928 announcement of this young businessman that he was going into farming created quite a stir in Winkler. Abe simply felt the town was not a place to raise his family. With less than a thousand residents, Winkler was not exactly a rural fleshpot of temptation. But Abe felt strongly that his children, the oldest of whom was then entering the troublesome teens, needed a wholesome outlet for energy and purposeful activity. This uncharacteristic retreat to safety underlined a contradiction in Abe Kroeker's life—progressive methods were fine in business and education, but when it came to his family, in the early years at least, Abe was staunchly conservative.

Using his equity in the family business, Abe purchased 360 acres six miles southeast of Winkler, adjacent to a farm owned by his younger brother Peter. Agriculture was relatively stable in 1928, and the new farm had clean fields and suitable buildings. Abe and Elizabeth and their children set to work producing raspberries, Yorkshire hogs, Aberdeen Angus cattle, grain, sheep, and poultry. This would provide the well-rounded work experience they considered essential for their growing family. They called their new enterprise Poplar Grove Farm.

Their timing couldn't have been worse. Myriad hazards lay on the immediate horizon, including an infestation of sow as well as Russian thistle, grasshoppers, drought, wind, and plummeting farm prices. The Great Depression had begun. At his and Elizabeth's golden wedding anniversary in 1964, Abe recalled that they had made the switch to farming "just in time to experience the dirty thirties, when drought and grasshoppers left us with practically no income. Elizabeth with the children and a half acre of raspberries and her twelve milk cows (which we managed to keep alive), did a good part of supplying food for the family."

Abe was not a quitter. Like entrepreneurs before and after him, he determined to find new ways of responding to the challenges he faced. One response was to break out of the farming patterns that had been rigidly followed for the fifty years since the region was settled— the standard cropping cycle of several successive years of wheat followed by a fallow year. "Dad had always been drawn to those who stimulated the mind and imagination, people who were not content to remain on well-trodden paths, notably Frederick Philip Grove, Reuben Torrey, Abram Unruh," recalls Walter. "Now that farm problems required imaginative and innovative solutions, he applied to them the bold and fresh approaches of his mentors. As a beginner in farming, he was unhampered by the baggage of narrow prejudiced views."[17]

The mentors Abe chose were specialists like Bill Breakey of the Morden Experimental Farm, located a few miles west of Winkler, as well as provincial agricultural representative Jack Crawford and agricultural professors Tom Harrison and Joe Ellis of the University of Manitoba. A fascinating synergy developed between Abe and these experts. He drew from them and applied their expertise. They in turn went out of their way for him because he was willing to test their theories on a commercial basis.

Neighboring farmers were amused when Abe Kroeker broke with traditional patterns. They laughed when he purchased their manure piles to fertilize his crops. "In 1930 Dad began using chemical fertilizer, with dramatic results," says Walter. "The next year one of the first fertilizer attachments was installed on his drill, and nitrogen phosphate pellets were applied to all seeded grain. The crop response was excellent, and proved to be a valuable object lesson to other farmers."

The experts were concerned about the long-term environmental effect of black summerfallow, which led to wind erosion. They favored instead balanced crop rotations that included corn as a row crop and legumes for soil fiber. On one of their visits to the Morden station Abe and Walter heard Jim Haney, a representative of International Harvester, extol the virtues of corn. If there was a salvation from drought and grasshoppers, he said, it was corn.

Abe recalled later: "On the way home I said to Walter, 'What do you say, shall we try corn?' His answer was, 'I don't care how hard we have to work in summer, as long as we can go to school in winter.' "

So in 1932 Abe and his family planted forty acres of corn, a big undertaking without proper machinery. "The whole family went out

Canada's first drying kiln (1936).

to weed corn at 6:00 a.m. till about 10:00 a.m.," Abe recalled. "Then, during the hottest part of the day, from 10:00 to 4:00 p.m., we did other work. From 4:00 until dark we again weeded corn."

Their neighbors weren't impressed. One morning when the family was on their way to the field, hoes in hand, a neighbor needled them, *Jo, Jo, Rachual halped plaunten oba nich weden* ("Greed helps to plant but not to weed"). The needling gave Abe and the whole family a shot in the arm. When Abe passed that neighbor's yard on his daily trip to the field, he'd remember the taunting and work even harder.

As the first farmer in the province to grow commercial corn, it was not easy for Abe to break with tradition and acquire the necessary equipment for the switch to row crops. But the Kroeker family persisted, obtaining two secondhand horse-drawn cultivators from "across the line" in North Dakota. "When fall came, the critics' tune changed. People saw that Kroeker didn't have to sell his pigs and cows for lack of feed. One or another might come for advice, while yet another would ask whether corn still left on the field could be spared for his stock. In short, others benefited from the Kroeker venture into row cropping."[18]

Not only did the corn produce an excellent crop, Walter remembers, but its stalks trapped drifting snow during the winter, providing adequate field moisture for a bountiful crop of wheat the next year when extreme drought brought general crop failure elsewhere. "The demonstration was so dramatic, and the results so widely promoted by Dad and farm periodicals, that this new cropping principle for southern Manitoba was accepted quickly and applied generally."[19] As a result, black summerfallow became a thing of the past in the Pembina Triangle, and the lessons learned from this first successful row crop set the stage for other innovative applications like sunflowers, sunflower oil processing, sugar beets, and potatoes.

Abe had launched a corn boom in southern Manitoba. Suddenly there was also a great demand for corn seed, which he and his sons set out to fill by growing seed corn the following season. Existing corn varieties matured too late for the early Manitoba winter, so they set to the task of cross-breeding a hybrid strain that produced earlier. Before long the Kroeker farm was providing a major part of the country's seed corn needs.

Another challenge was to develop new methods of drying the corn. Conventional methods were archaic, consisting of hanging individual cobs on nails set at an angle in 2 x 2's. The Kroekers adapted for local conditions a system of corn drying used at the University of Wisconsin; heated air was forced through slatted-floor bins containing cob corn. What resulted in 1936 was Canada's first corn-drying kiln. "This innovative project proved to be highly successful, and the development of a row-crop economy in the Pembina Triangle was assured."[20]

Farm periodicals took note, and Abe Kroeker's reputation spread. One visiting journalist observed that as a result of the innovative methods used in southern Manitoba, "corn is no longer a gamble . . . it is an investment." The writer went on rather melodramatically. "What most impressed me was the farm of A. A. Kroeker, a prosperous farmer south of Winkler. But he was not always prosperous. Wheat all but finished him. Like a drowning man grasping at a straw, he grasped at a corn straw, only perhaps it was a stalk. On this stalk, like Jack in the Bean Stalk, he hoisted himself up to affluence—and good crops."[21]

In 1942 an early frost devastated the corn, and Abe turned to commercial production of the potatoes he had been growing on a small scale. "In addition to the 'table' crop, he began growing seed potatoes, and developed a system for commercial-scale production of 'tuber-unit' Foundation seed. This seed found acceptance both for domestic and export markets, and the marketing success led to the establishment of a flourishing seed potato industry in Manitoba."[22]

His leadership led to potatoes becoming a major crop in Manitoba. From an importer of potatoes, Manitoba became an exporter, first to other parts of Canada as early as 1949 ("Manitoba 'Potato King' Ships Five Carloads East," said the newspaper headline) and later overseas. In time, large potato processors set up shop in Manitoba and today commercial production of French fries, instant and mashed potatoes, and chips is more concentrated in Manitoba than in any other Canadian province.

The Kroekers also led the way in storage technology. When the firm built a modern new potato storage building in 1956, it was the only one of its kind in western Canada. When they introduced onions to Manitoba in 1958, the early lessons learned in drying corn were applied. Kroekers' kiln-cured onions became popular across Canada and the United Kingdom. "The basic system is now in general use in Western Canada."[23]

Kroeker Farms Today

As the company grew and several sons assumed larger roles, corporate changes were made. Abe was ahead of his time in easing back on control of the company by implementing an early and orderly transition to the next generation. The business was incorporated as a family farm corporation in 1955 under the name A. A. Kroeker and Sons Ltd. In 1978 the name was changed to Kroeker Farms Limited.

Today, Kroeker Farms has some 9,000 acres (some of it rented) under cultivation in southern Manitoba. It employs eighty people year-round and another 100 on a seasonal basis. It is still the province's largest potato producer, including table stock, seed, and processing. It is also the province's only commercial grower of Spanish-type onions, supplying Manitoba's requirements as well as selling to neighboring provinces. "One real success today is our Spanish-type onions," says Donald, the youngest son and currently president and CEO. "We kept on working at it until we developed the technology to grow transplanted onions in such a way that they would develop to sizes comparable to those grown in Idaho and Washington."[24]

Kroeker Farms is also known for its sweet corn, much in demand in the grocery trade because an innovative hydro-cooling technique retains the product's freshness and taste for much longer than traditional harvesting methods. Some cereal crops continue to be grown, primarily for crop rotation purposes. The company is also the registered owner of K-Line Pigs, a successful line of breeding stock. The service division of the company looks after transporting the commodities, maintains equipment, and operates a farm garage, including a fabrication shop to build and modify equipment.

As with most businesses, there have been failures and missteps along the way. One was a potato chip venture in the early 1960s. Another was a failed 1970 expansion into Saskatchewan. Despite these "learning experiences," the farming venture begun by Abe Kroeker in 1928 grew into a firm that became known for innovation and leadership within the industry. "All in all, the Kroeker farming family has proved a decided asset to Winkler, bringing increased employment, greater volume of business and renown to the community," a Mennonite journalist wrote.[25]

Another journalist commented, "By example, and by advice on request, they are ready to help neighbors, and visitors to their farm from further afield, to improve their farming operations."[26] The company is still quick to adopt innovative ways to deal with complex situations, such as recent efforts to use "minimum tillage" techniques to improve environmental sustainability. The company's current mission statement still reflects Abe Kroeker's legacy: "To meet people's needs through innovative agriculture in a way that honors God."

Mr. Sunday School

As Abe's children shouldered more of the responsibility for running the farm, he was able to put increasing energy into church work. The pivot of his Mennonite Brethren Conference work was Christian education.

As a trainer of students for Sunday school teaching, he believed

Sunday school curriculum and methods should be tailored to the particular capacity and learning characteristics of each age-group. He began to promote this concept with zeal. Graded lessons were fully accepted in secular education, but in the Mennonite Brethren Conference they were a source of considerable controversy. Conference records show Abe promoting this concept as early as 1934. That year he was able to win over conference delegates, but there was still opposition to overcome. Some found the lessons too difficult. Not all teachers were willing to do the necessary preparation. Some children objected to "homework." Moreover, hadn't simple Bible stories been good enough for the previous generation?

Abe Kroeker persevered. His sister Nettie said, "Once Abe knew that his vision was from God, he would persist in his efforts until he succeeded."[27] It took ten years, but finally the graded lesson principle was adopted.

Abe Kroeker was ordained in the ministry by the Winkler Mennonite Brethren Church in 1941. In those days it was not unusual for a fully-employed businessman to receive such formal affirmation of ministerial gifts. Abe continued to straddle his two worlds—agribusiness and church.

From 1942 to 1956 he chaired the newly formed Canadian Conference Sunday School committee, traveling widely on its behalf. He organized and participated in Sunday school conventions and short courses for the various regions of the MB Church in Canada. When traveling, recalls son Peter, "He would go out of his way to see how churches in other denominations were organizing their Sunday school work."[28] The graded Sunday school lessons he brought into being required separate rooms for each class, and Abe urged churches to build education wings. Congregations he and Elizabeth attended after moving to the city in 1946 were some of the first MB churches to build such facilities. These activities earned Abe designations such as "Mr. Sunday School" and "the father of MB Sunday schools."

A related involvement was Christian camping. In the 1930s, Winkler Bible School had begun using a camp setting to expand its outreach to children. The school annually rented the grounds of the Canadian Sunday School Mission on the shore of Lake Winnipeg near Gimli, some sixty miles north of Winnipeg. A drawback was that the Mission needed the facilities for its own summer programs, so the only time slot available was quite early, before other programs got underway. From the standpoint of weather, this was not ideal.

"We were always looking out for property to buy as our own so we wouldn't have to hold the camp so early," Abe explained in the early 1970s. One day in 1939 Abe was in the drugstore in Gimli when he met an elderly Icelandic gentleman and mentioned his plans. It turned out the man had a piece of lake front land he might sell for a good cause like a Christian camp. Abe organized a group of ten men from Winkler who drove out to look at the land. It was a lovely quarter section with a vast sandy beach. The price was $1,000. The men each contributed $100 and bought the property.

Plans for the development of the camp were disrupted by World War II, which began that fall. Among other things, it was not considered wise to be constructing a camp for nonresistant Mennonites at a time other young people were going to war. By the time the war ended, many of the original backers had lost interest. Abe heard about another group of Winnipeg Mennonite Brethren who had independently been discussing a camp program. He threw in his lot with them, the original investors were bought out, and in 1949 Camp Arnes came into being. Today the camp ministers to more than a thousand young people annually.

He is remembered chiefly for his work in Christian education. But Abe also "furthered trends in the development of music in the Mennonite communities in Canada," writes Esther Horch. He was "an ardent supporter of music workshops held all over Canada in Mennonite communities, and in 1944 his influence led to the creation of a youthful Mennonite Symphony Orchestra."[29] For a number of years Abe also did some performing of his own. In 1925 he formed a gospel quartet with his younger brother Peter, a cousin, and a nephew. They traveled widely in Manitoba and North Dakota.

Music remained an interest of Abe's throughout his life. No family reunion or annual business meeting was complete without a musical component. In the early 1960s, when Abe and Elizabeth gave each of their three dozen grandchildren a $1,000 debenture as an "early inheritance," they stipulated that it should not be cashed in prior to maturity unless it went for education or music lessons.

Giving Generously

Despite their material success, Abe and Elizabeth Kroeker lived modestly. When they moved to Winnipeg in 1946, the frame house they purchased in Elmwood was anything but lavish. Several years later they moved into a new bungalow in East Kildonan. It was more upscale, but still distinctly middle class. When they died within eleven days of each other in 1981, after sixty-seven years of marriage, they left a relatively small estate. Most of what they had accumulated had long been passed on to others.

Some acts of generosity came to light only after their passing. One couple told youngest daughter Betty that they were still using a set of china that Abe and Elizabeth gave them when they arrived, penniless, from the old country. "Another man told me he was forever grateful to Dad for the faith he put in him when he couldn't get a bank loan to start a new business," says Betty. "Dad gave him the $3,000 to get started."[30]

Abe and Elizabeth were also generous to their own family. When the company was incorporated in 1955, all common shares went to their nine children. At one point they gave a major trip to each child's family, the only condition being that the two of them could go along. Though he had left Winkler nearly two decades earlier, Abe founded the Winkler Home for the Aged in 1964 and secured the necessary funds for its first senior citizen's home, Heritage Manor. He also initiated a larger facility, Centennial Heritage Apartments, a six-story senior citizen's home in Winkler.

Today the Kroeker Foundation, which owns shares in Kroeker Farms, carries on charitable works in its founder's name. The company meanwhile donates 20 percent of its profits to church-related causes, as well as giving away nearly 100 tons of produce a year to camps, Bible colleges, soup kitchens, and the annual Mennonite Central Committee auction.

All in the Family

Abe Kroeker's business success cannot be separated from his passion for his two "families"—his immediate biological family and his wider church family. In the early years every one of Abe and Elizabeth's nine children served their time at Poplar Grove Farm.

This, after all, was one of the reasons for starting the business in the first place—to provide purposeful activity in a family setting. But if family considerations were never far from mind when business decisions were made, the reverse was also true. In the early years, family members were expected to make significant sacrifices for the good of the larger enterprise. In Abe Kroeker's mind, the two were one.

When Walter was a young man, he had his eye on a forty-acre piece of land he wanted to purchase to start his own farm, but his father wouldn't loan the money. Later Abe purchased the land for himself. Greed was not the issue; rather, this was his way of exercising control to keep everyone together.

While Abe embraced modernity he wanted little of it for his children, at least not at first. In the early years he didn't want his children to be innovative and modern. Though he'd had a motorcycle as a youth, he never let his oldest son, Walter, have even a bicycle. "He didn't want me mobile," Walter recalls. "He was different in business than he was with his children. He was afraid of us tasting freedom."

Despite his progressive views in many areas of child psychology and education, Abe was a strong disciplinarian in his early years. While his children remember him as loving and generous, he had his stern moments. Once he returned from a trip to Chicago with a "special gift" for the children—a leather riding crop for disciplinary purposes. (One day it mysteriously disappeared; one of the older children buried it in the ground.)

As a young parent he feared worldly influences on his children. When the family went to Winnipeg for a day of shopping, Abe insisted that an older child check in with him every hour under the huge clock in Eaton's department store. Years later it was revealed that the motive was to make sure the child didn't have a large enough block of time to attend movies.

What does one make of these apparent contradictions? Perhaps it was Abe's way of dealing with his own fractured childhood. He lost his father at a young and impressionable age, and when his mother remarried he and his siblings felt pushed aside. His zeal to mold his own family into the cohesive community he himself had lacked may have made him all the more determined to keep his family on a short leash. But the leash lengthened as Abe mellowed and continued to develop. Youngest son, Donald, says he did not experience the strictness of his older siblings. He remembers Abe as a father who always went the second mile. "He was always very supportive; he trusted me and encouraged me. When I made mistakes, he never rubbed it in."

The Roots of Entrepreneurship

What explains Abe Kroeker's remarkable entrepreneurship, in both business and the church? How did a young Mennonite boy in a hidebound rural community slip the bonds of tradition?

One factor, as noted earlier, was the range of mentors he chose during his formative years. He was eager to learn from others. Humility and willingness to learn have been hidden ingredients of business success. In recent years this has been documented by, among others, Arizona business consultant Daniel Scully. Scully found that blue collar workers who start their own businesses are more likely to succeed than more sophisticated executive types because they are more willing to listen and take advice. "Humility gives them a much better chance of success," Scully says.[31]

Abe Kroeker wasn't exactly a blue collar worker when he launched what would became a major farming enterprise in 1928. But he was humble and willing to learn. "With little or no actual farming experience, he had difficulty coping with drought, dust storms, and economic woes," writes P. J. Peters. But as noted earlier, Abe turned to the experts at nearby Morden Experimental Station and faithfully attended their extension meetings. "Abe Kroeker became a convert to the gospel of crop rotations, field corn and legumes, all foreign to traditional farming practices of the area. He seldom did things 'by halves' and he revolutionized his farming program with characteristic enthusiasm and zeal."[32]

Abe also shared with most entrepreneurs a trait not easily defined or explained—good instinct and the courage to take risks. Mennonite Brethren patriarch A. H. Unruh, Abe's colleague at Winkler Bible School and later at Mennonite Brethren Bible College in Winnipeg, once said of him, "He sees the rabbit coming; I only see it when it's going away." One of his children notes that "he had the right instincts. He worked on intuition. He had an infallible evaluation of people the first time he saw them. He could discern the flash-in-the-pan people from those who had staying power. It was an invisible process."[33]

On the rare occasions when instincts failed him, Abe learned from his mistakes. One early business setback taught him a lesson that would long leave its mark. While a merchant in Winkler, he had invested in Union Traders, an automobile and machinery dealership. His cash investment wasn't huge, but the bank guarantees were significant. When the company failed he not only lost his investment but had to come up with his share of the guarantee. This was money he didn't have, and fulfilling his obligation was difficult. From this he learned two lessons. First, don't let other people handle your money. Second, avoid borrowing; when you take a risk, do it with your own money, not someone else's.

"Dad followed these precepts, with very minor exceptions, throughout his business career," recalls Walter. "From the early 1940s until the mid-1950s we could have grown much faster had it not been for Dad's conservative view of debt." When his sons assumed greater control of the company the restrictions were relaxed, but Abe would frequently remind them to keep an eye on their debt.

Abe also had a knack for infusing others with his own excitement. "In both agriculture and church work, Abram Kroeker was known as a motivator and entrepreneur, a man of vision not bound to tradition yet firmly committed to the fundamentals of the faith. He had a unique ability to recognize opportunities, accept challenges, impart his insights and infect those about him with his irrepressible enthusiasm."[34]

A significant factor in Abe Kroeker's success was that he always had a mission beyond profit. The conscious pursuit of profit will forever be a controversial topic among business analysts, but a growing chorus of voices is promoting the notion that to succeed over the long term a business must have a larger vision than mere profit. Leading entrepreneurs have promoted the view that profit is to business what breathing is to life: we must breathe in order to live, but breathing itself is not the chief goal of existence.

Abe Kroeker always had a larger mission in mind. While he tended his business interests with vigilance and energy, the larger issues in his life were his family, his church and his community. He once wrote, "We are living in times in which all of us should place our personal entrepreneurial interests in the background. Our rallying cry should be: 'Our best efforts for the Lord.' In that way we will help our neighbor and our country in the best possible way."[35]

3

Alta Schrock:
A Pragmatic Visionary

By Jack Dueck

Alta Schrock (b. 1911) expressed her entrepreneurial skills in truly unique ways. Unlike most entrepreneurs, she realized her dreams almost entirely within the context of her Mennonite faith community, devoting herself and her projects to the good of her fellow human beings. Yet like most entrepreneurs, she has done so with a pronounced individualistic and creative bent. There is clearly a tension in her story between the poles of communal norms and expectations, on the one hand, and individualistic drive and creativity, on the other. Her ability to balance the two is only one of her many remarkable traits.

In March 1991, Dr. Alta Schrock was inducted into the Maryland Women's Hall of Fame by the Maryland Commission for Women in a ceremony officiated by Governor Donald Schaefer. Remarking on her wide-ranging contributions to the tri-state Allegheny region and beyond, one speaker noted, "What is remarkable and significant about her many and varied contributions is that she was essentially a woman in a man's world. Be it in her church setting, in society, in pursuing a profession, or in business, the cultural and ethical milieu of her times saw these as areas for predominantly male roles. Today we recognize Alta Schrock's early emancipation and her positive and creative pursuit of a productive liberation."[1]

While most entrepreneurs, Mennonites included, pursue their projects first for private gain, Schrock's entrepreneurial mode has been to incarnate her beliefs, values, and dreams to the benefit of a surrounding community. Yet like most entrepreneurs, she has pursued her projects with a pronounced individualistic and charismatic approach. She has been a Mennonite entrepreneur marching to a different drummer. She has been a communal participant inspired by individualistic creativity, a consensus builder with a need to initiate and to control, a romantic botanist, a charismatic communalist, a childlike academic, a pragmatic visionary.

When looking at Schrock's life and career, a number of questions arise. To what can be attributed her unabated creative genius and its accompanying entrepreneurial ferment? Being a strong woman in a man's world, why did she not become a feminist? During her full career she frequently encountered either male dominance or male hindrances and even abuse. The horrendous capstone of this occurred in her brutal assault and rape in her own home in July 1979. Why was she not psychologically and spiritually debilitated? What religious faith, values, genetic inheritance, and upbringing made for her courage, centered stability, and creative living?

Family Background and Youth

In her acceptance speech upon induction into the Maryland Women's Hall of Fame, Schrock gave an explanation for her many accomplishments that went beyond her habit of attributing her success to God's leading and "opening doors" for her.[2] Among other things, she declared to the assembled politicians, professionals, church friends, and institutional leaders that "I'm here today because of my genes. I did what I did in life because of what I received from my an-

Alta on the left.

cestor Benedict Miller. . . . And it is up to each of us to live out our nature and our genes to the glory of the Creator and for the good of our
fellow humans."

Schrock's Amish Mennonite ancestors came to America in the
late 1700s from Switzerland.[3] One of the more outstanding, even
legendary, ancestors was Benedict Miller (1781-1837), who lived in
the counties Somerset, Pennsylvania, and Garrett, Maryland. Alta's
mother Amelia was a Benedict Miller descendant. Solidly Amish but
highly entrepreneurial and inventive, Benedict, his sons, and his
people were the progressives of their day. Benedict started a school in
his home and with his son Joel built the first school in the Springs,
Pennsylvania, area, for children of Mennonite and other backgrounds.
Although school was not compulsory in Garrett and Somerset
counties at the time, Miller recognized the human and social need
with his refrain, *die kinder mussa lerna* ("the children must learn").

Benedict aided immigrants, even personally redeeming inden-
tured servants off the boats in Baltimore. Numerous ancestors of area

families, of varied ethnic and religious backgrounds, had received their first year of room and board from the Miller family.[4] He was also involved in promoting mutual aid among Mennonites, relief work among the impoverished of the Allegheny mountain region, and in church-building and nurture, all within a wide radius of his home. While aiding new settlers in starting their farms, he also traveled on horseback as bishop and preacher of "good news" in localities as far as Ohio.

These powerful traits and values prevailed in subsequent generations. It is possible to trace an astounding trail of invention, aesthetic creativity, and benevolence stretching from Benedict's son Joel's furniture and inventive creations, to grandson Posey Sam's ornate and colorful sketches, and through the wide-ranging creativity and contributions of the present-day descendants.

Benedict's great-grandson, Jacob S. Miller, was Alta's grandfather. He farmed what became known as Strawberry Hill Farm located on Dorsey Hotel Road north of Grantsville. Jacob, in typical Miller fashion, was known far and wide for a variety of gifts and contributions. Not only did he husband the widest variety of apples in the area (up to eighty-three varieties), but he was also known for planting apple trees along the roadside for the hungry traveler. He was widely known for his horticultural avocation, and people sought his advice on matters ranging from planting to preparing wills. He settled estates, organized disaster service groups, sat on bank boards, served on juries, started a home and school for orphans, and ministered to the poor in the mountains, carrying provender from garden, kitchen, and smokehouse on horseback.

Alta Elizabeth Schrock was born into this remarkable lineage in 1911, the daughter of Alvin and Amelia Miller Schrock. At that time they were members of the strongly religious Conservative Amish church. (The Conservative Amish split from the Old Order Amish in the 1890s.) Alta appeared, unlike most in the Miller tribe, "an unpromising and sickly child." She didn't walk until nearly two years of age, and due to her frailty her mother delayed her school attendance for several years until Alta's younger sister, Naomi, turned five and was able to take care of her eight-year-old sister in school.

Alta was raised in a milieu in which entrepreneurial self-help and communal solidarity were not mutually exclusive. Theological tenets like submission to the church and a nonresistant (pacifist) lifestyle were given expression in daily practice. Yet there was plenty of room for individual entrepreneurial activity within this context, given the basic need for agricultural and pioneering survival. The Amish farmer enjoyed rugged independence and had an open door to inventiveness and innovation. The Miller clan thus naturally displayed a healthy sense of entrepreneurship in a variety of ways. Somehow this did not militate against mutuality, interdependence, and communal values.

Interviewees also maintain that gender roles were less chauvinistic and fit into a more natural matrix appropriate to agrarian life. While the men managed the fields and the barns, the women managed the household, food processing, and even livestock, whether in making cheese or preparing goose feathers for pillows. In some ways the management of a home, its supplies and their processing, and its seasonal projects involved skills of organization and innovation unsurpassed by the demand on men in the fields. Thus in Alta's youth the family was a microcosm of the larger communal life; it was an interdependent partnership relying on dependable work, individual management skills, innovation, and creative dexterity. Entrepreneurial gifts were a necessity and woven into the fabric of everyday life.

Alta grew up in a benign, supportive, and nonjudgmental home. In interviews she claims that it is difficult to remember any criticism or resistance from parents to her aggressive pursuit of projects and pushing out of the boundaries of role and gender. The parents fostered instead a love for human beings and a delight in the natural world. Afternoons might see them picnicking by a creek. On a recent rural sojourn with her we stopped at an old bridge where she fondly reminisced, "Here my father would stop the car and say, 'Now children, be quiet and smell and look and listen.' "

The parental encouragement heightened an already deep natural inclination and love of nature within her. When on a Sunday afternoon visit to cousins the children joined in games with their counterparts, Alta would be found climbing rock ledges in the forest. Illness caused her to withdraw from school in the midst of the seventh grade, but while recuperating Alta embarked on a systematic study of the flora and fauna that existed within a fifteen-mile radius of home. One observer noted that "she learned the habits and the habitats of all things rooted and footed."

This love of nature, with its attendant curiosity and desire for interaction with it, tended to give rise to all manner of projects. From her early years Alta was known as a doer, an independent dreamer immersed in plans to enact her dreams. Her vibrant creative vision always gave birth to yet another project; nothing ever remained purely on the level of reflection for Alta. When she envisioned her "Thoreau's cabin" in the woods where she would live in nature, observe it, and write about it, her parents stated that they simply could not afford the lumber. Alta, however, discovered that her father had some delinquent receivables on his feed milling books. She obtained her father's permission to accept collections in lumber for her proposed cabin.[5]

In this cabin she penned the weekly nature columns and articles for the *Meyersdale Republican* which were instrumental in getting her a scholarship to Waynesburg College in 1932. The cabin, christened "The Sanctuary," became the center for her own nature programs, poetry readings, and private nature studies. Today her sister Ada vividly remembers Coleridge's "Rime of the Ancient Mariner" intoned to the flickering of an oil lamp and the rhythm of summer rain on the cabin roof.

Academic Career

Although illness had at times interrupted her schooling, and she was uncertain about continuing, a good friend convinced Alta to attend the high school in Salisbury. Not only was high school unusual for Amish Mennonites at the time, it was even more so for a young woman. Attendance required a four-mile walk each way as there was no school transportation. But she walked the rails those high school years, memorizing poetry, investigating nature along the way, learning new vocabulary, and imagining future projects.

A high school acquaintance recalls, "She promoted the organization of a biology club, established a natural history museum in the school basement, procured and organized the planting of several thousand spruce trees on designated land, landscaped the school grounds and wrote nature essays for local publication."[6] She spent many hours over a microscope and collecting stones, twigs, bark, butterflies, and moths. In a contest sponsored by several Pennsylvania counties, she won a twenty-dollar gold piece for her collection of several hundred medicinal plants.

Alta completed high school in three-and-a-half years but never received a diploma. Story has it that the authorities claimed, "We operate a four-year program, and you have only been here for three-and-a-half years and so we will not give you a diploma." This pattern of accelerated accomplishment has characterized her entire life. When at Waynesburg College the annual citations and awards were given, Schrock was named "Busiest Girl on Campus." Not only did she organize students in a host of extracurricular projects, she was also a lab assistant and hand-painted hundreds of slides of wild flowers.

Gender was never a barrier; pragmatics determined plan and method. To manage the tree-planting project she wore the practical attire of shirt, britches, and boots "because snakes and brambles dictated common sense." Alta was once spotted by a Mennonite bishop wearing such "men's" attire. Since this was contrary to church codes, the Schrock home soon received an admonitory visit from the bishops. Her father, a quiet man, never questioned Alta's motives but pondered the matter for some time. When other occasions brought the bishops on similar calls, such as to rebuke her father's cut of hair, he gently declared that "enough is enough" and left the Conservative Amish church to join the Mennonite church in Springs.

Alta's pursuit of a college education and then a doctorate in science—not in nursing or home economics—certainly broke new ground. It appears that she was the first American Swiss Mennonite woman to earn a Ph.D. She persisted in a man's world throughout her academic career at Waynesburg, Cincinnati, Kent State, Oberlin, and Pittsburgh, winning the respect and friendship of many professional men and women, some of them internationally known scholars. Nonetheless, when she applied for university teaching positions, numerous responses recognized her prodigious gifts and strong credentials before adding, "But we don't hire women."

At Bluffton College, Ohio, though busy as dean of women, dorm matron, and instructor of biology, her zest for improvement projects resulted in many accomplishments, including a college arboretum. But she remembers that "it was a difficult time for women." In 1946 she joined the Goshen College faculty in Indiana. Here too her gender wasn't naturally welcome. Some male faculty preferred not to share an office with a woman, but no man there at the time asked if a woman wanted to share an office with a man.

What is remarkable is that instead of becoming cynical or strident about gender attitudes in churches and in institutions of higher learning, she worked enthusiastically with men and women so long as the project was worthy, challenging, and added to the good of the human community. For her the vision and the related project were all. When asked how she kept the joy in teaching all those years, she responds: "Oh, every new class was like opening a surprising Christmas package, with its varied precious students coming alive to personal growth and knowledge. Students always energized me and then nothing else mattered."

While in Goshen she established the "Fliederhof," which became a symbol of Christian hospitality and warm fellowship for many Goshen students. The C. J. Gunden barn had been offered for sale, so Alta took an option on it, intending to move and restore it into a house and a place for student fellowship. When another prospective buyer inquired of the current owner, he was told that the barn would likely become available soon as "no woman can move that barn." But move it she did, and it became a "friendship house" which has been described as a place "where young people have fellowshipped, discussed problems pertinent to Christian youth, and sung and prayed."[7]

While in Goshen, Alta also became a founder of the Mennonite Youth Village, a halfway house for troubled youth. Its founding is directly traceable to discussions which occurred before the sunken Fliederhof fireplace. She engaged in fundraising for the Youth Village and later also for Goshen College. It appears that her fundraising efforts were so energetic that at one point Goshen received a call from her to "send more receipts." She had access and credibility to engage a diverse number of people. Even the Amish allowed her to present to them the mission of Mennonite Youth Village, a cause to which they subsequently donated.

A Multifaceted Entrepreneur

Alta Schrock's visionary, innovative, and entrepreneurial zest enlarged all the boundaries touching her life. She worked in the Mennonite church and many other denominations on a plethora of projects, boldly taking on roles traditionally reserved for men and then enthusiastically marshaling men to run boards to oversee yet another project. In addition to her career as teacher and mentor in academic institutions in Washington, D.C., Pennsylvania, Ohio, and Indiana, she worked with the Mennonite Central Committee in post-World War II refugee work. She also did historical research in Europe and was peace-making envoy to a fractious group of Mennonites in Saskatchewan, Canada. She approached each new event or project with a sense of holiness. Her Christian calling and vision, expressed in an entrepreneurial nature and methodology, knew no secular or private gain and no artificial boundaries.

It is impossible in a short chapter to describe adequately all the major projects which Schrock helped found in the Allegheny region and beyond after her return to the area in the 1950s. The following chronological list, however, gives some idea of the breadth of her pragmatic vision.

Alta researching wildflowers.

1957 — Springs, Pa., Historical Society
  — Springs Museum of Casselman Valley
1958 — Penn Alps Incorporated
  — Springs Folk Festival (an annual event)
1960 — Council of the Alleghenies (cofounder)
1961 — Casselman Chronicle
1963 — The Highland Association (cofounder)
  — Journal of the Alleghenies (cofounder and editor)
1965 — Vista Volunteer Program (community cofounder)
1967 — Spruce Forest Artisan Village
1976 — Christian Outreach of Maryland
1977 — Casselwood Corporation
1988 — Miller House and Anabaptist Peace Center
1991 — Friedensheim

In addition to her role in founding the above organizations, Schrock also served on numerous area service boards, such as the Garrett County Community Action, a variety of church and educational organizations, and countless ad hoc committees addressing various needs. One of Schrock's best-known and most characteristic enterprises has been Penn Alps Incorporated. The original idea was to provide an outlet (and hence needed income) for area craftspeople. A restaurant was added to increase visitation. A historic inn was purchased to house the restaurant and craft shop, and a craft village was later added on the adjacent property near Grantsville, Maryland.

Along with the marketing of handicrafts made by local craftspeople, Penn Alps has been instrumental in reviving early arts and crafts of the area, including hand-spinning, wool dyeing with vegetable dyes, hand-loom weaving, and so on. Another enterprise was Casselwood Furniture, a spin-off of Penn Alps which specialized in early American furniture that "reflect[ed] the culture of the Alleghenies."[8] Friedensheim is a recent venture that seeks in a rural context to provide a place of refuge and spiritual and physical renewal for residents of the Grantsville area.

Some acquaintances have affectionately referred to Alta as a "genetic fallout," embodying in magnificent measure the creative, inventive, and compassionate Miller traits. However, as if to justify this entrepreneurial Mennonite to God and the religious constituency, some of her Christian friends recount her life and her projects in passive terms. Almost all references to genes, personality, character, propensities, entrepreneurial zeal, and creative fireworks are submerged under a shroud of religious passivity. These accounts have God as the benign master puppeteer and Alta as the manipulated object. A set of dominant formulae emerges. "God spoke to Alta—God led Alta—Alta heard the call—God opened the doors—Alta obediently walked through—to God be all the glory."

Even Schrock's own written and spoken accounts refer both to herself and to God in the third person. Ironically, the omniscient author's viewpoint renders both Alta and God as somewhat predetermined and passive participants. The reason for this may lie in the fundamental unease a devout pietistic or Anabaptist-Mennonite ethos has with the individualistic entrepreneurial shaping of external reality.

But whatever the case, numerous acquaintances have commented that while Alta prays about a project at night, by morning she feels free to intervene and see to its happening. All those not joining her have simply not yet heard "the call." One associate remarked that in this she is like Martin Luther, who ostensibly said, "Pray as if working will not avail; work as if prayer will not avail."

One interviewee and longtime friend commented that virtually all of Alta's dreams for organizations and projects have been initially impossible; the possible she left to others. Again and again good analysts have presented their best and sincere proof. It seemed folly, for example, to propose opening a craft store, a restaurant, and an artisan village—Penn Alps—in a small rural community. All indicators pointed to other locations, other times, other methods, other financial conditions. But no mere opinions, analyses, budget evidence, or even outright scoffing deter her once she catches a vision. To enact her vision she uses every persuasion she can muster, even if the final clincher is that the Lord himself told her to tackle this project.

Not all her projects have been successful. Casselwood Furniture and even Christian Outreach of Maryland floundered and became potential disasters, resulting in unfortunate ill-will on the part of co-workers and financial backers. But even in financial failure and in the face of sound contrary advice, Schrock never admits to a mistake in the envisioning and "call" of a project. God has given her the vision; he will see it turn to the good. The delightful irony is that even those organizations that did not flourish were picked up by others and ended up "to the good."

Opinions differ as to why her projects have not always succeeded, but there is some agreement in seeing the problem at least partly in her management style. Because she has a need to control management and operations, good managers often have left early and a sound management philosophy has seldom been instituted in operations she controls. But this is only one side of her character. One ingenious strength of her approach is that once she has envisioned a project, she has always been able to gather a group ready to serve as a board of advisers. Thus while the project may be conceived individualistically and charismatically, it proceeds under communal and consensus structure through a selected group.

In many cases this has worked well. In cases where her own management style and refusal to heed sound management counsel created problems, she nonetheless has always been able to find boards to join her process, even if they have not always addressed the need for concerted board decision and action. Like many entrepreneurs, Schrock has struggled to reconcile her own vision with the advice of others, which she has typically sought through boards of directors.

A significant factor in her good relationships, even as an inveterate individualistic entrepreneur, lies in the nature of her theological perspective. Alta has maintained a conservative stance regarding theological language, creed, and expressions of piety in prayer, song, and speech. Her willingness to work in male-dominated leadership structures has made her a nonabrasive and contributory presence. In all projects she has used the "right" language—sincerely so—and chosen to defer to men for leadership on the boards. Alta has a keen diplomatic sense for timing the selection of battles and for the best stances and means to win them. One former co-worker and supporter commented that "she is a manipulator 'par excellence' and probably unaware of it."

Clearly Alta is more than a pragmatic developer of projects. The projects are the results of intensely felt visions and creatively imagined castles. But like Thoreau, her mysticism is in part otherworldly, in part inner-directed, in part rooted in the physical world about her. She went into the cabin in the woods not to escape from the world but to understand it lovingly and to fortify her spirit. And she came out of the woods to endow those visions with social and physical form. All her life these two elements, the mystic communion with nature and its Creator, and the pragmatics of giving concrete form to the visions for the good of society have pervaded her daily living.

In building the consensus necessary for establishing her projects, Alta normally sets out to establish consensus *in advance* of calling the exploratory and foundational meetings. Thus consensus does not always grow out of deliberations of "the gathered church," with its divergent gifts and views brought into play, but by handpicked people who agree with Schrock in advance. Critics and naysayers are simply not invited.

Before these first meetings Alta will already have spent much time and energy soliciting potential project members. Out of this pre-organized consensus will often emerge a formal meeting, a chartered organization, a constitution, and a board of directors. When Alta claims that she works on an "Anabaptist consensus model," and invokes that approach once she has her select "fellowship" gathered for a particular organization, the premises become confused. She achieves legitimate and invaluable consensus similar to that gained by interested persons forming a club or a corporation by purchasing shares but unlike a more traditional meeting of the gathered church community.[9]

With the exception of organizations such as the Council of the Alleghenies, a cofounded and joint venture, Alta has seldom appeared in the initial official leadership positions on the board. Questions involving leadership roles—the sense of consensus and the need for direct involvement of men from church and community—she has met by taking a backseat in the board structure. This is not done cynically, for Alta genuinely respects business, organizational, and positional influence men can bring to her projects. For over three decades her projects would have been impossible without the key involvement of good men.[10]

Asked about this initial pattern of taking a backseat, she replies, "I did that to get the widest possible base of consensus and involvement for a project." The same approach, she adds, has worked in church conference work and in MCC. Asked how she gained consent on a certain matter she smiles and says, "I got [paramount church leader]

H. S. Bender to agree and to propose it." While teaching at Goshen College she also persuaded Bender, at that time dean of the Mennonite Biblical Seminary, to have her teach a course in "Agriculture for Service." He caught the vision, so she taught a class of fifteen men, the only woman in a male-dominated seminary.

Thus over the decades she has been able to locate and involve a large company of influential men in her many works. Her vision and her dynamic personality put her in the position of "master arranger." Many people agree that without her unique methodology of engineering consensus, and her ability to gain the involvement of key men, all her visions might have only resulted in a single dynamic sewing circle. Today, moving with the times, women form an integral part of leadership on her boards and committees.

As innovator, however, Alta has also realized that projects tend toward inertia, if not stalemate, at the hands of voluntary board members of nonprofit organizations. Since most of her projects have been entrepreneurial in methodology—involving capital, risk, and individual initiatives—how does she keep the entrepreneurial ferment alive?

Here another pattern emerges. The records of various organizations reveal that after the first several board meetings are conducted, boards on which Alta is member but not officer, someone proposes that Alta be appointed executive secretary of the organization—a position distinct from secretary treasurer. Although at times the language seems to indicate that this is to be reviewed annually, the term in fact becomes indefinite if not permanent. In the same way she appears as permanent museum curator, director of development, and so on, in other contexts.

The purpose of the executive secretary's position is to have someone with a controlling position on location. As such, in the Penn Alps situation, she was given check-signing authority and other implicit decision-making powers. When interviewed about this arrangement she commented, "It seemed important to the board to have someone on location to sign checks, keep things moving along, and to control the project." The defining lines between board and administrative duties often became completely blurred. Even today the boards she is involved with find it difficult to be visionary, policy-oriented, governing bodies. As entrepreneur she has spent a lifetime crossing over all the lines that make for a clear and effectively structured operations.

Alta has also kept control of projects by driving countless miles and donating immense time visiting with board members on the way she feels things should go at the next meeting. Once she has agreement, she has someone else present the agreed (her) view at the next board meeting.

Once when someone noted that Alta was uncharacteristically quiet and humble at board meetings, another responded, "That's because she's done her talking and convincing in advance." Visitors have nonetheless been impressed with her stated desire to do "whatever the board decides." One former colleague said with a twinkle in his eye, "She used every possible approach to good effect. Even when she got us to agree that we need to pray, she more often had in mind that the outcome would be for us to see the light, not for her to receive new light."

Over the years management responses to Alta's style have varied. With some administrators she has been a daily presence. In fact for many years she lived in the inn above the Penn Alps Restaurant and Craft Store, thus having immediate access to all operations and employees. Since Alta was engaged in virtually every sphere of activity, administrators found that a completely professional management profile was impossible to achieve.

Some managers, recognizing her constant involvement in operations, have settled for some specific areas as their own and allowed the other areas to be managed in ad hoc fashion. At Penn Alps one manager became comfortable primarily in the office; another chose to be head cook; another focused on buildings and grounds; others floated around amiably humoring Alta and the board.

Managers never become fully empowered because they need to interact with Alta and the varied signals she gives on a day-to-day basis. In some instances the classic manager-board reversals have occurred—managers have functioned more as board members while Alta, the board member, has functioned more as general manager. But over the years management according to a clear constitution, job descriptions, budgets, policies, and monthly board decisions have never been part of the matrix.

Alta has nonetheless found and attracted good people; her vision and her boundless creativity and force of personality become magnetic. But the pattern remains the same. At one juncture a new administrator was needed at Penn Alps. Again the Lord had shown her the right candidate for just this emergency. On her urging and conviction the man was hired. Not long after he was installed, board members received urgent calls from Alta. Now it seemed a serious mistake had been made, and both Alta and the Lord had changed their minds. The man would have to go.

"Why?" they asked.

"He's not for us—he's a military man."

"How so?"

"Well, he gives orders, he doesn't take them."

In some businesses, such as Casselwood Furniture, there was a constant stream of managers. Although relationships have generally remained cordial and some good friendships established (it is practically impossible not to like Alta), managers frequently have left because they were not allowed to function as managers. Although hired as managers, they soon discovered they had to consult her for extra hinges for one cabinet or a needed gallon of paint for another. Managers at Casselwood were not allowed to plan inventory, assembly process, or long-term marketing. If they questioned these limitations, a board chair would soon counsel that Alta ultimately "calls all these shots."

When managers have been given periodic free reign the results have been often and predictably disastrous. In each case managers have not been given a clear job description or trained. No solid guidelines and goals have been established or firm policies agreed on. Consequently since the board does not have a clear picture and methodology, managers cannot be evaluated and guided. So people see a seventy-nine-year-old woman driving the Casselwood Furniture truck to Oakland for lumber because "they [managers] just don't know how to buy lumber. The last time I sent a manager he purchased far too much."

Potentially effective Casselwood managers were never allowed to flourish. But when recovering alcoholics or rehabilitating drug addicts needed work, they were not only hired but given responsibility. Furniture disappeared, funds were mismanaged, and these people were dismissed. Promptings of the heart overruled sound, objective management approaches.

One consequence of this founder's sincere, free-wheeling entrepreneurial style, substituting for management and sound board governance, has been a string of financial emergencies. Frequently after much prayer with others and crisis solicitation, a friend will help bail out a situation. In 1985 the financial indicators predicted the demise, if not bankruptcy, of Penn Alps. At the time there were still no basic financial management tools in place. No real financial statements were available for use by the board. There were no cost ratios of labor and supplies, no inventory controls, no real menu planning, and no short- or long-term strategic plan in place. Yet that very year Alta's vision for a restored Markley Log House was in progress, with yet other projects on the burner. The boundless visionary and entrepreneurial spirit always prevailed undimmed.

The traits discussed here mirror the classic entrepreneurial prototype. However, the unique aspect of the Alta Schrock phenomenon is that while she has laid the foundations for her "castles" through entrepreneurial modes and techniques, the product has never been private gain. Not only has she not profited from them, but Alta has donated virtually all her time to the many projects. In fact when she was gainfully employed at Frostburg State University, 1960-77, she used this income to support her projects.

Someone calculated recently that if all the time and energy Schrock donated to all the organizations were assessed, the total would exceed $1,000,000. All her work has been characterized by its biblical and Christian humanitarian purpose. At a recent testimonial, Alta stated the *raison de'être* for her life and her projects: "To minister to people in the spiritual, economic, educational, and physical aspects of life."

A Storied Individual

Stories abound of Schrock's humor, compassion, creativity, and generosity of spirit. In one, several interested friends were dining with Alta when two expressed an idea they had for a project that involved her. Alta had not thought of it to date and now disagreed with it. They explained that they had given much serious thought and prayer to the project and now believed it was God's will.

Rapping the table emphatically, Alta exclaimed, "You're barking up the wrong tree."

Whereupon a listener remarked, "Why is it, Alta, that when you talk to God it's praying but when another does it, it's barking up the wrong tree?"

The room erupted in laughter, the heartiest coming from Alta. After the hilarity Alta proceeded to outline God's "real plan" in the matter.

Alta has often declared that in life's issues calendar and clock should be of lesser significance. She has a system of filing correspondence, journals, and memorabilia in what someone has called a "fluid proximity, spontaneous accessibility, and visual periphery." Her correspondence is pigeonholed about her rocker and telephone in an ever ascending oval cockpit.

A story bears out her tendency not to live by the calendar. One day she noted in her mail an announcement of a famous speaker's appearance at a nearby city. She and a friend journeyed there for the advertised time. It seemed they were early for their session at the local Holiday Inn, so they waited. But no one came, so they approached the desk clerk again stating their reasons for being there. Would the clerk check other inns to see if the session had been scheduled elsewhere in the city. Others had no record either. Finally the manager asked to see the brochure advertising the session. Reading it he stiffened and in an accusatory tone used for mere pranksters he exclaimed, "Girls, this session happened five years ago!"

At a business luncheon in eastern Maryland a business executive discovered that I was acquainted with Alta. He informed the table guests about this extraordinary woman and added, "Do you know what that woman did to me? She was the first person ever publicly to get me to my knees. I was living in Cumberland at the time in about 1959 and she would call anyone that came to mind for volunteer help in projects involving some dream about an Allegheny craft store and restaurant. When I arrived I was given an apron, a brush, and a bucket. I spent well past midnight scrubbing floors."

One evening I dropped in at Alta's house for a visit. After welcoming me she added, "Won't you come with me? I need to deliver a kitchen appliance to someone I'm helping in a difficult time." We loaded a small refrigerator onto an old truck and headed into the windy, rainy night, Alta at the wheel.

En route Alta told me of a young man in difficulty with drugs, alcohol, and the law. Alta had sought him out and become involved to the point that the judge, on Alta's recommendation, offered probation. Among other involvements, Alta became cosigner of his bank account. When we arrived at the apartment he was not home but neighbors suggested where we might find him. Following Alta into a smoky, dimly lit country bar, we walked among the tables looking for this young friend. Once we found him, Alta sat on a bar stool and discussed his affairs, oblivious to her surroundings.

In many visits and interviews I found great affection for Alta and appreciation for her many projects. Even those who have questioned her operational and management methods recognize her unique and immense contributions, such as the following.

In 1958 when she returned to the Allegheny area and opened a craft store, Alta was a pioneer in instituting a self-help philosophy as a complete program. She located artisans in the hills and encouraged them to produce more of the crafts they were gifted at or interested in learning. Then she arranged loans for access to spinning wheels, woodworking equipment, quilting frames. She provided the market outlet as well. Remembering this she commented, "You'd be amazed what people can do if you show them how."

She established formal classes for artisans to learn a trade. If they were unable to come because of a handicap, Alta arranged for visits to the homes. A Baltimore *Sunday Sun* reporter summed it up: "She has worn out one automobile, three sets of tires and a dozen pair of shoes seeking out mountain craftsmen, interesting them in her idea, getting them to work, and setting up markets to sell their products." To date, over 2000 Allegheny craftspeople—a fifth of them handicapped—have sent their wares for sale at the Penn Alps Craft Store.

She became a shining example to young people looking for meaning in life. To some contemporary church people she appeared an eccentric. But during the Vietnam War years and Johnson's Great Society times, many Mennonite young people were becoming aware that social justice was part of the biblical message. Many young people found their local churches too calm if not indifferent to the pain and suffering of the larger world. One returning Mennonite college student and war protester states that "Alta seemed to me to be the only Mennonite, and a woman at that, out there on the social and economic justice scene. I realized at that moment the dynamo at the center of all her work and life. She didn't wear her faith on her sleeve." Soon he too became involved in a work putting belief and values into action.

Another returning college student who found Alta a key encouragement in choosing a social service profession testified that "Alta made her life her argument and statement of faith. . . . Hers was a shoe-leather Christianity . . . for me she stood tall even sitting down. She was not ashamed or apologetic for being a Mennonite, a woman, a Christian, or a Miller descendant but lived out her vision and faith in all these. She was no respecter of persons or of issues, relating to the down and out, the university professor, the dishwasher, the Washington politician, the shoeless, the children and youth—all with the same joy and positive outlook to innate potential."

Conclusion

Alta touched on the keystone of her life and faith when she concluded her induction speech at the Maryland Women's Hall of Fame ceremony. "Although I don't feel worthy of this honor which the governor and this organization confer on me today, I would like to share with you what lay at the foundation of all the Lord permitted me to do. And it is the way the Creator wants all of us to live and work. I did it all for the greatest resource in these mountains: for the people in all walks of life, for their economic, spiritual, social, aesthetic, and educational good. As people are of real value so we value their real stories, their history, their habitats, their natural environment, the religious gatherings, [and] their ability to generate economic self-help. . . ."

Although many of her projects have benefited the region immensely and will compound that benefit for subsequent generations, there are people who have negative feelings about her work. Some no doubt have fastened on some aspect of her fundraising or promotion of a project, or have been puzzled by her various juggling acts. Seeing the larger picture is not easy. One pastor commented, "People somehow have a need to see a symmetrical picture of their heroes. The real biblical heroes would also make them uneasy."

Alta responds to this situation by saying, "It's almost impossible to be a pioneer and not be misunderstood." Alta has clearly been a catalyst, and catalytic reactions can be volatile. "I believe I was a fire builder, putting fires under people, getting them to move . . . but I was only an instrument. Where there is no vision the people perish, as the Bible says. The Lord gave me a vision and I was able to rally the people around it."

Dr. Alta Schrock is not symmetrical and perfect, not a papier-mâché saint. She is a person who has dared to achieve great things for and with her fellow humans on this earth. So how can a mere teller of lives weigh the spirit? For the mystery and magic of spirit is that it always transcends the material world and its rationally decipherable processes. Alta Schrock may not have been a magician, but the lamps she rubbed have shed a profound and enriching light.

4

Jacob Redekop:
An "Up-Front"
Mennonite Entrepreneur

BY VIC KRAHN

If the career of Alta Schrock represents a tendency on the part of at least some Swiss Mennonites toward humble submission to the faith community, Jacob Redekop (b. 1930) embodies the strongly independent character often seen among Russian Mennonites. Yet Jacob also has, in his own way, strongly supported the work of the church. His experience of alienation from both the legal system and some members of the church community exhibits some of the problems inherent in juggling the values of the world of business and those of a strong faith community.

JACOB REDEKOP is a successful Mennonite entrepreneur who does not mince words. He is not afraid to admit that he enjoys making money and living relatively well, and that successful businesspeople have an important role to play in the Mennonite church and in building Mennonite institutions.

Jacob exudes blunt integrity in all he does. If on the one hand he appears the classic self-interested entrepreneur, on the other he does not shy away from stewardship responsibilities associated with his faith, and he actively participates in the building of Mennonite institutions. His disapproval of the legal system as a proper form of conflict resolution among Christians, despite his own reluctant use of the system, illustrated Jacob's candor regarding anything he is involved in. Honest disclosure of the truth (as he sees it), however painful, is a guiding principle for Jacob.[1]

Early Years

Jacob Redekop was born on October 29, 1930, in the village of Nieder Chortiza, in a Mennonite colony situated in the southern region of the Ukraine. He was second of four children (Mary, Jacob, John and Peter) born to Jacob and Mary (Gunther) Redekop. Life in the Ukraine was harsh, as both parents had to work from morning till night in order to keep enough food on the table.

Jacob's first distinct childhood memory reaches back to when he was five years old and to an incident that points to an adventurous, risk-taking character. He had been allowed to accompany his parents to a field some distance from their house, where grain was being harvested. Soon he became a nuisance, so his parents sent him home with someone who was leaving in a horse-drawn wagon. They dropped him off near his home, but instead of walking the short distance to his house he turned and headed back to the field to have another ride home. He loved animals and had thoroughly enjoyed the ride. He took a roundabout route so no one would spot him, and by the time he arrived the only person there was a night-watchman. He eventually made it home, but the deed did not go unpunished.

The severe living conditions of Jacob's childhood worsened in 1938, when his father was taken by the Soviet secret police and imprisoned for eight months. Jacob's father was one of two men from the village, out of eighty, who came back to their homes; the rest were sent to Siberia. As times were tough, his father decided that he would sell the lumber from their barn to raise extra cash. While tearing down

the barn a beam fell on his back, breaking it and permanently dam-
aging his spinal cord. This had an important effect upon Jacob, as his
father relied on Jacob's physical and financial strength until Jacob was
in his twenties.

The family left Russia in 1943 and lived in Dresden, Germany, for
a few months, until the German government sent them to work on
farms in Yugoslavia. In 1944 they left Yugoslavia for Austria, where at
the age of fourteen Jacob dug trenches for the German army. This lasted for only four weeks, as the war was ending, and Jacob was fortunate enough to make it back to his family.

As the German army retreated, the Redekop family went with it,
hoping to make it to the Western zone and avoid Siberia. They managed to reach Tamsweg, the location of a German prisoner of war
camp. Here the Redekops lived with six other families in a burned-out
factory. To survive the Redekop boys caught loose horses and either
traded them to the farmers or killed them for food.

From Tamsweg they made their way to Salzburg, where the Red
Cross provided them with food and a place to sleep. The Red Cross
also obtained clearance for the Redekops and many other displaced
Mennonites to go to Holland, the country from which their ancestors
had emigrated.

In December 1947, the family sailed to Canada. On landing in
Halifax they boarded a train for Winnipeg, Manitoba. Jacob Redekop's
uncle lived in a little village near Steinbach. For the seventeen-year-
old Jacob, the following months were a time of transition from childhood to adulthood. While Jacob's father and two younger brothers
took over a little farm in Kliefeld, Manitoba, and his sister worked in
Winnipeg, Jacob worked in a lumber camp in northern Ontario.

With only a minimal amount of clothing and old thin blankets,
Jacob traveled to camp in the back of a pickup truck, in the middle of a
Canadian winter. As he was the youngest (and shortest) in the camp,
Jacob found himself at the bottom of the pecking order. Each small
shack had a wood stove and a limited number of bunks. The Canadian
boys slept on the top bunks with their warm feather blankets near the
hot stove. Jacob slept on the ground with his three thin blankets. On
many a frosty morning Jacob woke to a frozen pillow. Being a sociable
person among quiet men who had no social life to speak of, Jacob was
lonely.

This lumber camp experience was the first real challenge Jacob remembers as setting a course for his life. In comparison to those first few months in Canada, the struggles Jacob later experienced were minimal. By April, when Jacob left the camp, he had saved about $450, which went a long way toward paying off the $850 debt his family had incurred in their passage to Canada.

That same month the family moved to Yarrow, B.C., where they spent the summer picking berries, working in the hop yards, and re-building river dikes. By the fall of 1948 they had saved enough money to pay off the Canada trip debt and make a down payment on their first farm in the Clearbrook area. Jacob continued to help his family fi-nancially over the next few years. His jobs included working at CP Rail, a sawmill, and Roger's Sugar.

Along with the responsibility of a job, Jacob was obligated to work on the family farm whenever possible, due to his father's crip-pling. It was not until Jacob reached age twenty-one that he began keeping the money he made, although he would lend it to his father at low interest.

During these first few years in Canada, Jacob and cousin Jake Wall were involved in various activities to raise extra cash. For exam-ple, they would butcher a few cows and peddle the meat, or buy pota-toes in Cloverdale and sell them in Clearbrook. Their families needed every penny each member could raise. While working at these odd jobs, Jacob knew his true goal was to become a businessman. Once he began dreaming about entering business, he could not get the thought out of his mind, because every day that he realized he hated working for other people.

Farming

Early in 1954, Jacob's father offered him a brooder barn where he could raise chickens to earn extra money. When Jacob and Hilda Ol-fert decided in summer 1954 to marry, Jacob's father gave him $3,000 to help them buy a little farm. The five-acre farm, with its old house, was bought for $5,500. Jacob borrowed an extra $1,000 from the bank and built his first chicken barn for 500 chickens.

For the next sixteen years Jacob continually expanded his chicken business. However, in 1957 the price of eggs was low and various diseases afflicted his chickens. Jacob's major buyer went bankrupt, leaving him with a large debt. Throughout this difficult time, Jacob supplemented the farm income by working at mills and on a pipeline, completing all his farmwork in the early morning and late at night. Jacob acknowledges that during these years his wife did much of the work on the farm, in addition to almost singlehandedly raising their five children (Rick, Ruth, Ernie, Rob, and James).

In 1965 Jacob and his brother John started an egg grading station, which involved grading, packing, and selling their own eggs. They continued to expand their own layer production capacity to produce enough eggs for their grading plant. Throughout most of the 1960s and 1970s, the two brothers were the largest egg producers west of Ontario, with 150,000 layers.

The egg grading business turned out to be more of a headache than a profitable business, as the brothers often had to undersell, which meant financial losses. However, the egg processing plant paid off in an indirect way. To retain a large share of the egg market, the two brothers had increased their egg production. Thus when the egg marketing boards were established in 1964, their farms increased in value. In addition to managing the grading plant, Jacob was selling poultry equipment and medications. He acknowledges that he would have been better off monetarily if he had been solely involved in selling equipment and medications.

Diversification

The poultry business was only the first step in Jacob's business career. In the late 1960s, Jacob and his brother John had expanded their business activities to include building and land development. It was at this time that the Wall & Redekop Corporation was started by Pete Wall (Jacob's first cousin), and Pete and John Redekop (siblings) as the major shareholders. Jacob Redekop became the next largest shareholder with 40,000 shares. The Wall & Redekop Corporation initially owned a lumberyard and was involved in building apartments. Later land development was included.

Jacob found this time difficult because of his independent nature and his desire to control whatever venture he is involved in. Jacob describes himself as being "too much of an independent person to report to others. I myself have always wanted to be independent because in this way I can involve my children in any way I want."

The disturbing element of Jacob's relationship with the Wall & Redekop Corporation was one of ethics, not working relationships. The directors of the company were paying themselves substantial wages and directors fees, building up large inventories in apartment buildings, and traveling for personal pleasure—yet charging all this to the company expense accounts. These practices meant that dividends for other shareholders fell below expectations.

After discussing this situation with his brothers, a deal was reached whereby Jacob sold his shares to them at one dollar above market value, which was half the book value of the shares. When Jacob was bought out in 1978, he had been in the corporation for ten years. After averaging out the income from the money he had invested in the corporation, he netted a one percent return.

In another venture, Jacob acquired 45 percent of the shares in a chick hatchery business. Mickey Sanders, a young Catholic man who owned the other shares, was a good manager who invested cautiously. Though Jacob and Sanders operated on different levels, Jacob being the visionary and Sanders the practical manager, they always resolved their differences. This turned out to be the best partnership Jacob has had, because even with his brothers there have been times of difficulty resolving issues due to philosophical differences. The hatchery business was a solid investment with steady profits, and it was not until 1987 that Jacob sold his shares in the enterprise.

In the mid-1970s, Jacob and his brother John sold the egg processing plant, by then the second largest in British Columbia, to Kelly Douglas (Super-Value). Jacob had a three-year management contract with them, but by the time he was six months into the contract, he knew it was time to get out. First the union came in, which caused new workplace dynamics. Jacob had worked with some employees for seven or eight years, and now the union told the employees not to talk to him. Second, Jacob realized that he was "in over his head" bureaucratically, finding it difficult to write the many reports the head office demanded. "I asked them to relieve me. This was done within six weeks. This was the best thing that happened to me. It almost destroyed me. I got myself into something, it was more than I could bite." While Jacob and his brother lost $5000 in the sale of the plant, they had created a new outlet for their eggs.

After selling the egg processing plant, Jacob concentrated on developing Triple-R-Construction. The company consisted of Jacob, his brother John, and Berend Reitsma, Jacob's foreman from the egg processing plant. It became involved in everything from building houses and rental apartments to developing smaller subdivisions. Jacob received a good income from this company, enabling him to spend more time with his family.

Since the Wall & Redekop Corporation had a lumberyard, and his brothers were now major shareholders, they wanted Jacob to buy all of his supplies from them. The difficulty with this arrangement was that Jacob was charged more for the materials because they had to be delivered from the lumberyard in Vancouver to Clearbrook, where most of Jacob's developments were located. Jacob could have purchased the same materials cheaper from a lumberyard in Clearbrook.

For this reason Jacob and Don Martin jointly opened their own lumberyard in Clearbrook. Jacob's only regret concerning this venture is that he never invited brother John to participate in the business. Jacob concludes that he has probably paid for this mistake, as the lumberyard has never been exceptionally profitable. Jacob attempts to live by the principle that "what goes around must come around." He believes omitting John has come around to haunt him many times.

During the 1970s, Jacob formed numerous companies and partnerships. With the creation of these companies Jacob recognized that he had to become more selective when taking on partners. "I found . . . that my partnerships were the type where I was always the main source of supply, and the blood to keep the heartbeat going. It was [at] this time of my life that I realized that if I was to continue in business I would have to form different types of partnerships." Thus Jacob concluded some of his partnerships, allowing him to be independent once again.

While the profits in the lumberyard were never substantial, they were steady. However, in the early 1980s the recession caused a significant slowdown which nearly wiped out many of Jacob's business ventures. The lumberyard was the first of Jacob's businesses to experience financial difficulty, first with a $500,000 loss in accounts receivable. Jacob felt he could not approach his brothers for help since he had formed the lumberyard against their wishes. Added to this was the financial stress of sustaining some of Jacob's numerous business partners who had become very weak. As the opportunities arose, Jacob severed these business relationships.

The early 1980s were tough, not only due to the losses in the lumberyard but also because Jacob was part of a group of businessmen who had committed themselves to relocating the Mennonite Educational Institute, a private Mennonite high school. Development of a multi-unit residential complex was begun on the former school property, and shortly after construction on the second phase began, the recession hit. For about a year interest rates were 22 percent, which resulted in interest payments of $20,000 a month. In addition, Jacob was nearing completion of building his home, which was costing him half a million dollars.

The difficulties of these years were a new experience for Jacob. While in business he had only encountered short economic slowdowns, nothing of this magnitude. Until this point, whatever Jacob's companies had been involved in had been profitable. Jacob had been careless in the sense that he had left himself wide open for disaster, as each company was heavily financed to allow maximum expansion. Jacob made these years even tougher for himself by refusing to ask others for help.

The banks were now hesitant to lend Jacob more money, and they requested reports every three months. At one point Jacob became so tired of their demands that he responded, "Why not leave me alone and let me try to get rid of these problems rather than sitting and working out statements?" Jacob could not afford to have an accountant draw up the financial statements or projections, nor did he have anyone on payroll capable of this. Jacob had to complete the statements himself, which meant they were written with only a rudimentary understanding of accounting practices. Fortunately the local bank managers, who trusted and believed that he would keep his word and pay back his debts, gave Jacob the breathing room he needed to make it through.

To reduce the debt load it was necessary for Jacob to sell some of his best properties. However, his problems only escalated when this resulted in a tax bill for Jacob and his brother John of over $1,000,000. The positive effect of this was that they had lost such a considerable amount of money that they could write off the majority of the tax bill! Jacob was worried that the tax department would choose to assess him. He knew that would put him in a desperate situation, since he had pulled $400,000 out of the company to build the family house when the market was at its peak.

This nightmare was realized in 1989, when Jacob was audited by the tax department. The audit took three months to complete, due to the many partnerships and the way in which money had been shuffled around. By the time it was over, Jacob owed Revenue Canada $500,000.

Community Work

Throughout his life Jacob has been involved in what he terms "community work," which he defines as anything that concerns the Mennonite community. All of Jacob's community work has been church related. He has been involved with the Mennonite Educational Institute (MEI), Columbia Bible College (CBC), the Mennonite Foundation (a charitable Mennonite organization), and three Mennonite congregations. The primary foci of these involvements have been finances and construction projects.

Jacob was on the MEI Board for ten years, during which time the new school building was being constructed. Jacob's interest in this project was not only the well-being and future of the MEI but also financial gain. It was this project which almost caused Triple-R Construction to go bankrupt. Jacob was also one of three individuals instrumental in starting Friends of MEI, an organization which donated $380,000 toward building the new MEI school building. In addition to their monetary support, they shared their construction expertise and business knowledge.

As a board member of the Mennonite Foundation for thirteen years, Jacob has been able to witness the organization grow. He was vice-chair for two years, chair for three years, and director for four years. The members wanted him to be chair again, but Jacob declined. He felt there were others better suited for the job.

Jacob's involvement with the Columbia Bible College (CBC—a joint Mennonite Brethren/General Conference Mennonite venture in Clearbrook) has been in an advisory role. In recent years the college has substantially expanded its physical plant, and Jacob has been involved in this work. His involvement in his local churches has been either with church finances or building projects. Jacob hesitates to take on the role of chair in committees because he knows that involves writing reports. If he takes such a position, his wife, Hilda, has to help write the reports. Since Jacob puts off the task until the last minute, this usually becomes an inconvenience for Hilda.

The Friends of the Conference (of the Mennonites in British Columbia) was a committee Jacob was instrumental in forming. He was frustrated by the lack of direction and action the Conference Missions and Service Committee displayed, and the hesitation exhibited by the Finance committee whenever church planting was discussed. Jacob's dissatisfaction led him to see Peter Kehler, the conference minister, with whom he discussed supporting the conference in an informal way.

In the beginning of 1988 the Friends of the Conference became a reality. There were eight couples at the initial supper meeting, and after four meetings attendance was over 100. Jacob points out that it is not for economic reasons that they need 100 members, as any one of them could donate substantial amounts of money. The purpose of the group is to have fun, listen to a speaker and special music, raise money for the conference, and enjoy the fellowship and support of other businesspeople.

To date the Friends of the conference have raised over $60,000 for the church planting programs of the Conference of Mennonites in British Columbia. They have also committed themselves to raising between $30,000 and $50,000 a year, which is budgeted for a church planter. These monies are not included in the conference budget but are channeled through the conference treasury as part of the books. The first venture the Friends of the Conference have committed themselves to is a church building program in Vernon, B.C., where the money will be offered as an interest-free loan.

Jacob has also found support and enjoyment by attending the annual Entrepreneur Meetings held in Kansas and Arizona. Jacob sees this gathering of businesspeople as one of the more positive experiences which businesspeople can have in Mennonite circles.

In 1988 the Canadian Conference fundraiser approached Jacob and his brothers Pete and John to see if they would liquidate a $250,000 debt against the conference office building in Winnipeg. After checking to make sure that the building in question was well-built, the brothers agreed to liquidate the debt. Jacob is rather modest about himself being used as an example of business support for the church, but he is convinced that the role which businesspeople play in the continuation and support of the work of the Mennonite conferences needs to be recognized. Without the businesspeople willing to put their funds behind projects, the conferences would not have grown in the same way.

Jacob and his brother John have always prioritized their support of Mennonite Institutions. First is the local church, followed by the B.C. Conference, the Canadian Conference, and finally the General (North American) Conference. Jacob finds it frustrating when projects which do not make sense or have not been properly researched get steamrolled through the institutional network, leaving the conference to face the consequences. The Mennonite Central Committee (MCC, a Mennonite relief agency) is also given top priority in Jacob's giving since it was this organization which assisted his family in Europe.

Jacob does not believe in supporting organizations in which he has little voice and is therefore selective when donating money to non-Mennonite institutions. Jacob is committed to supporting the Mennonite institutions, as he considers this the primary way the Mennonite faith is maintained. Three non-Mennonite organizations which Jacob has supported include the Terry Winter organization, the local Community Services, and the National Institute for the Blind.

In responding to the philosophical "question of stewardship" Jacob expressed some frustration. First, during the recession of the early eighties Jacob continued to give at the same level as he had before experiencing financial hardship. He continued to meet the financial commitments he had made to his home congregation, Emmanuel Mennonite Church. Jacob points out that the most difficult people to collect money from were those least affected by the recession. Jacob's bankers considered him foolish to continue giving to the church at such a high rate when he had to borrow an additional amount each month to meet his interest payments.[2]

In the last five years Jacob's stewardship level has ranged between 10 and 20 percent of his income. This is not something which Jacob advertises, yet he is willing to share this information if someone asks. Jacob realizes it is easier for him to give $10,000 or $20,000 than it is for many others to give $2,000. If Jacob is expecting to collect some monies for a charitable cause, he deems it imperative that he be the first to write out his check, and if others want to know how much he gave, they have that right.

Jacob adopted this principle from his father, who collected money for numerous organizations. When fundraising opportunities arose, Jacob's father always went to his sons first, telling them that they needed to make a donation. Jacob now does this with his own children, as he wants to ensure that his children are following through on their commitments.

Unsurprisingly, Jacob has never heard any opposition to his giving of large sums of money to the various Mennonite institutions. Where Jacob has encountered negative responses is in relation to his standard of living, as people believe he does not have the right to live at his level. The estimated value of Jacob's home, on top of a hill overlooking the Fraser Valley, exceeds $500,000. Jacob boasts that the combination of building and location make it one of the best homes in the Abbotsford area. Jacob admits he has a problem justifying the house from a stewardship perspective. For vehicles, Jacob limits the amount he invests, choosing in the past to own three vehicles which total $100,000 rather than buying one Mercedes which alone is worth that amount. This is one area in which Jacob has made a conscious decision to limit his spending. However, he admits that he has of late overstepped his own boundaries by buying his wife a new Jaguar.

Various individuals have challenged Jacob's concept of stewardship. They insist that if he makes a million dollars a year, he should be willing to donate all of his post-tax dollars, except for $50,000 (the average wage of a member of their church), to charitable causes. Jacob views this rationale as naive for numerous reasons. First, why should he take all of the risks involved in making this kind of money, and not benefit or enjoy it except in a limited way? Second, there would not be any money to invest and to back up those investments if something went wrong. If he lived by this principle he would have lost everything in the early eighties and would not have had an opportunity to recover his losses. Had he lost everything, would there have been church members willing to extend him the amount of credit needed to get back into development? Jacob's guess is that no one would have made such an offer.

Jacob does not feel he uses wealth to achieve status. He has many friends who do not share his income level. While Jacob takes pleasure in giving, he recognizes that part of his motivation comes from being able to live a good and comfortable life, and he is honest about it.

Congregational Involvement

For the past ten years Jacob has been an active member of the finance and building committees of the Emmanuel Mennonite Church. Jacob's responsibility as a finance committee member has included meeting the church budget. He approaches members who are able to give on a larger scale, as he feels that some of the people who are salaried are not comfortable discussing their giving practices with him. Jacob finds it disturbing when families whose joint incomes range from $50,000 to $100,000 do not respond positively to requests for donations. Jacob's impression is that these individuals consider it the responsibility of families like his to bear the majority of the budget requirements of the church.

Jacob is aware that some people resent him because of his wealth. Such sentiments are expected, but he feels they create a problem when people accuse him of using his financial resources to gain power in the church. "Wealth would give me power if I wanted to purposely withdraw my finances and say look, if you do not do this then I will do that. I have never used that power," he asserts. "I will not say that I never have [used finances as power], because I am sure that it has come out sometime. I am quite noisy when I speak out and I would say that some people are probably scared of me. I would not want this to happen, and no one should be scared of me."

Jacob's comments indicate a dilemma faced by many Christian entrepreneurs. In business their success depends on aggressive, decisive behavior. The church community operates more by consensus and seeks to give all individuals, regardless of ability, a chance to be heard, which can make for a tedious decision-making process. It is sometimes difficult to move between these two worlds.

Business Ethics

While suspicion of successful businesspeople is present both in the Mennonite world and in the wider society, Jacob respects most people in business and does not deal with those he does not respect. He knows business and nonbusiness people alike who, whether they are selling a product or service, try to wring out of each person the last possible penny. Jacob does not identify with this attitude, one he is convinced does not belong in Christian business.

Jacob's concern to demonstrate fairness in business dealings is illustrated by events in the early 1980s, when he was experiencing financial difficulty. At that time many elderly Mennonites wanted to purchase a condominium in the high-rise complex being built on the site of the old MEI. When the economy crashed, and with it the local real-estate market, these elderly people were left with their homes up for sale and a nonrefundable down payment holding their condominium. Despite his legal right to do so, Jacob did not take advantage of their situation. Instead he worked with individuals to make financing possible, or he just refunded their deposits.[3]

Jacob maintains he has never knowingly and ultimately taken advantage of someone. He admits that over the course of his business dealings he may have taken advantage of individuals. But when made aware of the wrongdoing, he did everything in his power to correct it. Jacob believes his business practices are ethical, for after doing business in the Fraser Valley since 1956, he can walk down the street with a clear conscience, his head up, knowing no one will come up to him and give him an "earful."

Jacob acknowledges only one never-settled disagreement. One of Jacob's companies bid on a job, suggesting they had a certain level of expertise. When the job was complete, neither he nor the vendor were satisfied with the results, for two reasons. First, Jacob's superintendent likely exaggerated the experience of their company and what it could accomplish. Second, the vendor (a Christian) was inexperienced in this type of development and made poor decisions.

On completion of the job there was a $40,000 discrepancy in the billing amount, due to decisions made by both parties. Jacob offered to cover the costs of his company's mistakes and suggested it would only be right for the vendor to cover costs of his mistakes. But the vendor refused to acknowledge his errors, leaving Jacob with the full bill. On many occasions Jacob tried to work it out but to no avail. Some urged Jacob to take the individual to court, but Jacob does not believe Christians should settle disputes using legal means.

The Legal System

Before 1988, Jacob had been directly involved in only one court case. He had made an $8,000 handshake deal, but before completion of the deal, the person died. This person had been in partnership with another individual who did not accept that the handshake deal had been made. Therefore, he demanded that Jacob turn over the $8,000 being held in trust. When Jacob refused, the partner sued.

In discussing with his lawyer the possibility of going to court, Jacob realized the partner was financially troubled, thus the courts would likely rule in his favor. The case was therefore settled out of court, with each party receiving $4,000. From his share Jacob paid his lawyer $1,500, leaving him only $2,500 from an original $8,000.

Many times buyers of homes or condominiums built by one of Jacob's companies have threatened to sue Jacob due to the company's inability to fix a leak in a roof. Jacob's standard response, besides making further attempts to fix the leak, is to ask for patience in finding the leak and to note that court action will do neither party any good. "The judge is not going to come and fix the leak." By responding in such a manner, Jacob has been able to avoid the court system.

Jacob aims to evade the courts but has used them twice. In one case Revenue Canada reassessed assets Jacob had transferred to his children in 1981. Jacob could not afford to pay the $70,000 assessment which came in 1984. As a result, on the advice of his accountant, he filed a notice of objection. Jacob lost the court case because of a technicality in one sentence of the objection notice. After two-and-a-half years, the two parties settled for half the original amount—yet interest, lawyer costs, and accountant fees cost Jacob almost as much as the original assessment. Jacob was not unduly upset about losing the case, however, because it had been a gamble in the first place. Although the outcome was negative, the case did give Jacob enough time to recover from the recession so he could afford to pay the bill.

The second case involved a hog farm owned and managed by his son Rob. This case underscores Jacob's dislike and mistrust of the legal system. Rob started hog farming in 1981. In his early years he was as successful as most of the other hog farmers in the area. For the first few years of operation Rob had been buying his hog feed from a mill which had a good reputation. Jacob then asked Rob to purchase his feed from Wall & Redekop Feeds. "I told Rob it looked silly. My brother is in the business. Why should I not support him? They had a good reputation in all of the other feeds."

Rob took his father's advice and switched feed companies. Shortly after he began to have difficulties with his hogs. Although they were not able conclusively to pinpoint the problem, Jacob thinks it stemmed from ingredients in the feed. One result was a lengthened growth time for the pigs, another was a health problem with sows. Jacob estimates the total losses incurred by the feed problem to have been around $200,000.

When confronted with this information, Wall & Redekop gave Jacob the name of the firm's insurance company, which refused to accept the claim. Rob needed his father's support to prepare a court case, as he alone did not have the finances. To the elder Jacob this indicates that only the wealthy or those who have access to capital can use the judicial system to its fullest potential. "A judicial system is not just, if one's cash flow dictates whether one can seek justice."

After months of gathering evidence, the case went to court. The proceedings lasted thirteen days. Jacob felt they established a strong case. After three months, the judge decided against Rob. Jacob is still bitter, particularly about the fact that Wall & Redekop "did not back us one bit. They just said you go and fight the insurance company. They did not mind selling us the feed and collecting from us but when it came to say, look, there was something wrong, they did not say it."

Many in and beyond the Mennonite community could not understand why one brother would take another brother and cousins to court. For Jacob, it was because they refused to deal with the issue except through the judicial system. Thus Jacob, who always tried to live by the spirit of the law—evidenced by his scant court experience—felt that to seek justice he had to take Wall & Redekop to court.

But it was not something he did with gusto. "I personally feel that, let's face it, the court situation usually comes out of anger somewhere along the line," he said. "I think it pays sometimes to sit and evaluate. The winners are the lawyers and only the lawyers because they charge an arm and a leg. I wish Rob could have won, because he needed it.

"In the future," he stressed, "I will be very careful before I ever go to court. I would not recommend [it to] anyone else. In thirty years I have never been there, and now in one year I have two cases. I have lost both of them, and that is nothing to brag about or be proud of."

Jacob's experience raises some of the most fundamental issues surrounding the legal system, including the problem of access and the difference between the letter and spirit of the law—between what is "right" and what is "legal."

Goals

Jacob views his accumulation of wealth as stockpiling equity for the future, to ensure a comfortable lifestyle in his later years. One principle guiding his pursuit of this goal has been to use as little of his own money as possible and let the bank finance the rest. By taking risks one can spread oneself farther with the possibility of making more money.

This practice was successful until the recession in the early 1980s. Jacob began to panic, for he was fifty years old, and his primary skills were in poultry farming and land development. Without financial strength it is impossible to develop property. Jacob was fortunate to survive, but the experience led him to alter his philosophy.

After regaining his financial strength by the later 1980s, Jacob decided to change the direction and purpose of his investments. At the end of the recession he still had enough assets that he could have lived comfortably without additional income, yet this would have reduced his support of charitable organizations. "This [retirement] would restrict my donations towards the conference, church, and all of the other things I support. But I enjoy supporting them, and I must say that whenever I write out a check, though some people say it hurts them, it does not bother me. I enjoy doing that."

Jacob has made a conscious decision to invest only in short-range projects so as not to build up more equity. This allows him to divide up his cash from each individual project and donate it to various causes. Jacob does not try to hide the fact that he enjoys making money and having the capacity to give it to Mennonite institutions. Although he does not agree with everything being done or promoted by Mennonite churches and institutions, he is convinced that Mennonites need to support and be proud of them.

"Nor do I exactly believe too strongly this system that the Bible states that your left hand should not know what your right hand is doing. I think that there is nothing wrong about having a little bit of pride in what you are doing. You should motivate other people to do so as well and therefore you have to tell them that. Maybe you do not have to brag about it, but I think you have to let them know that this is what makes my system tick."

Jacob believes that in failing to acknowledge and recognize the successful businessperson the church is alienating a vital part of its membership. After years of his own alienation, Jacob Redekop believes businesspeople are now starting to be accepted at the local levels, which is a positive step in building the kingdom of God.

5

Emanuel E. Mullet:
In Partnership with People and the Land

By Willis J. Sommer

Emanuel Mullet (b. 1910) grew up in an Amish community and joined a Conservative Mennonite church. Already in his youth his innovative spirit led him to the margins of acceptable Amish/Mennonite activity. His entrepreneurial career has been lived in tense yet creative partnership with his faith community, and interestingly, with the "land," something important both to the traditional Amish/Mennonite way of life as well as an emerging environmental movement. Throughout Mullet's fascinating career in horse trading, strip mining, and manufacturing, he has lived his life with one foot in the conservative Amish/Mennonite world and the other in the world of business.

THE STEREOTYPICAL IMAGE of a horse trader or a strip miner is not usually a positive one. If successful, the person is generally believed either dishonest or shady. Yet in Holmes County, Ohio, there resides a person who does not fit this stereotype. Emanuel E. Mullet was a successful horse trader and strip miner who incorporated honesty, openness, and integrity into his dealings. Mullet's success in horse trading and strip mining allowed him to expand and diversify into other ventures including restaurants, nursing homes, overhead garage door factories, a tile factory, a community sale barn, horse farms, racehorses, and more. His experience illustrates the positive results and the difficulties of incorporating Christian principles into the economic environment.[1]

A Young Entrepreneur

Emanuel was born into an Amish family in 1910, the first child of Eli and Anna Mullet. The family moved frequently, usually on the fringes of the Holmes County Amish area where land prices were lower. Emanuel attended small, one-room public schools where he was one of two or three Amish children in the student body. He never felt accepted by the other schoolchildren and because of dress and language often felt inferior. Often at noon or recess he would work in a farmer's field next to the school rather than participate in activities with the other children. After finishing seventh grade, he left school to help his father on the farm.[2]

Emanuel's father worked hard as a farmer, but never seemed to achieve much success. Emanuel's mother was more firm, and a better financier than his father. In Emanuel's words, "My father was a good man. He taught me a lot about being honest and fair. I don't want to take an inch of credit away from him. My mother was more of a promoter. I always say that I got the motor from my mom and the governor from my dad."[3]

As a youngster Emanuel had a love for horses that continued throughout his life. He became knowledgeable about them and was good at selecting horses suitable for a specific purpose. Most of Emanuel's experiences with horses were positive, though one of his early experiences was not. One day Eli Mullet used Emanuel's pony to travel to town. Someone asked if the pony was for sale. Thinking this would end the discussion, Emanuel's father gave a price higher than the cost of a good buggy horse. It was accepted. Both Emanuel and his father were disappointed. However, a deal had been made. Emanuel learned that once a deal is made, you live with it.

From that experience Emanuel began to see the potential economic benefit of buying and selling or trading horses. In his later teens he began buying horses, retraining and breaking them, and selling them to others. While the Amish were using all-purpose horses to pull their buggies, Mullet wondered why standard bred racehorses, pacers, and trotters no longer fit for racing could not be retrained to pull buggies. Emanuel would hitch rides on trucks to racehorse centers, buy a horse, and lead it home. Seeking horses with the right temperament, he would buy them after studying pedigrees.

He selected the first buyers of his horses carefully and gave the buyer an admonition. "If the horse does not turn out well, tell me. If the horse is satisfactory, tell others." It was an admonition that Emanuel would use in later ventures. If the racehorses could not be satisfactorily retrained for buggy use, then Emanuel sold them to private riding clubs and stables. Emanuel introduced standard bred horses to the Amish. (Today nearly all buggy horses are from standard bred stock.) Since automobiles were becoming more prevalent, Emanuel also began buying and refurbishing old buggies no longer needed by new car owners. The "new" buggies were sold to the Amish.

Two of Emanuel's common business practices were evident in these first ventures. One was, "Buy a good item in an area where it is not in demand and place the item in an area where it is in demand." A second practice was never coaxing an unwilling seller to part with an item until he was ready. If the seller had to be coaxed, the price was too high. By the time the seller was ready to part with the item, the price would be lower, since the owner would have less need for the item.

Though not as evident, another practice Emanuel used was not negotiating over price, or as he called it, "chiseling." Emanuel knew the value of a racehorse no longer fit for racing, and of buggies no longer being used for transportation. He could buy them at low prices and sell them at competitive market prices in areas where horses and buggies were in demand.

While Emanuel farmed with his father and dealt in horses, he began dating Alma Swartzentruber. Emanuel and Alma were married in December 1934, after he joined the Conservative Mennonite Church. For a honeymoon trip, Emanuel and Alma traveled to northern Indiana and Illinois to visit relatives.

Like many entrepreneurs, Emanuel also used a personal trip, even his honeymoon, as an opportunity to conduct business. Alma surely knew what being the wife of an entrepreneur meant after this trip. He delivered a horse in Indiana and took a side trip to St. Louis to buy draft horses. The St. Louis horses turned out to be mules, and of no value in Holmes County.

Returning from his unsuccessful St. Louis venture, Emanuel met Alma in Illinois. They were returning to relatives in Indiana when their car missed a turn in the road and jumped a ditch, coming to a stop in a wheat field. Emanuel and Alma were delayed a week while repairs were made to the car's damaged frame. While walking the streets of Topeka, Indiana, Emanuel met a man who volunteered that this was an excellent area to buy draft horses, since tractors were becoming more widely used.

As the two men traveled the area, Emanuel bought twenty-one roan Belgian draft horses and shipped them back to Holmes County. The horses were resold on arrival in Holmes County. This transaction started ten years of buying draft horses in areas of no demand and selling them in areas of high demand. In 1942, Mullet sold 726 draft horses at private auction. About a year after their marriage, Emanuel and Alma, helped by their parents, bought a farm near Alma's parents. The farm provided an excellent environment for his horse business. Several years later a second farm was bought and the first farm sold.

Expansion

Emanuel became involved in smaller ventures in addition to horse trading. He began working with his brother Atlee, who had a talent working with machinery. Emanuel provided funds to buy a small crawler tractor with Atlee providing the labor to run it. Projects included logging operations and cleanup operations at Dundee Coal, a local mining concern. When an opportunity arose to haul coal for Dundee, the brothers bought a truck. The coal-hauling then expanded to several dump trucks. Considerable debt was incurred as they expanded. The brothers had a thin profit margin, so they were continually at risk of failure. But by the time Dundee Coal was sold and renamed Copperhead Mines, the Mullet brothers owned all the pit and highway trucks used by Copperhead Mines.

When Emanuel bought a second farm, he was unaware that coal had been deep-mined from land on the farm. After discovering the mine entry, Emanuel had his farm drilled to determine possibilities for mining the coal. The results of the survey indicated large amounts of coal nearer the surface than in most coalfields. Emanuel and Atlee sold some of their trucks, bought mining equipment, and started the Trail Ridge Mine Company. Like many entrepreneurial ventures, it was undercapitalized and never achieved operational success. After a short time the mining company was sold. The sale left Emanuel and Alma financially strong, with no debts, two farms (the first farm was rebought) and considerable money in the bank. Yet Emanuel was unhappy. "I was idle for a year. It was no good for me. I thought I was happy, but I wasn't. I was unsatisfied."

A friend suggested that he investigate a coalfield near Mt. Eaton. Emanuel and Atlee investigated the field, bought the farm on which it was located, and leased two others which also had coalfields. Thus began Mullet Coal and Clay. Although the brothers started from scratch, the company was doing well by the late 1940s. In 1949 they formed Holmes Limestone Company in Berlin, Ohio, to handle limestone mining.

Prosperity often brings problems, and it did to Mullet Coal and Clay. According to Emanuel, "Atlee and I got along well until we were out of debt. But when things were paid off we had problems. I don't blame anybody." Each was a strong-willed entrepreneur who had different visions of what direction their ventures should take. The differences could not be reconciled. In 1952, the brothers split the company. Emanuel received Holmes Limestone Company and a small pallet company in Mt. Hope, Ohio, and Atlee assumed control of Mullet Coal and Clay. The brothers would later attempt other joint ventures, but they encountered many of the same problems as earlier.[4]

During and after the split, Holmes Limestone Company was losing money. Emanuel needed funds to buy land that would insure future limestone supplies, for more and bigger equipment in the operation, and for an inventory of limestone available for sale. But he had reached his credit limit. He was depressed over what appeared to be the collapse of Holmes Limestone. "I felt all alone. I felt whipped. I would get spells of energy, but that was rare," he says. "I looked at myself and thought, 'maybe I did some things to deserve this.' I meditated and confessed to things that I may have done, and admitted that maybe I was a little greedy. I was out of the land of honey and in the desert. With the help of others I finally plunged into the work again." A close friend counseled Emanuel to persevere. With Emanuel's individual stamina and the help of a limestone dealer cosigning a note, Holmes Limestone was able to move out of debt.

Several years later, Emanuel Mullet began coal operations with two other partners in a venture called Hardy Coal Company. With another partner, Mullet bought the Copperhead Mines where the Mullet brothers had earlier hauled coal. The Copperhead buy was not without problems. Mullet's Copperhead partner lived outside the Holmes County area and did not appreciate local needs and interests. In addition, the previous owners of Copperhead were a factor in management, since they were not open to changes in the loan repayment schedule when funds were especially tight. Apparently, the previous owners were hoping Mullet would default on the notes.

After refinancing the notes, however, Emanuel was able to pay off the original loan, solving one problem. Emanuel then bought additional mines and bought or leased more land to insure future supplies of coal. After initial struggles, the coal mines were prospering, though with one negative result—stripped land was worthless for any farm use or practically any other use.

A Question of Stewardship

Problems resulting from stripping came to a head for Hardy Coal in the late 1960s, when a farm came up for sale on which Hardy had a lease for the coal. The farm, sold subject to the lease, was bought by an Old Order Amish farmer who did not want the farm stripped. Emanuel's partner wanted stripping to begin immediately. Emanuel hesitated, understanding the local community and church concerns. The dispute went to court, which determined the lease valid. Stripping began, but because of the hard feelings involved, particularly in the Amish community, Hardy Coal was sold when an offer was received.

This particular sale was difficult for Mullet. It had taken much time and energy to make the mine succeed. Now that it was successful, it was difficult to sell. Pastor Joe Yoder remembers working with

Emanuel trying to balance economics, church, and community interests in resolving this dilemma. The process took time. "He often had tears in his eyes as we sat together trying to figure out what to do. He wanted to do what was right in the eyes of the church and community. At the expense of economics, he sold the mine so that more hurt in the community would not be incurred."[5]

Emanuel also had other mines, and he knew that Holmes County land contained considerable coal. However, much of this land was owned by the Amish who would not allow strip mining on their farms. Throughout his coal mining experience, Emanuel felt guilty for the lack of stewardship of the land involved in strip mining. The guilt was similar to what he felt as a teenager when his family moved to a new farm that had an outcrop of limestone. At that time, Emanuel calculated the size of the outcrop and realized its economic potential if the limestone were mined and sold. He began dreaming of the possibilities, yet tempered that dream when he recognized the land would no longer serve for farm use.

Three factors converged in the late 1950s to change Emanuel's method of strip mining. The first, involving economics and public relations, had to do with Emanuel's need to buy or lease land for strip mining. Amish farmers would not participate in mining projects and would make group bids on available farms to prevent Emanuel from buying them. "My Amish friends used to look down on me." It was clear to Emanuel that buying or leasing Amish farms would not be possible unless their productivity could be restored once the coal was removed. According to Emanuel, "In a way the Amish really did me a favor, as well as themselves. They made me come up with a method of stripping that would be acceptable . . . or I would never touch the coal.[6]

Second, the strip mining industry was getting unfavorable publicity in the press. Articles concerning destruction of the land from strip mining were particularly critical of the industry. In addition to articles appearing in the general press, William Stauffer, a local pastor and conservationist, wrote letters to the *Sugar Creek Budget* criticizing specifically Emanuel's strip mining methods. As Stauffer put it, "I was a thorn in his flesh on the reclamation issue."[7] The negative publicity was a major concern for Emanuel.

The third factor had to do with the development of technology.

Through a mutual acquaintance, Emanuel met Joe Erb, an Amish excavator. Together they developed a method of replacing topsoil and subsoil after the coal had been removed. New technology and larger equipment that replaced dragline shovels permitted development of this method. The new method started slowly, with some of Emanuel's colleagues doubting it would succeed.

Emanuel and Erb formed Charm Mining, near Charm, Ohio, and used the new method to strip mine one small farm. It took several years to judge the success of the method, but productivity was restored. The success of the pilot farm made it considerably easier for the process to blossom. Charm Mining merged into Holmes Limestone Company. While the new method proved more costly due to the reclamation costs, the process could still be competitive with other companies because less dirt per ton of coal had to be moved.

In most situations, the restored farms were more productive than before the mining operations occurred. Henry Stutzman, an Amish farmer stated, "They took about fifteen feet off the top of that knob up there when they mined it. Now the slope is more gentle and easier to work. He made my land 100 percent better. It holds moisture better than before. Everybody says that."[8]

William Stauffer also praised the reclamation work. "It is the best around and Emanuel deserves credit for it." State regulatory officials visited the restored land and incorporated Emanuel's methods into new legislation regulating strip mining. In 1972, Ohio law was amended, requiring all strip mine operators to replace top soil after removing coal or other minerals. Not required was the multilayer soil replacement Emanuel used but new federal regulations will enforce a similar method on land categorized as "prime farm lands."[9]

Emanuel has received numerous awards for his land reclamation efforts. According to daughter Ruby Hostetler, the award that pleased Emanuel most was being honored as "Coal Man of the Year" at the 1986 Ohio Mining and Reclamation yearly meeting.

A Partnership Model

Emanuel and the Holmes Limestone management team resolved the land stewardship problem by returning the land to farmable use. This also helped the company economically. Additional management practices illustrate Christian principles. Because of the need for a ready supply of coal and timely trading of farms, Holmes Limestone had to contract with a farmer, including royalties, in advance of actually mining the farm. But the selling price of the coal might fluctuate when the coal was actually mined. According to Levi Beachy, retired Holmes Limestone land buyer, if the price of the coal increased substantially, Emanuel often unilaterally increased the royalty amount paid to the farmer, even if the farmer did not request it. Another practice noted by Beachy was Emanuel's desire to customize transactions to each farmer's individual needs rather than using standardized contracts.[10]

A comment made by Emanuel in earlier interviews provides some rationale for making unilateral contract changes. "I usually say a strip miner in farm country has to be a farmer [as well as] a strip miner. Strip miners have to know farming to do it right. They have to work with farmers. It is a partnership." Son Merle suggests that finding coal was not his dad's greatest talent; it was his ability to meet and work with farmers in a personal way.[11] While this provided obvious benefit to the farmers, it was an administrative and financial headache for the Holmes Limestone management team, who had to develop and understand many different contracts.

Emanuel altered some individual contracts in favor of the farmer if it helped develop community relations. Joe Yoder recalled an incident in which Holmes Limestone had a lease with an Amish farmer to mine half of his farm land. The farmer requested that the other half also be mined. However, due to the terrain of the surrounding land, it could not be mined unless a neighboring farm was mined at the same time. Arrangements were made to lease the neighboring farm.

The farmer received additional royalties from the other half of his farm plus royalties for the neighboring farm coal which had to be transported over his land. The initial contract required returning the land to farmable condition in two years from the start of mining. The land was returned to farmable condition in that period except for a lane necessary to transport the neighbor's coal. The Amish farmer felt he deserved additional compensation since the original contract was not fulfilled. After consulting with Yoder, and wanting to maintain positive relationships, Emanuel agreed to an additional payment.

Since coal in the ground is considered real estate, Emanuel developed a procedure for tax-free farm exchanges for the farmers involved. An Amish farmer received a comparable farm for his current farm. After mining the coal and restoring the land, Emanuel had another farm ready for tax-free exchange. In other situations farms owned by Holmes Limestone were leased to Amish farmers while their particular farms were being mined. After mining was completed, the farmer returned to his reclaimed farmland. In both situations, the farmer received royalties for the coal mined from his farm.

Emanuel always felt he should mine using the best technology possible. He would do more than the regulations required, thus anticipating future regulations. For example, he bought a wash plant so he could understand its operation, and began washing coal before it was a requirement. Emanuel noted, "I am not against doing what we know how to do." But he would get upset when the Environmental Protection Agency would suggest or require something for which technology did not exist.

Because of the reclamation efforts, the coal mining projects continued to grow, bringing financial success. This allowed Emanuel to consider additional entrepreneurial ventures. While the coal and limestone business involved daily management of operations, the additional ventures did not require daily supervision, since the ventures were done in partnership with other persons who assumed general management of the businesses. Often individuals with creative ideas would present them to Emanuel for financial backing. Rather than loaning money for the venture, he would provide investment capital and become a partner.

Not all ideas were judged prudent, and Emanuel often asked others for advice before deciding on an investment. For example, one individual requested capital for developing a wood chipping machine. Emanuel asked Joe Yoder to buy and use one in cleaning hedge rows to judge its usefulness. After a period of usage, Yoder said it would be a good machine if certain changes were made. The changes were suggested to the individual, but he elected not to alter the machine. Emanuel did not make the investment.

If Emanuel was excited about a particular product, he expressed interest in buying the company. If the company was bought, he kept key managers involved in running it. In other areas Emanuel would start a business from scratch or buy an existing business if it complemented one of his other businesses or met a need in the local community. In most ventures, but not all, Emanuel retained majority ownership control. Rather than describe all Emanuel's additional entrepreneurial ventures, one of each type will be reviewed.[12]

An example of buying an existing business to complement the coal and limestone business was the purchase of Deco-Tile, Dalton, Ohio in 1956. With several additional investors, including brother Atlee, Emanuel bought Deco-Tile to process the clay mined from the coal mining operations. Emanuel wanted to supply steel mills with tiles able to withstand high temperature pressures necessary in the mills. Unfortunately the process for manufacturing the tile could not be immediately perfected. As a result Deco-Tile was near bankruptcy. Emanuel made another decision typical of his ventures—he hired a trusted friend and relative to manage the plant. In time, as that person acquired production experience, conditions did improve and profitability was reached for Deco-Tile.

A church relations problem arose with Deco-Tile, because the oven kilns had to be run seven days a week to maintain constant temperatures. Emanuel compared the Sunday work with Sunday farm chores. With profitability, however, came tension in the church. As long as Deco-Tile was not profitable no one seemed to be bothered, but with profits the Sunday work became a concern. Efforts to satisfy the concerns were not successful. Rather than allowing the concerns and tension to continue, Emanuel and the other investors sold the plant in 1967.

In 1955, Emanuel was intrigued with a bifold garage door manufactured by Wayne Door, a small firm in Mt. Hope, Ohio. The firm was owned and managed by Ervin Hostetler, an Amish man Emanuel learned to know while associated with Mullet Coal and Clay. Believing the bifold door had great potential, Emanuel made an offer for the company which Hostetler accepted. Hostetler continued to manage the business and was offered stock in the company but declined in favor of receiving a share of the operating profits.

Because of the limitations of the bifold door, Wayne Door (later Wayne-Dalton) began making sectional overhead track doors. Later the company made insulated garage doors along with other types of doors. The company quickly grew as major building programs began

Emanuel standing by the Wayne-Dalton building.

in 1959. Expenditures for the building were covered by company profits.[13] Through expanding into other geographic areas and buying other existing door manufacturers, Wayne-Dalton has become the largest garage door manufacturer in the United States.

In 1961 Emanuel, along with a son-in-law, saw an opportunity to meet a community need for a nursing home. This took place when a motel in Dalton, partly remodeled for nursing care, became available at auction. Emanuel and his son-in-law formed a partnership, bought the motel, and finished the necessary remodeling. The nursing home proved successful. When a larger and eventually more complete retirement living center was wanted, the nursing home was sold and the partnership developed a retirement center in Walnut Creek, Ohio.

The new facility included duplex apartments, helped-care apartments, and nursing care. The Walnut Creek retirement center celebrated its twentieth year in 1991 and continues to expand as needs warrant. Other immediate Mullet family members participate in the partnership.

Finally, Emanuel's entry into the restaurant business occurred in 1969, when an individual needing financial help for the purchase of a restaurant in Walnut Creek approached Emanuel. Emanuel did not want to loan money, but both he and another immediate family member were interested in becoming partners in the purchase. A three-way partnership was formed, and the Der Dutchman restaurant was bought. Der Dutchman needed to expand quickly to meet the increased demand.

Restaurants were also bought or started in other locations. Seven restaurants located in Ohio, Indiana, and Florida are currently owned by a Mullet family partnership. Similar motifs and styles exist in each restaurant, with gift shops and bakeries included in several locations.

Analysis

Emanuel's personal character provides background for understanding his thinking and success as an entrepreneur. He came from a poor Amish farm family that never had resources to meet other than basic family needs. Emanuel noticed material possessions of others. For example, Wayne Mullet remembers that while other kids growing up had change for a bottle of pop, Emanuel never did.[14] Emanuel began to see money as the source of prestige and power.

Clearly, one of Emanuel's goals was to achieve financial success. Yet his success would not lead to major changes in consumption or lifestyle. His goal simply was to acquire money. Various individuals commented that Emanuel's real enjoyment was "letting the money grow in his businesses." The excitement and challenge was making money, not spending it. Emanuel enjoyed challenges and said, "I like to do the things people say cannot be done."

When he was fourteen, for example, he became part of a road improvement crew, pulling tree stumps and widening roads, by convincing the crew chief to let him show how he could handle his horses and do the other tasks. He was assigned to work with the best teamster on the job. Four horses were used as a team in pulling out stumps. According to Emanuel, "The horses had to pull together smoothly, or you were in serious trouble. I still use this example in business today . . . this job is too big for you and it is too big for me . . . let's do it together."

Emanuel also notes that he is stubborn and does not like failures. "I'm a hard loser. I push to the end. [But] I don't think I fight dirty." During his days of active business leadership he had a knack for recognizing a need for change in the middle of a venture and could turn what seemed a sure failure into a success. When asked the secret of Emanuel's success, his daughter Ruby Hostetler replied, "He had determination to see an idea through; he would not quit or give up until the idea succeeded."[15]

Emanuel's personal characteristics fostered business practices that also contributed to his success. He was truthful and honest in negotiations and dealings. His word was good. Wayne Mullet remembers Emanuel saying, "If you are honest, you do not need to remember what you said earlier. If you are not truthful and honest, you will spend a lot of time trying to remember what you said earlier and somebody will catch you when you aren't consistent." Various colleagues remember Emanuel as tough but fair in work. Retired land buyer Levi Beachy suggests Emanuel's policy was a "fair deal for both parties or no deal. Each party should know the whole deal."

If business or personnel problems arose, Emanuel wanted them on the table and quickly resolved. He did not like to admit he was wrong but would do so. Emanuel had an ability to listen to others and

sort through the key issues with them. Emanuel could see future opportunities and risks and the economic potential of those opportunities.

Emanuel did not like competition and often worried about it, particularly in later years. Instead of meeting competition directly in the
marketplace, he would attempt joint ventures with competitors which
often were not in the best interests of his particular company.
Emanuel also kept his various enterprises independent of each other
with no transferring of funds (though he admits funds were transferred early in his experiences, causing financial problems). Each entity had to stand on its own.

Emanuel's concern for diversification and independence resulted
from his desire to spread his risk. If one venture failed or did not do
well, the operations of the other businesses would not be affected. His
first lesson in understanding diversification came at a young age while
he was gathering eggs on his parents' farm. Once he collected and
placed all of the eggs in one basket so that the eggs were higher than
the upper rim of the basket. He waited until he knew his father would
see him before carrying them to the house. Rather than praising
Emanuel, his father scolded him, "If you fall there is a good chance
many of the eggs will break. If you place the eggs in two baskets, there
will be less chance the eggs will break." In later life Emanuel clearly
didn't "put all his eggs in one basket."

Emanuel sought ways to keep personnel involved and interested
in the businesses, since he relied heavily on them. Profit-sharing and
stock ownership were always offered to key personnel. Piecework
wages were offered to encourage productivity. Emanuel believed a
key to success was lower profit per item with high turnover. Profits
were reinvested in the entity rather than distributed to the stockholders or partners. Emanuel takes pride in relating that many ventures
grew and developed with internally generated funds, not through additional external funds.

Emanuel was not a detail person; he was a dreamer, a visionary.
"I dream, and if you do not put feet or action under dreams, you might
as well not dream. I am not a detail man, I blaze the trail . . . nobody
beats me in dreaming." He constantly dreamed and set new goals to
reach. But to accomplish his goals, Emanuel had to have the right mix
of support staff. The ideas and dreams were meaningless without a

partner or colleague who could move them to fruition. Emanuel's success lay in finding the right person for a task or developing a partnership with a good management team that supported the goals of the organization. Ervin Hostetler states, "Emanuel was a sharp man. The key was finding the right person. He believed you can be a challenge in any competitive business there is, if you have the right people."

With few exceptions, Emanuel connected with people with whom he was familiar. He developed an intuitive knowledge about people in his earlier horse transactions and used that knowledge to find the right people for later ventures. He studied the family histories of potential colleagues like he studied the pedigrees of horses. According to Alma Mullet, he would continually look for honesty in the individual with whom he might work.[16]

Emanuel would observe how individuals worked in other situations before placing them in key positions. Cousin Wayne Mullet moved into Deco-Tile to assume a management position without prior knowledge of tile making. He was a farmer who several years earlier had asked Emanuel for a farm to rent. After renting an available Mullet farm for a year, Wayne was invited to rent Emanuel and Alma's home farm. A short time later, Emanuel asked Wayne to become associated with Deco-Tile, including a share of ownership. "It was clear, in fact Emanuel even told me, that I was being observed on how I did things around the farm," says Wayne. "He . . . gave me more opportunity than I probably should have had, but he thought I could do it."

Pastor Joe Yoder has a similar story. Yoder is supervisor of the rental properties of Holmes Limestone, including farms and other rental properties, and also pastor of Emanuel and Alma Mullet's church, Light in the Valley Chapel near Walnut Creek. According to Yoder, "It was clear I was observed in my pastor position, particularly in how I made decisions and handled conflict." After a time, Yoder was invited to join Holmes Limestone. Yoder was concerned that he did not have the proper background for the position and that the rental property work might conflict with his church work. But the decision to work with the company turned out to be one he could live with—Yoder has finished fourteen years with Holmes Limestone. According to Yoder, "I can serve the company as well as serving the church. It has caused no problems. I would do it again."

Most of Emanuel's key colleagues were or are local community people, often of Amish family background who have proven themselves in some way. Emanuel gave them opportunities and if successful additional responsibilities. Emanuel allowed managers and key people to function on their own as long as the bottom line was profitable and they were meeting company goals. He would allow for honest mistakes since that showed initiative to try something new. If a person could not fill a need for which he was hired, he would often be moved to another position. Wayne remembers Emanuel saying, "If you get a good man, keep him; if he has a weakness, find a better slot for him—find a slot where he is useful." Others recall his saying, "Hitch the right man to the right job."

In Holmes Limestone, the controlling entity of Emanuel's mining interests, several key individuals in addition to Emanuel formed the management team. There was not always consensus among them. Some on the team would oppose Emanuel or suggest other approaches. Emanuel welcomed differing opinions and often changed his mind after hearing them. More conservative fiscal approaches of members of the team often conflicted with Emanuel's desire to take on more risk and potentially costlier programs. The discussion process ultimately strengthened the company.

Alma Mullet: A Parallel Story

Emanuel spent considerable time on his economic endeavors, which suggests other areas in his life may have suffered. Several interviewees suggested that Emanuel did not play or relax; he only worked. He did not or could not appreciate the lighter things in life. This characteristic carried over to family life.

Parallel to the Emanuel Mullet story is another story, and that is the experience of Alma Mullet, who nearly singlehandedly raised a family of nine children and became a successful entrepreneur in her own right. As Emanuel's ventures developed, Alma was required to become a bookkeeper as well as housewife and mother.

Emanuel and Alma's marriage had a difficult beginning. Emanuel had an alcohol problem and his first job at a sawmill exacerbated the problem, since the sawmill owner was an alcoholic. Moving to their first farm allowed Emanuel to expand his horse dealing and, with his mind occupied, to refrain from alcohol. Alcohol would, however, continue to be an intermittent problem for many years. Later, Emanuel would provide help to recovering alcoholics, since he understood the difficulties and problems they faced.

Like many entrepreneurs, Emanuel often made aggressive, quick decisions without consulting others. For example, Alma was not aware of Emanuel's interest in the second farm buy, until he announced that they were moving. "I was disappointed. I did not want to move. I did not know he was going to do it. With five children, I made the best of it." Alma's tasks as housewife, mother, and bookkeeper continued to increase as additional children were born and Emanuel's various business ventures increased.

Emanuel's ventures required that evenings be for business rather than family. Considerable travel was needed to arrange buys of both horses and coal. With her family responsibilities, Alma would periodically fall behind in the bookkeeping work and occasionally misplace a needed paper, or it would be assumed that she misplaced the paper. She would bear the brunt of Emanuel's criticism for this. Alma did eventually receive additional help, and after several more years the office and bookkeeping work was removed to a centralized office.

Although Emanuel participated in day family trips and family games played in the evenings, responsibility for child rearing, including discipline, rested mainly on Alma's shoulders. Emanuel comments, "I can't explain what she went through, but I know she went through a lot bringing up the children. She did a good job. She was patient and calm." When Alma wanted help from the older children, Emanuel required their help in a business or suggested they be placed in work situations with other families.

Such a family situation is not atypical of Amish and Mennonite families of the same era, but it does appear that Emanuel's entrepreneurial ambitions affected family life. Yoder recalls Emanuel acknowledging regret for not being a better family man. While Emanuel obviously provided economic benefit to his family and a management mentality to his children, primarily Alma provided them with moral values, integrity, and the sense of family cohesiveness obvious in their support of each other in times of difficulty. She has been the family's rock.

Alma Mullet did not have major input into Emanuel's various ventures in his early years in business. She encouraged him in those ventures since it kept him focused on business matters and lessened the alcohol problem. Alma would periodically discuss issues with Emanuel, but he made final decisions. Later, however, Alma found him more flexible in the decision-making process. He would invite interaction and comments from her before making decisions.

As Emanuel's ventures grew, Alma wanted to increase their giving to the church. Emanuel wanted to get things paid for before increasing their giving. But as debts were paid off new debt was incurred, making it impossible to increase giving. Alma, however, was able to address her concern when the Helping Hands Quilt Craft Foundation was incorporated to distribute the profits from her quilt shop to charitable and community causes. The quilt shop, which started in Emanuel and Alma's home, moved to Berlin, Ohio, in May 1974. The Foundation also receives contributions from several other Mullet businesses.

Foundation contributions have been given to half-way houses for former prisoners, children's homes in Ohio and Pennsylvania, and a Mennonite Hospital and orphanage in India. Contributions have included both major gifts and regular routine operating subsidy gifts. Contributions have also been given to the Mission Board of the Conservative Mennonite Church. Generally the Foundation has supported programs that provide help to "underdogs" in society (a term Emanuel feels describes him). The Foundation provided funds for development of a community park for the village of Mt. Hope, Ohio. Because the Helping Hands Quilt Shop provides much of the Foundation's resources, Alma's efforts deserve credit for the Mt. Hope park.

Several expansions of the quilt shop have occurred. Many people make quilts and help in the shop. In addition to quilts, small gifts, quilt kits, and fabrics are available for purchase. Alma continues to provide energetic management, coordination of personnel, and supervision of work done in the homes for the shop.

Alma's dream was to become a schoolteacher. Due to the economic situation of her parents, she received only an eighth-grade education, which prevented her being a teacher. She did, however, become a capable businessperson who attained considerable success in her quilt shop.

Church and Religious Life

Religion has played a major role in Emanuel's life. He began receiving instruction in the Amish church in his early twenties. The death of a close friend in an accident provided the impetus to begin instruction. At the same time he was dating Alma Swartzentruber, a member of the Conservative Mennonite Church. After considerable thought and discussion with both his father and Alma's, Emanuel joined the instruction class of the Conservative Mennonite Church. He joined that church on completion of the instruction class.

Emanuel is viewed as a Christian by the people who know him. Wayne Mullet comments, "Everybody knew he was a dedicated Christian; it was the way he talked and conducted his life." Levi Beachy adds, "He used Christian principles and values in his work." Lloyd Mischler, driver for Emanuel, believes Emanuel exhibited Christian principles in his treatment of employees and that this continues in the present organizations. Mischler says, "I am treated by Emanuel and the Mullet family better than I have been anywhere else. They make you feel that you are a vital part of the team. They will do anything for you that is possible. I think they do this for all employees."[17]

While basic Christian principles were prevalent from the beginning of Emanuel's entrepreneurial ventures, nearly all interviewees commented that something happened in midlife that deepened his Christian faith and values. They could see a difference in his attitude toward family, church, and the needy. His conversion helped keep earlier alcohol and health problems under control. Alma suggests that several events occurred during the 1950s which could have affected and consolidated this change. Emanuel had a thyroid condition in 1952, leaving him with a lack of energy. At the same time he was deeply concerned with the financial difficulty of Holmes Limestone.

The two conditions brought a period of depression. As the thyroid condition and the financial health of Holmes Limestone improved, Emanuel was able to work out of the depression and began to be more flexible in working with people. "I never lost my faith in the Supreme Being. But it was a period of testing," Emanuel explains. "God had to test me and ask, 'Emanuel, how do you act when you are in the mud? How do you survive? Do you lose your faith or do you

Emanuel receives award of Coal Man of the Year.

Emanuel with contractors at Memory Park.

trust me?' I asked many times, 'Where did I go wrong? Who did I hurt? I want to apologize.' It was a time of atonement."

A trip Emanuel and Alma took to the Middle East expanded his knowledge of the Bible. As a result he became more active in starting mission churches and broadened his knowledge of management styles available to promote new ideas. In the late 1950s he was a candidate for ordination three times but was not chosen in the lot. Although he was disappointed, Emanuel had worked at personal preparation and study for possible ordination which provided him with a deeper understanding of Christian faith.

Emanuel also commented on these changes in earlier interviews but did not suggest specific reasons for life changes. He did, however, provide a brief explanation of his faith. "A number of years ago I accepted the Lord as my partner. I try to live as a Christian and I have faith that God knows what I am trying to do. I feel that if I treat my fellow man fairly that the Lord will be fair to me. I have a theory that he controls the spigot, and our actions determine the flow."[18] Wayne also remembers Emanuel commenting, "Whatever we accumulate, we are still stewards of the Lord." And in one interview Emanuel noted, "Money isn't always good. I think it is a test. If I do not stay the same as if I didn't have it, then it isn't right to have it."

There was some tension in the Mullet's church as the Mullet enterprises enjoyed economic success. A few members believed the Mullets could not have attained that economic success honestly. A number of accusations were made. The bishop was called in for membership meetings to determine the merit of the accusations. Emanuel and Alma were open and not defensive in the meetings and were willing to admit and correct a wrong if substantiated. The bishop found no merit for the accusations.

According to current pastor Yoder, the episode had two positive results. The Mullets became much stronger in their faith. And the truth helped the church gain a better understanding of the role of money. Yoder remembers a phrase used by Emanuel Mullet in summarizing this situation, "Stick to the truth and what is right, and you will never have to back down." Alma remembers the membership meetings as a time in which they were alone with little support from others in the church community. Even after it was over it took time to work through what had occurred. Emanuel felt that living a consistent, conscientious Christian life smoothed many of the tension areas. "I had to prove myself—not getting a big hat and a big head, staying honest, associating with church members, helping them. It took a long time to accomplish this."

Emanuel and Alma have provided considerable support for building and expansion programs by making land available for new church buildings and providing support for their construction. Emanuel has served in numerous church roles, including trustee and treasurer.

The Mullet enterprises are a major economic force in the local communities. The reputations of the businesses are strong. The various businesses employ hundreds of workers and provide opportunities particularly for Amish workers to remain in their home communities. Other community businesses are also supported by the Mullet enterprises through purchases of materials and supplies furnished by others. Though there may be individual envy of the economic success of the various businesses, those businesses and the Mullet family are respected in the local community.

Although Emanuel and Alma had the economic means to live a more affluent lifestyle, they chose a simpler approach, consistent with their Christian principles. Merle Mullet states, "I always respected my parents for not living an affluent lifestyle. It also helped the community to understand them." Emanuel and Alma have helped or influenced many community people, and helped numerous communities to grow and develop. According to Lloyd Mischler, "When Emanuel Mullet makes short trips from the nursing home, everybody visits with him; they have appreciated what he has done."

Prospect

In earlier interviews Emanuel offered several personal reflections about his entrepreneurial experiences. Particularly gratifying was the sense of character and the work environment developed in each business using Christian principles and practices. According to Emanuel, "My goal and hope for the future of all of the companies is that they continue to run with integrity and honesty, fairness and truthfulness, and will have a good reputation and testimony of ethical operations."

A second reflection concerned the involvement of his children in the businesses. Both Emanuel and Alma are happy their sons, daughters, and sons-in-law are an integral part of the continuing operations of the Mullet businesses. Alma is proud that the children are in the family businesses and managing them well. The managerial involvement of the sons and daughters is an intriguing aspect of the Mullet story. The managerial intuitiveness of Emanuel and the moral integrity of Alma have given their children solid resources for continuing the economic successes Emanuel pioneered.

A third reflection concerned Emanuel's goal of keeping the businesses family-controlled. "I would like to see the companies continued in a family-controlled business, at least not in the open market. This is a closed community. Management needs to understand the community before it makes decisions." Emanuel feared outside ownership would not attempt to understand the local community and its interest but work only for its own economic gain.

Implicit in Emanuel's statement is another reason for his success. He respected the Holmes County social environment in which he worked. For example, he bought and leased land from the Amish, but in the process allowed for their individual needs. He hired Amish or individuals of Amish background for his factories and management positions. With his own Amish heritage, he knew the Amish in a way others could not. As an entrepreneur, Emanuel might have succeeded in a different locale, but he probably would not have accomplished as much as he did in Holmes County. He did not move beyond the environment he knew.

The Mullet businesses are positioned for the future, although there are potential risks. The expansion of Wayne-Dalton Doors, for example, has moved it beyond the local environment into the larger marketplace. This growth required expansion of the workforce beyond the Amish community, creating a different work environment. The growth also brings a different type of competitive pressure to Wayne-Dalton in maintaining market share. The challenge for Wayne-Dalton is addressing these risks in a manner that permits the character and principles instilled by Emanuel and his management team to continue. Wayne-Dalton has the potential to provide examples of creative, innovative leadership to the industry as it continues to grow.

In his career as entrepreneur, Emanuel experienced success but also failure. He has had to deal with conflicts and tensions. He faced challenges as he tried to balance economic activity with his Christian faith, his church, the needs of his family, the natural environment, and the interests of his local community. Mullet's genius consisted in his ability to go beyond a mechanical "balancing act" by integrating many of these potentially conflicting interests into a relatively harmonious whole. As such the Emanuel Mullet story is an excellent example of responsible entrepreneurship, of a partnership with people and the land.

6

Kurt Janz:
The Struggling Phoenix

By Joanna Buhr

Having grown up in German Prussia, Kurt Janz (b. 1934) and his family experienced upheaval under Hitler and fled to Canada in 1951. Once in Calgary, Alberta, Janz wasted little time building a construction empire that grew with the postwar upswing. During the recession of the early 1980s, Janz found himself bankrupt. The personal devastation was colossal, and he experienced a fair amount of rejection and insensitivity in the community and even in his own congregation. Yet Janz also received support as he struggled to regain his equilibrium. The story of Janz's rise and subsequent fall in fortune illustrates, among other things, the tensions and ambiguities which face aggressive Mennonite entrepreneurs.

DURING THE BOOM YEARS of the 1970s and early 1980s, many Calgarians referred to Tower Construction as the "Mennonite Mafia" in recognition of its power and remarkable level of success. Kurt Janz, dominant partner in this multifaceted company, commanded the respect, admiration, and in some cases envy of observers. But bankruptcy during the recession of the early 1980s brought new challenges and struggles to Kurt. His story is that of a "high-flier" brought low, only to be reborn, like the Phoenix of ancient Greek mythology, from the ashes of his defeat. It is a story of struggles with himself and with his faith community, with success and with failure.

Childhood

Kurt was born on May 17, 1934, in the farming community of Lakendorf, East Prussia, to Bernard and Erna (Lange) Janz. As the third of six brothers born in a span of only nine years, Kurt never lacked for companionship. Despite being a middle child and already showing signs of being short, his competitive nature and perpetual good humor ensured a strong position in the sibling infrastructure.

Kurt's great-grandfather had homesteaded in the area in the 1860s and '70s, but Lakendorf was not a Mennonite community. The nearest Mennonite church was a good distance away, so the Janz clan attended only intermittently. Kurt recalls however that the pleasant ride and change of scenery made church attendance preferable to the services held at home, which featured lengthy readings from the *Prediger Bucher*, a rather dry collection of printed sermons.

Education was important to Kurt's parents, who wanted each of their children to complete high school—a total of ten years of schooling. The local school, however, offered only the first four grades. To help bring about their continued studies, the boys had to leave home and board with relatives in a nearby town. Despite the interruptions and displacements of World War II, Kurt completed his formal education in only nine years. This was due mainly to his academic abilities and enthusiasm for the classroom experience.

Kurt's early years at home had a deep and lasting impact. Parents, grandmother, and several hired hands living under the Janz roof ensured numerous authority figures for the growing children. The boys were raised to be rigorously obedient. This authoritarian style of leadership, in which the "rod was not spared," had a strong influence on the boys' behavior. In the chaotic environment of the refugee camp at Grunau, Germany, following the war, a neighboring family noted the respect and prompt obedience evident in the Janz family. But despite these expectations, Kurt adored his father, and the strong bonds which developed between father and son in later years attest to their mutual respect and commitment.[1]

Kurt's father was a humble, unassuming person, thorough in all his endeavors, well-liked, and affirming of everyone he met. In our conversations, Kurt made frequent reference to his father and wanting to be remembered as being like him. The senior Janz was a role model for his son's professional life. Kurt admired his father's business skills, his organization, and fastidious attention to detail—characteristics which helped his modest success as a farmer. Kurt also observed the freedom and independence enjoyed by those engaged in farming, and resolved that he too would one day be self-employed.

Kurt was only five when the outbreak of World War II cast a dark shadow on his community. Although no soldiers were posted nearby during the early years of the war, the elder Janz family members watched the progress of German forces as reported by the media. Given their proximity to the Russian border, an atmosphere of fear prevailed as neighbors pointed accusing fingers at those deemed not to have demonstrated appropriate commitment to the German cause.

The threat of concentration camps for Jews as well as those regarded as dissidents hung heavily in the air. Tension escalated in the small community as Kurt's father persisted in his refusal to join the Nazi Party, due to his reservations about Hitler's policies. In an attempt to deflect accusing fingers, Janz rigidly met farm production quotas. While political discussions were reserved for adult ears, reverberations reached the Janz children, dampening their enthusiasm for membership in Hitler's Youth.

Despite rising anxiety as the combat zone drew nearer, civilian retreat remained inconceivable. By retreat they would be acknowledging the possibility of defeat for the German forces—a treasonous admission. Not until October 18, 1944, only days in advance of the Russian army, was the official order given permitting flight to the west. While parents feared the worst, the children reveled in the excitement of travel, new sights, and "camping out." After a treacherous flight, the refugees were resettled north of Hamburg in a farming community called Holstein. This would be their home for the next seven years.

Through the efforts of the Mennonite Central Committee (MCC), a Mennonite relief organization, and individuals such as C. F. Klassen, contact was made with the scattered Mennonite refugee families throughout Germany. In the Holstein area, monthly meetings served to reinforce spiritual values. It was here that Kurt was baptized, as he made a public commitment to the Mennonite faith. Kurt remembers how the distribution of material goods donated by their coreligionists in America affirmed a sense of identification with a large and vibrant international Mennonite community. The monthly meetings were also used to disseminate information about possible destinations for those considering leaving war-torn Europe. In light of the limited economic opportunities for their children in Germany, the Janz family decided to go to Canada.

Opportunities in Canada

Kurt considers the date of departure—December 9, 1951—to have been "one of the happiest days of my life." The family was pleasantly surprised to find a house and friendly people waiting for them in Coaldale, Alberta, where they had been assigned a sugar beet labor contract. But given the seasonality of farm labor, Kurt and his two older brothers found employment elsewhere—first as section men for the Canadian Pacific Railway and later (by 1952) in the Calgary construction industry.

In the postwar economic surge, work was plentiful and salaries rising. During the first year of employment in Canada, the three eldest brothers saved almost enough to pay off the family travel debts. After only two years, the young men proudly welcomed their parents to a newly constructed home in Calgary they had built themselves in off hours. For the first time in many years the entire Janz family lived together under one roof. This arrangement continued until each son in turn married and established a home.

The postwar economic situation offered some unique opportunities to immigrants and native-born alike. The Canadian government was determined to avoid the slump which had followed World War I. Unemployment and inflation after that war had precipitated labor conflict and political upheaval. A repetition of the social and economic devastation of the era was unacceptable to leaders and the general public alike. Thus well before the end of hostilities in Europe, the federal government was making plans for postwar economic reconstruction. The automotive industry, which had not been producing civilian motor vehicles since 1942, and residential construction, which had been strongly curtailed during the war, were expected to span the gap in peacetime.

In determining the structure of the postwar housing construction industry, the federal government assumed initiatives such as the passage of a new National Housing Act and the creation of the Central Mortgage and Housing Corporation. The opportunities available through this legislation ensured that single family housing would dominate the urban landscape. The absence of any effectively enforced building codes or standards enabled individuals to construct their own homes virtually without intervention and, in the process, gain valuable skills which could be used in the workplace.[2]

Traditionally, Mennonites had avoided urban centers. However, privately owned homes in residential areas allowed a degree of separation from "worldly influences" and hence gave cities a measure of acceptability. Mennonites thus joined the migration to the cities to capitalize on the tremendous new opportunities. With gradually accumulated capital, experience, and confidence, a fledgling entrepreneur could hire additional labor to multiply his efforts. Continued Mennonite immigration to Canada throughout the 1940s and 1950s provided a reliable pool of highly motivated labor.

The Janz family had always expected Coaldale to be a temporary location. They had hoped to save enough money to buy a farm. But agricultural conditions in Western Canada had changed since the war. Inflated land prices and increased mechanization demanded greater capital investment. Although Kurt shared with his father a tremendous love for the land, another entrepreneurial pursuit beckoned. The booming construction industry proved too tempting for a young man impatient to make his mark on the world.

The construction industry in Calgary seemed to offer unlimited potential. Even Father Janz joined his sons in finding employment in the building trade. Having spent one year as an apprentice cabinetmaker in Germany, Kurt was hired as a finish carpenter by Engineered Homes, one of the largest general contracting companies in Calgary at the time. But after two years with Engineered Homes, Kurt felt "stuck." His ambition was stymied. When his boss refused to give him the raise he felt he deserved, Kurt quit and went to work for two fellow German Mennonite immigrants, Rudy Janssen and Gerhard Bartel. Like many others in the industry, Janssen and Bartel had formed their own cribbing and framing subcontracting company, J. A. Builders.[3]

The postwar immigrants were largely responsible for the growing trend toward subcontracting. With their energy and drive, many immigrants grew restless in the constraints of wage employment. General contractors feared the loss of skilled labor, so they encouraged the formation of subcontracting companies. It was an ideal solution; speed and quality of workmanship were often increased and costs reduced for general contractors. At the same time, ambitious tradespeople could maintain their level of interest and motivation. "The harder you worked, the more you made."[4]

And Kurt worked hard, at least partly because he dreamed of owning a car—not just any car but a certain 1956 Pontiac from Stampede Motors listed at $3600. "That car hardly let me sleep." In an unusual move, Kurt impulsively made the down payment without consulting his family, and proudly drove home his new set of "wheels." As a young man who had lived most of his life in a hand-to-mouth existence as a refugee, money and the things that money could buy were important to him.

Work and acquisitions, however, were not Kurt's sole focus. From his early days, the church and his Christian faith have played an important role in Kurt's life. In Scarboro Mennonite Church (later to become First Mennonite Church), begun only a few years earlier in 1946, Kurt remembers a strong, cohesive bond among the young people. This bond was bolstered by a shared faith, a common language (German), ambition, and the desire to have a good time. They all tended to work long hours throughout the week, but Sundays were reserved for fun and relaxation with one another. This pattern continued even after various members of the group married and settled down with families of their own.[5]

Kurt had met Ruth Bartel while in the refugee camp in Grunau, Germany, as they were both awaiting clearance for admission into Canada. Ruth remembers Kurt and his brother Art as always having fun, constantly initiating activities. Kurt was a "real go-getter." A special friendship developed between the two young people during the trip to their new homes. But when the Janz family left the train and headed toward Coaldale, the Bartels continued on to the Fraser Valley in British Columbia, where relatives awaited them. It would be four years before Kurt and Ruth would meet again.

In the fall of 1955, on a trip to British Columbia with a friend, Kurt sought out Ruth in Vancouver, where she worked as a housekeeper. Despite the fact that Ruth was dating another young man, Kurt set out to win the heart of this rather shy young woman. After his return to Alberta, Kurt began a persistent correspondence with Ruth. She was initially unsure what to do. But the arrival of a dozen long stemmed red roses for Valentine's Day convinced Ruth she ought to give this relationship serious consideration. Throughout the courtship, Kurt demonstrated the decisive action combined with panache that would become his signature style. Finally in August 1957 the outgoing groom exchanged vows with his more quiet bride. The young couple made their home in Calgary, where they were to raise four children— Bernie, Margaret, Arne, and Edgar.

Accepting employment with J. A. Builders was a positive step for the enterprising Kurt. After working as laborers for about a year, Kurt and his friend Paul Bartel received a crew of their own. Here the goal of self-employment began to take shape. With limited technical knowledge but high motivation, they worked long hours and learned fast. Kurt remembers the satisfaction he felt after completing his first set of steps and seeing them fit properly.

A New Partnership

When the J. A. Builders partnership between Rudy Janssen and Gerhard Bartel dissolved in 1956, Rudy offered partnerships to Kurt and his brother Alfred. Because Rudy feared the Janz brothers might strike out on their own, Rudy invited Kurt to become a partner with him in the newly formed Tower Construction Company, while Alfred became a partner in J. A. Builders. Work was plentiful and they expanded operations significantly. But after a few years, the relationship between Kurt and Rudy became strained due to a perceived failure of the elder partner to adequately acknowledge joint efforts. In the spring of 1961, Alfred traded shares with Rudy, leaving the two brothers fully in control of Tower Construction.

The decision to move into an independent operation had been carefully calculated. In the short term, the new owners of Tower Construction took over contracts which had been awarded to J. A. Builders. Paying Rudy a flat fee for each job, they ensured a steady income while they established an independent reputation. In a year they had their "foot in the door" with Keith Construction, the largest and most respected quality builder in Calgary at that time. With Kurt responsible for framing and Alfred in charge of cribbing crews, they provided steady employment for their eleven to twelve workers on a year-round basis. At differing times their father and several brothers were on the payroll.

Kurt was wary of fifty/fifty partnerships because he believed one person always has to be final boss. With this in mind he proposed to Alfred a sixty/forty arrangement. As the major partner, Kurt was prepared to assume the additional responsibility for invoicing, book work, and keeping tools in shape. Initially he received a slightly higher salary, but the partners soon equalized monthly incomes. Annual bonuses, however, continued to be paid on a sixty/forty basis.

The partners consulted one another on all major decisions, but Kurt's word was final. The arrangement worked well and arguments were rarely personal. Only in the later years, when the economy plummeted, was there a tendency for Kurt as boss to be blamed for faulty decisions. The partnership would last for almost twenty-five years, 1961–1984.

Interviewees suggest that as a leader Kurt demonstrates the potentially contradictory qualities of a benevolent dictator and facilitator. On the one hand he adamantly believes persons in charge must be decisive. He admits to becoming quite frustrated when others accept responsibility, then fail to carry through commitments. But co-workers also speak of his willingness to cooperate and confer with others. Kurt regards himself as a patient man, although he's prepared to admit that not all would see him as such. He tries to be fair and appreciative of the efforts of others but also believes you don't get more than you expect from people; consequently, high standards are essential.

This leadership style carried over into his family. In the days he was running a large business, he sometimes found it hard to shift gears at home. "I'd have a busy day, giving orders . . . and I'd start doing that at home . . . Ruth had to put her foot down." Looking back he suspects he may have been too harsh with his children; he admits he was easily frustrated when obedience was not prompt.

Other family members, however, recall a father who left all business behind at the office, not even accepting business calls at home. Ruth could expect a devoted husband who communicated well with his family. The children could count on their father's enthusiastic participation in a variety of activities including football, swimming, skiing, and table top games. Sundays were reserved for the family.

Kurt exercised his leadership skills at church as well. At varying points Kurt was Sunday school superintendent, congregational chair, and church leader (during the years when the pastor was granted a sabbatical to further his studies). He also served on the finance committee for the provincial Mennonite conference and sat on numerous boards for both church and secular organizations. But Kurt did not confine his involvement to high profile positions. He was also continuously active in the choir, in home Bible study groups, and as a teacher in the German language Sunday school class. Kurt's optimism and perceptive qualities endeared him to his church family.[6]

New Ventures

After ten years in partnership together, Kurt and Alfred decided to expand into general contracting. The timing was optimal. Alberta was entering its greatest boom period ever. The 1971–1981 explosion in the province was the product not so much of local conditions as of Organization of Petroleum Exporting Countries' (OPEC) decision to increase oil prices. When, as a result, the demand for Alberta oil skyrocketed, people and capital flooded into the province, contributing to the general economic boom.[7]

Alberta became the wealthiest province in Canada, with the highest per capita income. The province's two major cities, Calgary and Edmonton, where growth was most dramatic, became classic boom towns. New suburbs mushroomed, housing and land values escalated dramatically, and downtown highrise construction was extensive. By 1978 the building industry had reached staggering proportions—$1 billion in annual activity.[8]

As they moved into general contracting, the two partners reorganized their business, splitting it into three primary companies: Tower Construction Calgary (which became the labor arm); Janz Construction Ltd. (the commercial arm); and Tower Construction Ltd. (which remained the parent company with management and any unionized contracts on its payroll).

A few years later they started Horton Building Supplies to provide themselves with rough lumber and finishing materials. Before long, however, demand for their services led to a fifty/fifty split between themselves and other building contractors. The strong economy and numerous opportunities led to further expansion into subcontracting companies, such as plumbing and electrical, an excavating company, and numerous joint ventures in the development and holding of properties. At their peak in the early 1980s, Kurt and Alfred had some twenty-three companies, which they thought "fit together very nicely."

In retrospect Kurt acknowledges that managing three primary companies plus twenty subsidiaries with only two partners probably meant spreading themselves too thin. Although they engaged the support of several managers for specific operations, "Now when I look back it looks like a gigantic task," he says. "But when you're right in the midst of it, it doesn't seem all that much. . . . When things are going well, it takes less time to manage. Then you're looking for opportunities. . . . It's only when you've got a sick company that it takes a lot of input."

There were several reasons for the rapid expansion of subsidiary companies. Tax shelters offered through the federal government's Multi-Unit Residential Building (MURB) program facilitated growth. Tower had also acquired many key personnel, and subsidiary companies provided a way for these individuals to become part of the operation without Kurt and Alfred relinquishing shares in the parent corporations.[9] "I always remembered the reason I left Rudy," Kurt notes. "I didn't want that to happen to us, so we involved people."

Being an employer provided Kurt with the opportunity to live out his personal faith. He found that he became a counselor, financial adviser, lending institution, and even a mediator in domestic disputes. When he considered getting out of labor management, which was frequently more of a headache than an asset, the sense of responsibility for his employees kept him going. What would happen to workers in their fifties who had served faithfully for ten or more years? Who would hire them? His peers accused him of being "stupid." "When things got slack I didn't lay guys off. I'd take on work at a lower price to keep everyone working. We didn't make any money on it. But others lost their key people," he responds. "When things got busy they had to train new guys and that cost them money. Most of our guys knew that if there was work to be had, they'd be working."

As an employer, one of Kurt's primary challenges was to circumvent infighting and rivalry between the various subsidiaries. To bolster cohesion, the company held periodic employee banquets, annual family picnics, and ski trips. In an attempt to keep a "large company operating with [the] efficiency of a small company," Kurt had to keep reminding everyone that they were all working together for the same company, and that success for one entailed greater profits for all. To this end Kurt and Alfred set up "profit centers," whereby different groups were established, each setting their goals for the year. "Everyone knew that if he worked hard and his group did well, he would be rewarded."

With the help of 150 to 200 employees, productivity soared. In their peak years, between 1980 and early 1982, the 150 to 200 housing units constructed on an annual basis represented only about half of company energies. The commercial arm contributed about 25 percent of production. The remaining effort by the labor arm consisted of ongoing cribbing and framing contracts.

A major problem facing the construction industry during the boom years of the 1970s was the shortage of serviced lots. With the key to success resting on availability of land, Tower assumed a multi-pronged approach. They initiated residential development on acreages outside city limits, began their own development projects in bedroom communities a few miles out of Calgary, and undertook numerous multi-unit residential complexes. In addition, Kurt was a driving force behind the establishment of a new land development company, Market Place Properties and Investments.

Despite heavy commitments on the job, at home, and elsewhere, Kurt continued to contribute to the church through his gifts of leadership and finances. But being a successful businessman in First Mennonite Church created tensions. A small but vocal contingent in the church was constantly urging simplicity of lifestyle and taking what Kurt felt were "potshots" at the more successful businesspeople in the church. There seemed to be an implicit assumption that if one had become wealthy, it must be as a result of dishonesty, abuse of employees, or a low quality product—one should feel guilty about wealth.

This attitude caused Kurt considerable frustration. He urged a recognition of the ability to make money as one of many equally valued gifts of the Spirit essential to carry out the program of the church. The body of the church has many members, and each should be appreciated for its unique contribution to the whole. He suggested that placing an additional emphasis on stewardship of money as well as abilities regardless of age or personal circumstance would be one way to deflect undue attention from the wealthy and to encourage all members to assume their respective responsibilities.

In 1980 Kurt and Alfred decided to restructure their organization in an attempt to streamline operations and regain full control of the operation. Since the two partners no longer wanted their own estates to grow, they placed existing projects under a holding company called Janz Investments Ltd. Shares in this new company were distributed evenly, with one third going to Kurt and Alfred, one third to their wives, and the final third placed in their children's names.

This new arrangement had many positive dimensions. By spreading their income among more individuals taxed at a lower rate, some taxes could be avoided. Another positive result was that under the parameters of the new arrangement, the banks decided to release wives from personal guarantees. This meant their primary residences, long in their wives' names, could be protected regardless of what happened to the companies. The major problem with the new arrangement was the fact that everything was tied together in such a way that when the recession hit and their empire began to crumble, even clear-title properties could not be liquidated to bail out other holdings.

Recession and Receivership

From the beginning Kurt had been aware of the need to protect operations from business downturns through a strategy of alternating expansion and retrenchment and through maintaining sufficient reserves to ride out slow periods. This cautious approach was insufficient, however, to protect the Tower operation during the recession of the early 1980s. Falling interest rates, softening world oil prices, and an economic recession affecting the entire Western world led to distress throughout the Alberta economy. The boom quickly ended.

During 1982 and 1983, many oil companies and related service businesses laid off employees.[10] The malaise in Alberta's key industry was quickly reflected in other sectors of the economy. Even though the construction industry tried desperately to regroup, it found itself in a free fall situation. Customers quit buying. Those who had purchased often turned their backs on contracts and on sizable downpayments. As sales collapsed and purchasers walked away from their deposits, mortgage companies refused to honor funding commitments to builders. The builders in turn were left with massive financial commitments and no cash flow. Furthermore, banks severely curtailed builders' established lines of credit, causing various land development companies dependent on builders to collapse.

According to Janz, "Had the recession occurred a year earlier or a year later, we wouldn't have gotten into trouble." Tower Construction had just embarked on four new joint ventures—buildings in the $2-3 million range. With builders going bankrupt in droves, Kurt hired an accounting firm in the spring of 1983 to put together a survival proposal to take to the bank. Of the various scenarios, they determined to sell off their land and holdings as the market could absorb them, instead of attempting to unload everything at once. Both the Bank of Commerce and the Treasury Branch assured Kurt and Alfred of full support.

Despite their best efforts, Tower eventually found itself in a hopeless situation. In August 1982, a nearly completed condominium complex in Calgary's Beltline community burned to the ground. Although the building was insured, the company took a considerable loss. The sale of another condominium complex in the same area fell through that fall, leaving Tower holding a half-million dollar second mortgage on that property alone, which was subsequently lost by the rapid fall of property values. Another half-million dollars Tower was carrying on residential homes was lost through foreclosures. The recession affected other dimensions of Kurt and Alfred's operation negatively as well.

Thus even though payments were current, in December 1983 the Bank of Commerce put Janz Construction into receivership. Early in the new year, Kurt set up an appointment with the Treasury Branch to discuss plans for the future of the Tower operation. The bank managers assured Kurt of their support but also affirmed the need to restructure and downsize operations. Together they drew up a new five-year proposal.

But when Kurt and his lawyer met with the Treasury Branch management to sign the new contract on January 25, 1984, they were shocked beyond belief to hear that the bank had reconsidered. Kurt vividly recalls, "Instead of returning home that night with a new deal, we were put into receivership." In shock and disbelief, Kurt broke down and wept.

The next few days passed in slow motion. A trip to the lawyer's office formalized the "voluntary receivership." A stunned huddle of staff received Kurt's announcement of the bank's decision. The following morning, the receiver showed up at the office to change the locks and label the assets in preparation for auction disposal.

The speed of events left no time for Kurt to contemplate his own response to the situation. In the days that followed, he mechanically responded to assigned tasks. The weekend after the receivership, Kurt performed his duties as First Mennonite Church chairman at the annual congregational meetings. In retrospect, he's not certain he could do it again but at the time "I had a lot of strength and I've got to give God the praise."

Kurt was not alone in his numbness. The entire industry was in shock. Kurt's troubles were only symbolic of the larger scenario. But even though many builders found themselves in similar straits, shock and pride prevented the formation of a much-needed support system.

The Janz family's home congregation did not respond much better to the crisis. Much of the congregation was involved in construction and severely affected by the industry's downturn.[11] The pastor found himself tongue-tied as he sought to balance an awkward array of conflicting interests and pain. In several sermons he tried to address the "tough times" and suggest how one might cope with adversity and disappointments in life. One Treasury Branch district manager, who was directly involved in the bank's decision to force Tower Construction into bankruptcy, was also a member of the congregation. And several subcontractors in the church lost significant amounts of money in Tower's demise. Such factors further complicated the situation. The church council discussed the "problem" on numerous occasions but with no formal recommendations.

Friends and co-workers likewise had difficulty generating appropriate responses. In fairness, Tower employees tried to be supportive but generally found meaningful comfort elusive. Some Tower employees recognized that if "the top of the totem pole gets hurt, it trickles down and those below also get hurt."[12] Others blamed Kurt. They resented the fact that he retained his home and cottage, which had been registered in his wife's name. They felt that as a Christian Kurt should make good his debts by selling those remaining properties. What they failed to realize was that banks and mortgage companies, as secured creditors, have prior claim to any additional revenue generated.

A variety of hurtful comments reached the ears of Kurt and his wife, Ruth. "Fortunately you don't get to hear most of what people say behind your back. Some said, 'I used to respect Kurt but now I can't respect him any more.' They obviously saw it as being my fault."[13] Even some well-meaning friends demonstrated lack of sensitivity in relaying gossip spread by others.

The financial pressure strained all relationships, including family. In the Kurt/Alfred partnership, Kurt had traditionally provided the drive to push on toward new challenges. Alfred, on the other hand, would have been content to remain relatively small. Tensions emerged over the fact that had the company remained smaller, it might have experienced fewer difficulties. But with time and mutual effort, the two brothers have resolved their differences.

The stress between the two brothers, however, paled in comparison to how Alfred's wife, Ingrid, responded. She blamed Kurt for their misfortune, convinced that it was solely his ambition which had led to the economic disaster and had placed their lifestyle and futures in jeopardy. Despite the passing of time and numerous overtures on the part of both Kurt and Ruth, tensions remain today.[14]

Starting Over

Fortunately the strained relations with Ingrid were the exception rather than the rule in the family. Kurt credits his wife's support as being a primary source of support in the difficult days and months following bankruptcy. When news of the bank's decision reached the

Fraser Valley in British Columbia, Ruth's father came to lend moral support. The four Janz children likewise rallied around their parents. The crisis and the struggle to rebuild their lives were a family bonding experience. Kurt expresses his gratitude that there has been no hint of resentment that if "Dad hadn't fouled up we'd all be on easy street."

In an interview conducted by the Canadian Broadcasting Corporation (CBC) in the days between the receivership and the auction, Kurt said he considered himself fortunate to have lost nothing of value—only money. In comparison with those who under similar circumstances ended their lives, gave up the faith, or saw their marriages disintegrate, Kurt affirmed his gratitude for health, family, and faith. He was also grateful that his father, having passed away in 1982, did not live to see his failure.

There were those outside the family who also reached out to Kurt and his family. Two Mennonite pastors from the city as well as Ruth's parents' pastor in Chilliwack, British Columbia, made visits and phone calls. One First Mennonite congregational member who had worked for Tower refused to submit an invoice on Kurt's first house when he started building again. (A few months after the bankruptcy, Kurt began building again under the name of California Homes Ltd.) "I'll do this one for free because I want to give you a start." A Christian brother signed a $30,000 guarantee to the New Home Warranty Program, which enabled Kurt to reestablish himself in construction. Other persons approached with open-ended offers of help, although Kurt's pride kept him from accepting.

Nonchurch people also lent moral support. "We had a tenant in the building. He was an insurance agent in a wheelchair with MS. . . . He sent amusing cards and always had something encouraging to say." On occasion, individuals who had experienced bankruptcy a few years earlier would come into Kurt's office with the reassurance that "it's not as bad as you think right now. Give it time." Most social contact, however, was awkward.

Kurt accepts responsibility for much of this awkwardness. "What do you say to someone who just blew it?" He found himself falling into a pattern of self-imposed isolation. "Your mind tends to work overtime. People who have made remarks about you, you stay away from them. Then you think 'Who are their friends?' So you stay away from them as well and the circle becomes bigger and eventually you've got a lot of people you try to avoid."

122-unit condo project by Tower construction.

Janz Construction project: apartment block for rental purposes.

Not only the social setting contributed to Kurt's sense of isolation and persecution. Repeated grillings as the banks searched for hidden assets, and nasty encounters with collection agency representatives, continued for years. Kurt said, "Every time the telephone rings, every time someone comes to the door, you wonder who it is and what they've got up their sleeve this time."[15]

In his struggle to cope with personal and financial trauma, Kurt pored over the Bible and his church's hymnal, discovering in the process a new depth of meaning. Here he found a lifeline. But though some individuals treated Kurt in a Christian way, disappointment lingers in Kurt's voice when he refers to the church and his crisis.

More support could have been given, more tact and awareness of pain exhibited.

Despite the financial and emotional setbacks, Kurt found no time for self-pity. When the receiver asked him to oversee completion of the numerous houses Tower had in various stages of construction, Kurt agreed. On an interim basis he also served as property manager for the receiver. In some ways it was a relief to find himself performing many of the same duties as before without the financial pressures.

After about three months, however, Kurt activated California Homes Ltd., a previously inactive division of Tower Construction. Under the auspices of this new company, Kurt purchased several incomplete houses abandoned by their respective contractors. He never seriously considered working for someone else or even leaving the industry. After thirty-two years in the construction business as his own boss, it was in his blood. Although his spirit had been thoroughly shaken, Kurt knew he still had the technical and interpersonal skills required in the industry. His competitive nature and will to survive rose to the challenge.

But jumping back into the ring presented numerous unanticipated challenges. Although he no longer had aspirations of significant expansion, he found that even building twenty-five to thirty houses a year was no longer feasible. A limited operating line of credit, plus difficulty with subcontractors, hindered operations.[16] Kurt also found himself and his product maligned by competing salespersons, who warned potential customers of his past difficulties.

After years of focusing on the big picture in management, as a small builder Kurt found himself closer to the action. He was forced to deal personally with onsite difficulties, rather than delegating them to an employee. He willingly admits that many of the petty problems he encounters frustrate him. Although he has maintained the work discipline which is part of his heritage and personal disposition, much of the joy he used to find in work has disappeared. Now he finds himself looking forward to weekends and escape to their cabin at Fairmont, British Columbia, as never before.

In addition to the specific problems Kurt met as he struggled to reenter the industry, the recession had dealt the Calgary construction world a blow from which it would not quickly recover. In the highly competitive market which has persisted throughout recent years, the only way to sustain production and profits is through volume. This places much pressure on smaller builders. Whereas previously smaller operators could compete as custom builders, in the post-boom market the overall quality of construction has improved, and small builders cannot offer many more features than their larger, more cost-efficient competitors.

The distress Kurt continues to encounter in his working world seems to confirm his sense of failure. Although he continues to present himself with his customary smile, he has found himself masking a great deal of inner pain. The emotional strain has taken its toll on Kurt's traditionally optimistic spirit, and he struggles to maintain perspective. His own diminished stamina causes him to wonder if his father-in-law's stroke in the fall of 1984 and his brother Alfred's recent heart attack were at least partially induced by the additional stress of the bankruptcy experience. It is in such moments, when guilt still looms heavily, that Kurt is grateful for the strength he has found in his faith and in the support of his wife, Ruth.

Although she never had a strong interest in business, Ruth was actively involved in office tasks in the early years of the Tower operation. Ruth actively opposed Kurt's considerable expansion on grounds that a smaller operation would free time for family. Kurt, on the other hand, would not hear of it. The excitement, the challenge, and the rewards were too tempting. As the company expanded well beyond her own comfort level, she gave up her office tasks to focus on family and home. Since Tower's bankruptcy in 1984, however, she has resumed her involvement, not only as a faithful pillar of support, but also in a practical sense, performing whatever tasks are required—from cleaning houses prior to occupancy to offering critiques of prospective house plans.

Having experienced both the highs and the lows of the economic scale, Kurt is philosophical about the relationship between financial success and public leadership. He sees leadership happening almost automatically through a process of natural selection—as one gains expertise, responsibility tends to follow. Others, however, state emphatically that Kurt is being altogether too modest. They are quick to point out Kurt's leadership attributes, such as his sense of vision and his capacity to convert that vision into a shared objective. As a committed Christian with a strong sense of stewardship in the use of his time, money, and gifts, he has demonstrated willingness to further the work of the church in its many dimensions.

Despite encouragement to maintain involvement, Kurt and Ruth both withdrew from active church life following bankruptcy. Remaining in the shadows reflected not only a damaged ego and loss of self-confidence, it was also a strategy to allow healing and to give Kurt the time to reestablish his new business ventures. Although healing is gradually occurring, Kurt and Ruth still maintain a low profile in relation to the church and its programs.

Assessment

In assessing his own attitudes toward work and the entrepreneurial experience, Kurt recalls that working hard was always equated with godliness. But work has not been without tangible rewards. It has, for the most part, provided a generous lifestyle for Kurt and his family, along with challenges, opportunity for innovation, and the satisfaction of completing a task. He admits that these divergent rewards probably led him to work to excess at times but he never considered himself a workaholic. "To me it wasn't really work: I just enjoyed it so

Kurt Janz' family.

much. I never felt that work was an obsession."

The bankruptcy has dampened this enthusiasm. Although he admits he would be lost without work, he no longer finds himself consumed by the job. Not working or even working at a leisurely pace is not an option, however, given the need to provide for himself and his family's future retirement.

Despite his financial reversal, Kurt still adamantly maintains that the entrepreneurial experience provides the best opportunities in the workforce. Although hard work is essential, there is also a range of freedom available to the self-employed that is not possible for the salaried worker. This freedom at least partly eliminates the need to impress others, granting greater liberty to behave according to conscience. Freedom is also evident in the increased opportunities for generosity and practical demonstrations of faith as an employer, a church member, a friend, and a concerned citizen.

Whether it entailed providing an advance to the wife of an employee who gambled away his paycheck, putting up bail for an alcoholic worker, giving a job to an ex-convict, going out of his way to create summer jobs for students, or releasing employees (with pay) to teach vacation Bible school, Kurt tried actively to demonstrate his faith. A former colleague confirmed that although Kurt did not "go around preaching or handing out tracts," his associates knew where he stood in relation to his faith.

Reflecting on his life, Kurt has few regrets. He appreciates driving by projects he has completed, and he looks forward to someday giving his grandchildren a tour. Sometimes he's amazed at the courage and the confidence he and Alfred demonstrated when the Tower star was at its zenith. "We must have had a lot of guts —stupid maybe but at the time it was good fun." But while he's proud of his achievements, at the same time he finds it difficult not to berate himself. Had he been less exuberant in his actions, more cautious in the past, less caught up in the thrill of the moment, more aware of the fickleness of the marketplace, life might be much easier now.

External circumstances have formed a unique framework for the life of Kurt Janz. They include World War II, evacuation, immigration to a new homeland, the postwar economic explosion in Canada, the astounding opportunities in Alberta during the 1970s, and the recession of the early 1980s, which decimated the provincial economy and the lives of thousands of citizens.

But it is in the response to circumstances that the true quality of the individual is revealed. Kurt is an extraordinary man. In many ways he epitomizes the entrepreneurial personality. He has demonstrated a highly motivated, achievement-oriented disposition with the capacity and the desire to work independently and respond innovatively to fluctuating social and economic conditions. His good humor, his positive attitude, interpersonal skills, vision, and ability to capitalize on opportunities have ensured a prominent position for him in both business and church.

He has, however, another remarkable characteristic—the capacity to focus completely on the task at hand. While at the helm of his large company during his twelve-hour work days, outside thoughts disappeared. Similarly, when he headed home, he demonstrated the ability to leave the job totally behind and focus with the same passion on family and voluntary responsibilities at church and elsewhere. Individuals imbued with the entrepreneurial spirit are usually more narrowly obsessed with work.

But while undoubtedly exceptional, Kurt is human. Prior to his financial reversal, there were times he demonstrated confidence bordering on arrogance. It is difficult not to be proud when all evidence seems to confirm your astute judgment and "Midas touch." In more recent years, he struggles with cynicism. Yet this same man would like to be remembered not primarily for ventures in the business community but for being, like his father, a faithful Christian, humble, unassuming, thorough in all his endeavors, well liked by all and affirming of everyone he meets. He would genuinely like to be a person who enjoys life regardless of circumstances. The indelible impact of his "failure," however, ensures that this remains a constant battle.

He continues to mask many wounds to his self-confidence. But in moments of reflection one can see that the spark of vitality has not been extinguished. "I'd like just one more kick at the can—I'm waiting for the economy to perk up one more time and give me a bit of a boost and then I'll just step aside. . . ." In the subdued but not extinguished spirit, the renewed appreciation for the love and support of family and close friends, the gratitude for the faithful presence of God in his life—one can see the struggle for rebirth from ashes.[17]

7

Frieda Marie Kaufman:
Builder of Institutions and Lives

BY KATIE FUNK WIEBE

*Beginning as a private nurse, Sister Frieda Marie Kaufman (1883-1944)
was the driving force behind the establishment of the deaconess movement in the Mennonite community. She spearheaded the establishment of
the Bethel Deaconess Home in Newton, Kansas, in 1908. Sister Frieda
exhibited a devout faith, strong leadership, hard work, and ingenuity in
realizing her goals. Like most entrepreneurs, her pioneering efforts involved struggles and personal risk, including to her health. Her story is
an example of entrepreneurial abilities exercised almost entirely within
the church, clearly the most acceptable venue for independent women of
her time and place.*

IN THE 1943 EDITION of *Who's Who Among the Mennonites*, Sister Frieda
Marie Kaufman is listed as Deaconess, Mother of Bethel Deaconess
Home and Hospital in Newton, Kansas, and credited with sharing in

the organization and building of Bethel Hospital in Mountain Lake, Minnesota, and the Bethel Home for the Aged in Newton. Also noted is her editing of *In the Service of the King*, the organ of the Bethel Deaconess Home and Hospital.

Other sources reveal she was involved in a number of building projects, including the new wing of the Bethel Hospital in 1913; Sarepta, the student nurses residence; and the educational wing of the First Mennonite Church in Newton. She actively promoted Bethel College and organized the first Sunday school teacher's training class among General Conference Mennonites at the First Mennonite Church in Newton. She wrote *Auf Wanderweg*, a travelogue of her journey to Europe in 1934, and contributed numerous articles to various publications. The Sister Frieda Kaufman Memorial Chapel was dedicated in 1953, in honor of her significant contributions to the Mennonites of Kansas.

It would be difficult to tally the amount of money she raised for the various building projects, the addresses she delivered, and the Bible lessons and courses in nursing and the deaconess movement she taught. Her influence on the spiritual and vocational formation of the young women who joined the deaconess movement or entered nurses training was formidable. So was her effect on hospital patients during the thirty-five years she was "sister-in-charge" of the Bethel Deaconess Home and superintendent of the Bethel Deaconess Hospital.

At her funeral on August 10, 1944, Rev. H. J. Dyck quoted an earlier citation, read when she received the honorary degree of Doctor of Humane Letters from Bethel College. "Sister Frieda, more than any other, has been instrumental in establishing the deaconess cause in the Mennonite Church of North America," he quoted. "Women who have known her as a teacher and counselor have caught a vision that has enabled them to go to France, to Belgium, to India, to China, to Africa, to the plateau of Tibet in order to carry through the medium of nursing the torch of God's redemptive love."[1]

Frieda is an outstanding example of a woman who boldly met the challenge of her time, particularly as it related to single women looking for a spiritual ministry. She was ready to become a deaconess even before the church was ready for her. Yet in the final years before her death at age sixty, she was aware that the deaconess movement into which she had poured her strength for so many years would probably not survive the postwar era, though the nursing school and hospital would continue to expand.

Obituaries speak of her as a woman of "keen insight and vision," a "truly great woman," and "a builder of houses and lives." She never invested much of her own money in her enterprises, for she never had more than a small allowance. But she invested her life for a cause she believed in firmly. She was not an entrepreneur in the sense of developing a moneymaking enterprise but in the sense of a pioneer who, with the resources available, built institutions and shaped lives in the Mennonite world.

Childhood

Sister Frieda Kaufman's childhood reveals factors that led to her becoming a deaconess. She was born to John and Marie Kaufman on October 23, 1883, the last of nine children. Three brothers and three sisters died before she was born, some in infancy and some of diphtheria epidemics, so her family knew the pain of illness and death.

Frieda Kaufman at age eleven.

Frieda Kaufman at approximately age seven; taken 1890 in Germany. In her own handwriting at a later time: "Father picked me up from a sand heap where I was playing, and had a wandering photographer take my picture. That is why I look so unkempt. Mother was quite shocked."

Female religious figures were a prominent feature of her early childhood. She attended a kindergarten conducted by Lutheran deaconesses. Then for nearly a year the family lived in an almost entirely Catholic community, and seven-year-old Frieda spent much of her time playing in the home of a group of nuns who lived across the street from the Kaufmans. They enjoyed the young girl and allowed her to help with the kindergarten children of the parochial school. "Under these influences, she decided to become a sister, a desire she never lost," wrote Sister Lena Mae Smith, her longtime co-worker.

Other factors also directed her to deaconess service. On her mother's death at age twelve she felt bereft, for her two sisters soon married, and a Mr. and Mrs. Schowalter lived with her father. She wrote, "This changed my youth, and I had a very hard adjustment to make." She was a lonely child. Following catechism and a conversion experience, she was baptized and determined to spend the rest of her life "as a handmaiden of the Lord."

The Deaconess Movement

While still in her teens, Frieda was fortunate to have several mentors who were interested in the deaconess movement. One was Rev. David Goerz of Newton, Kansas, who as early as 1890 advocated deaconess work as a branch of home missions to General Conference Mennonites. The church was somewhat open to such a venture and for about ten years discussed it periodically in conference sessions. Then in 1903 the Bethel Deaconess Home and Hospital Society was organized. The charter states the purpose of this institution as "the establishment and maintenance of a training school to educate and train nurses and deaconesses in a hospital to be erected for that purpose in connection with said school."

The American deaconess movement had been growing from the later nineteenth century on. "Nearly sixty training institutions were opened in the United States between 1880 and 1915 for laypeople, mostly for women, that emphasized the acquisition of skills and practical experience, particularly in the areas of Bible teaching and missions," writes Virginia Lieson Brereton. Growth of the deaconess movement at first was slow, but when it gained a foothold in the Methodist church it became widespread. These training schools were not "hotbeds of feminism," for the emphasis was always on "woman's responsibility, not her rights; on service to the cause of Christ, not leadership of it."[2]

Historian James Juhnke sees the entrepreneurial spirit present in David Goerz, who besides being on the board of the new Society was cofounder and business manager of Bethel College, rather than in the women directing the hospitals and deaconess homes in Kansas and elsewhere.[3] He views the Mennonite deaconess movement as the frontline in the development of Mennonite health-care institutions. He notes that the movement brought together two resources: volunteer labor of single women (deaconesses working for subsistence or nurses working for minimal wages), and the energies of entrepreneurial, community-building churchmen.

Sister Frieda Kaufman; taken at Halstead, Kan.

In Juhnke's view, Frieda's lifework combined higher education, health care, and mission work in the Mennonite denomination. He adds that the deaconesses "enjoyed more responsibility and honor than Mennonite women could find anywhere else among their people except in urban or overseas missions. . . . The theory seems to have been that for success there had to be dedicated women for compassionate labor, and businesslike men for promotion and fund-raising."[4]

Yet without women like Frieda, who were willing to devote their lives and reputations to build a deaconess institution, Goerz and the board would have been severely handicapped. Such women were the entrepreneurs in the sense of risking money, sometimes beginning projects even before the money was subscribed. Frieda was an entrepreneur in that she risked becoming involved in an untried enterprise in the Mennonite community. She took the vows of the diaconate even before she knew whether there was going to be an opportunity to test her skills in the Mennonite Church.

Another early mentor for Frieda, besides Goerz, was Mrs. K. M. Krehbiel, who together with Frieda undertook the care of an elderly

Deaconesses at the front entrance of the deaconess home adjacent to Bethel Deaconess Hospital, Newton, Kansas, in March 1911. Left to right (in white garb): Sister Catherine Voth, Sister Frieda Kaufman, and Sister Lydia Goertz. The deaconess in the black garb may be Sister Greta Luken of Cincinnati, who visited the Newton deaconesses in 1911. She apparently functioned in the role of a deaconess mother to the Newton group.

woman who needed home nursing. The older Mrs. Krehbiel encouraged the sixteen-year-old Frieda to tell Goerz about her aspirations to become a deaconess. But Frieda was too young to be accepted into specialized training as a deaconess, so Goerz suggested she attend Bethel College. This she did from 1900-1902, followed by two years at the German Deaconess Home and Hospital in Cincinnati, Ohio.

On November 14, 1902, in Cincinnati, the nineteen-year-old Frieda was invested and donned the deaconess garb, to be known henceforth officially as "Sister Frieda." Thereafter she returned to Kansas to begin duty as a private nurse in homes in the Newton area. She worked in this capacity for four years, until the church community was ready to launch the new deaconess institution.

A New Institution

This finally occurred in 1908. In June of that year, Sister Frieda, Sister Catherine Voth, and Sister Ida Epp were ordained and installed into full-time service at the new Bethel Deaconess Home and Hospital, and the work began.[5] They knelt before the altar and vowed "obedience, willingness, and faithfulness to God in the calling of deaconesses." The first patient was admitted on June 21 and the first infant born on June 23. On September 28 the first three women were admitted to the deaconess training course.

Frieda was only twenty-five when she accepted the position of sister-in-charge of the deaconess home and superintendent of the hospital, with its myriad responsibilities. Behind her lay only four years of academic training and four years of private nursing to prepare her for the administrative responsibilities. She had enthusiasm for the task, a sense of calling, and a willingness to work. Frieda's sister once said of her, "Just let Frieda try herself at the most unpleasant and disagreeable tasks; she always has said that she wants to become a deaconess."

She had been a good private nurse before the deaconess home was opened, working long hours and serving whomever needed her. She had had difficulty at first getting anyone to pay her for her services, even as little as $1.50 per day "under our people" and $2.00 per day *unter Fremden* (under strangers). This was because nursing was considered housework, not a profession. In many homes she had to combat ignorance and superstition, yet her reputation for excellent care opened door after door to her.

But now, as sister-in-charge of the deaconess home and hospital, she was challenged with developing a health-care institution as well as offering single women and young childless widows opportunities to find a mission. In the early days it was not customary to bring the sick to a hospital except when very ill, so patients had to be convinced to come. The church also had to be convinced of the concept of deaconesses.

Mrs. Wilhelmina (Bernard) Warkentin of Newton became an important mentor for the young deaconess-mother, who still needed mothering herself. Frieda's diaries often mention going to Mrs. Warkentin for the evening or night. At her older friend's death in 1932, Frieda wrote, "That mother heart has ceased to beat for us." She missed her dearly. Thereafter Frieda does not mention any particular person in whom she confided other than her co-workers, especially Sister Lena Mae Smith.

The early years were busy with organizational activity. In 1910 the Women's Auxiliary was organized, with Mrs. Warkentin as president. Construction began on a new building for the deaconess home, funds for which Mrs. Warkentin had donated. As people began to accept the hospital as a place to go when ill, there was soon need for a maternity annex. Hard on the heels of these construction projects came a request from Mountain Lake, Minnesota, to the Newton board to help establish a deaconess home there.

The young deaconess was involved in all these ventures. During 1911-1930, Sister Frieda gave much "time, thought, and direction" to the hospital and home for aged in Mountain Lake. This work, which caused her much concern, was finally turned over to an elected board in 1930.

In late 1909 Frieda suffered from the first of recurring periods of emotional and physical exhaustion. She took a six-month leave-of-absence for rest and recuperation. At Excelsior Springs the treatment included baths, massage, and sixteen glasses of spring water daily. She was diagnosed as having chronic appendicitis. Some of her anguish about her physical condition is revealed in a letter written to the Cincinnati sisters with whom she had trained. She confided that she had expected to die on December 31, 1909. They should not be surprised if they heard of her sudden death. She also confided that she had seen a nerve specialist.

In other letters to these sisters, she unburdened her heart about the pressures of directing a growing institution. Sister Catherine was out in private nursing continually, the house was overflowing with patients, and six sisters were to be "put in their garb," which meant extra sewing. She hints at the administrative responsibility. "In an older institution there is usually someone to help with such things, in the beginning so much appears to be lacking and people must be drilled and trained into their place." But she wanted them to know she was not complaining.

In January of 1910, while still absent from her responsibilities, she wrote to these friends that she was trying to give her burdens "to stronger shoulders." She was not "like Sister Marie Baugertes [of the Cincinnati home], afraid to let anyone else share responsibility; but after one has shifted the load and still the slightest strain upsets one, it is so discouraging. . . . He will give me my allotted portion of those qualifications which I need to serve him as he would have me do." Was she too young and too inexperienced for the administrative load? Was the strain too much? Did her zeal surpass her strength?

Nearly thirty years later, when a male administrator was appointed, Frieda wrote a job description of her work as sister-in-charge of the hospital. It includes all matters pertaining to the sisterhood; director of religious life of patients, sisters, student nurses, and other personnel; director of public relations; and supervisor of the sewing room and dry goods. The details of her assignment look beyond human capability, yet she omitted one assignment. In the fall of 1910, when she returned to Bethel, one of her first tasks was fundraising for the maternity annex to the hospital. This involved traveling to nearby Mennonite communities and soliciting donations door-to-door.

During these early years, numerous requests came to Frieda: from Rosthern, Saskatchewan, for an English/German-speaking nurse; from Freeman, South Dakota, a call to establish a deaconess branch there; from Reedley, California, for names of sisters to work in their hospital; from Bluffton, Ohio, to send deaconesses to them. She was always forced to answer that no sisters were available to send elsewhere. The largest number of deaconesses at any one time was thirty.[6]

The Mennonite communities were gradually accepting deaconesses as hospital workers, but the supply was limited. Too few women were committing themselves to diaconate service. Frieda defined a deaconess as a "servant of the church, who in the spirit of Jesus Christ and for his sake spends her whole time in serving those who are sick or poor or morally in danger. She not only nurses them but takes care of them as a Christian, in order that they may be saved through faith in Jesus Christ." She insisted that a woman feel called to the task and dedicate herself totally to it. She had little use for those who looked fondly back on their previous lives.

How did the institution encourage work in the diaconate? At the beginning women read in church publications of the need for household helpers at the hospital, and some applied. While there they caught the vision of deaconess work. Others came specifically for deaconess training. The first student records are sketchy or nonexistent, but from what is available, it is clear the women who came in the first decades were not young, inexperienced visionaries. Their average age was closer to thirty than to twenty, although a few as young as eighteen or nineteen applied.

The older ones had probably faced the reality that marriage was not for them. Although celibacy was not part of the deaconess vow, constituency members and candidates sometimes thought it was. The educational background of many was limited. Some had only grammar school, others a few years of high school or Bible school and college. But these educational limitations were overlooked if the woman came with a strong sense of calling and the physical strength to do the work.

A Fading Dream

In the latter 1930s and early 1940s, until her death in 1944, Frieda's actions and correspondence indicate she was aware that the dream of an expanded deaconess movement, which had looked promising when she first began her work, was fading. In 1956 Sister Lena Mae reported that up to then, a total of sixty-two sisters had become members of the Bethel Deaconess sisterhood, with twenty-six still associated with it. This number probably includes both ordained and unordained sisters.

Clearly not all women who joined the diaconate remained with it. In fact Frieda faced disappointment in a deaconess candidate at the beginning of her career. In a letter written in 1908, even before the deaconess movement was publicly launched, she poured out her distress that one woman had left the patient under her care, taken the first train for Oklahoma, and married a widower with children before a probate judge. "What a blow for us and what a disgrace to the work. . . . Won't the evil tongues wag?" She had already given six years of hard work for the cause. Why should she have to see the work suffer now at the hand of "one who evidently was only half with it"?

In a letter written early in 1913, Sister Frieda responded to news of the resignation of one of the sisters at the German Deaconess Home in Cincinnati. "It is very hard for me to see one after another of the old sisters drop out of the ranks of the work, which is so dear, so dear to my heart and life." In June of that year she wrote again that she firmly believed that those who left the work were never "real deaconesses at heart. . . . There are many who think they had a call into the work, who probably misunderstood the Master at the time." A sense of spiritual calling, she firmly believed, was needed to sustain one during difficult times.

In another letter to the Cincinnati sisters, she writes, "Inspiration is good and we must have it, but I have noticed that the people who seem to be inspired all the time sometimes accomplish less in the long run than those who plod along and do the little they can in a wholehearted way." Was she rationalizing the difficulties the diaconate was experiencing? In 1914 she wrote to these friends that she was sometimes tempted to withdraw from the diaconate but was always ashamed of the feeling.

In 1919-20, fifteen deaconesses finished their program at Bethel. Thirteen had dropped out, citing illness, marriage, lack of education, need to take care of parents, and inability to handle the discipline or the work. Hours were long for sisters-in-training, and living conditions and regulations strict. They were always reminded that the school's main purpose was not to train nurses but to help the needy. Nursing was but one facet of their tasks, which included housekeeping (kitchen and laundry duty), spiritual ministry to the sick, and general mission work as needed.

Struggles

In late 1928 Frieda suffered a second serious illness which required her to give up her work again for a time. But when she returned, in January of 1929, there was obviously some awkwardness between herself and the other sisters. "From every angle I feel that the sisters want me to take up my responsibilities," she wrote. "No one wishes to say the last word. Oh how I will need wisdom and discretion to move aright these days. . . . God could not steer me to constructive action before. I would only try to load more and more upon myself and thereby made myself more unfit for a leader. I was too burdened with details which I could never finish or complete. He is going to put a stop to this all and I want to learn my lesson."

During these years of building the deaconess movement, her greatest strength was as a nurturer of lives, though she had to be involved in all aspects of the work, including the physical labor of cleaning and gardening. One of her greatest weaknesses appears to have been inability to delegate tasks to others, reflecting a general lack of organizational and administrative skills.

Reading the sporadic entries in her diaries for 1924-44, one senses the tremendous burden she carried, and that it was not apparent to others. When the hospital was small, her tasks were numerous, but as it grew she kept giving herself more tasks without assigning to others the more menial ones—such as cleaning and laundry, and particularly the gardening she loved. Thus entries mention that she involved herself with fixing a smokestack, supervising carpentry and landscaping work, quite a bit of cleaning, butchering animals, arrangements for prayer meetings, bookkeeping, meeting with various people including architects, and on and on.

Her diaries reveal that at times she was desperately trying to hold everything together but not succeeding. Her problems were compounded by other factors, including various teaching duties, the separation of the Mountain Lake institution from the Bethel Deaconess Home and Hospital Society, a fire in the deaconess home which destroyed a portion of the roof and damaged fourteen rooms, the death of Wilhelmina Warkentin in 1932, and sickness among the sisters as well as her own struggles with health. Another factor which probably contributed to her overwork and overinvolvement in detailed and

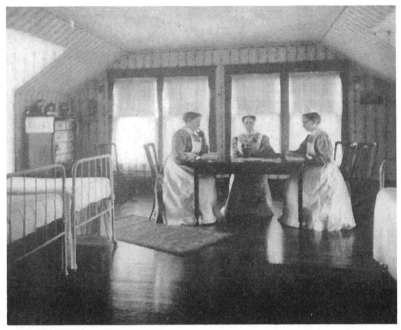

Sisters' room in deaconess home.

menial tasks was the economic situation of the Great Depression years
—the burden on everyone was heavy.

Yet she planned a trip to Europe, saving her pennies for years for
the longed-for journey. At the $300 mark she decided her trip was a
selfish indulgence and wanted to give the money to missionaries, but
they refused. She continued her saving. Whenever she saw a picture
of a Scotchman, she would smile and say, "I wonder if we're related."
When she finally reached the thousand-dollar mark, someone gave
her another thousand dollars, so she contributed her savings to missions, then took the trip.

On her return from Europe the situation did not improve. Frieda
recorded "weariness, desperately tired, bad nights." In March of 1935
she tried to lead a prayer meeting at church but felt herself "at the
verge of a nervous breakdown, [with] pain in chest and general distress. . . ." In 1936 she resigned as sister-in-charge and superintendent, but the other sisters (ordained and unordained) made a request
to the board that she remain but be given an assistant and time off for

rest. On June 6, 1936, Sister Lena Mae visited her in the evening and told her of this response to her resignation. "I am surprised and sleep poorly," she wrote. She stayed on. The following year she was granted an extended leave for reasons of health.

As Frieda struggled with health problems, she relinquished administrative duties first. On September 1, 1938, H. J. Andres took over as administrator. He wrote, "This step might be considered as the beginning of the transition from a deaconess-directed program for our institutions."

What might have happened to the home and hospital had a woman remained in the position of hospital superintendent? Juhnke notes that "the social and educational system had failed to prepare and legitimate young women for management."[7] It is ironic that earlier in 1938 the doctors agreed to form an onsite clinic, which in Andres' words "was the culmination of a dream long fostered by Sister Frieda."

Other Mennonite institutions were also facing loss of support. As early as 1929 a letter to Frieda from a Sister Magdalene at Beatrice, Nebraska, endorses the same idea. "At present our hopes and aspirations for [our] institution lie low. Most of all we need a real deaconess father, who would devote his life in the interest of deaconess work," Sister Magdalene wrote. "But this can hardly be stated publicly because it would reflect on our [Beatrice] board."

Several times men had been called to serve as superintendent of the Newton hospital but with prescribed duties leaning more toward the spiritual ministry among the patients and personnel than administrative responsibility or day-to-day details.

If, according to Frieda, the institution couldn't survive without male leadership, it also needed more deaconess candidates. In an address to the Ladies Aid Societies meeting at the General Conference of Mennonites at Perkasie, Pennsylvania, given probably in the late 1930s, Frieda passionately explained what a deaconess was and stressed the need for complete dedication to the task. "A deaconess is not made in a day, there is no shortcut route which will bring the same results with less claim on the life." She asked for the women's support for the deaconess cause, especially for fifty more "consecrated deaconesses."

At the annual meeting of the home and hospital in 1939 she tried to show those present the difference between a deaconess and a

Christian nurse. A deaconess could be a nurse, but she was not a nurse who occasionally reads the word of God and prays with a patient. "All Christian nurses do that. A deaconess is first and foremost a Christian woman who wishes to serve in the ministry of good works under the auspices and direction of her church."

In 1941 Frieda began editing *In the Service of the King*, a periodical designed to establish closer contact with supporters of the deaconess institutions and to encourage new converts to the cause. Each issue carried a continued account of the development of the deaconess movement and the Bethel institutions, as well as current news. But deaconess candidates did not appear in large numbers, although the number of nursing students continued to increase.

Final Years

On June 7, 1943, Frieda handed in her resignation to the hospital's board of directors. Her resignation, citing "a progressive and recurrent physical disorder" as its primary cause, was accepted. Later that year she wrote, "Our organization has been unable to gain a real foothold in the United States, where compared to the thousands of Roman Catholic sisters, there are few Protestant sisterhoods. . . . The Mennonite church in its simple pattern of the apostolic church organization does not offer favorable soil which would prosper an organization like a deaconess sister-hood." What she meant by "apostolic church organization" is not clear, yet it was likely stated with a sense that female leadership in a "female" task had not succeeded, for she added, "History reveals the fact that men must furnish the leadership and direct the work if the organized female diaconate shall prosper."

One of her biographers, Alice Claassen, writes that the last year of her life was marked by a quietness and a resignation to anything that life might bring. Previously, she had struggled against the thought of old age, but in the last months had cast all her cares upon her Lord. She was suffering from heart problems and diabetes and was on a strict diet, though she loved to eat. She knew deep inner peace and radiated a quiet joy to others.

She died a year-and-a-half after her resignation. A sister in the diaconate said that on the last day of her life Frieda worked in her office for a while, went to her room, then went to another room, fell on the bed and died with the words, "Please forgive me for all I've done."

Earlier, in November 1942, she had sketched a brief outline of her life with funeral suggestions. She concluded with the words, "My life was filled with great joy and some deep grief. The bitterest of all has been the ever-growing realization that I have woefully failed in living up to the great possibilities which surrounded my life through the grace of God." She affirmed her faith in the "wondrous cross" on Calvary and asked forgiveness for all her wrongs.

A Builder of Institutions and Lives

What personal characteristics led to the enormous recognition of Frieda as a successful "builder of institutions and lives"? Former students and sisters who knew her well describe Frieda frequently as "motherly." She was full-figured—at age fifty-seven, in 1939, her driver's license lists her weight as 200 pounds and her height as 5'7." Her hair was parted in the center and neatly drawn into a bun.

Her warm nurturing of students, deaconesses, and patients seems to have been her outstanding trait as sister-in-charge. She promoted "mothering" as the main obligation of all women and particularly of deaconesses. In an address to home economics students, she said that "a satisfied and happy woman is one who develops the mother spirit in her heart." This mother spirit can be directed to her own children, teaching other women's children, working in homes for children, taking care of "the sick, unfortunate, deficient, dependent, the aged." If these are absent, "She can mother a garden—anything which has life and a need!"

Students felt that at Bethel "we were one big family." The members of this island of women living in a man's world enjoyed their life together, which was patterned as much after home life as possible under the supportive role of a strong mother-figure.[8] Nursing students who knew Frieda speak of her extra efforts to make their lives as homelike as possible. Communion, birthdays, investment services, ordinations, and anniversaries were always celebrative occasions.

Christmas was made particularly festive for the students who had to remain at the hospital. There were gifts, decorations, food preparations, the memorizing of Advent verses, visits to the local jail and with friends, and a grand finale in the evening. Christmas at Bethel meant secrets just like in a family, ending with the unveiling of the manger scene in the dining room.

Left to right (back row): Sister Lydia Goertz, Sister Susanna Berg, Sister Elise Wiebe, Sister Elizabeth Harms, Sister Katharine Eitzen, Sister Maria Froese, Sister Anna Janz; (middle): Sister Margaret Franz, Sister Susie Quiring, Sister Bertha Schmidt; (front): Sister Frieda Kaufman, Sister Catherine Voth, Sister Ida Epp, Sister Hillegonda van der Smissen.

Frieda's office door always stood open so that as the nurses went to and from their rooms at the home they felt assured that "with the Lord's help all was well." She was lighthearted, spontaneous, good-humored, and a good counselor, ending interviews with appropriate Scripture and prayer for guidance. Her strong mothering instinct carried over to the hospital patients as well. At least twice a week she sat at their bedside, reading the Bible and praying with them. "Before a patient left the hospital, Sister Frieda knew their likes and dislikes, favorite foods, hobbies, songs, poems, and Scripture passages." She enjoyed telling them humorous stories. Letters from former patients on file thank her for her interest in them.

Her pastoral and nurturing spirit carried over to sisters who left the institution to work elsewhere. Many letters of advice and comfort went to the sisters sent to Mountain Lake, who endured difficult experiences there. It could be that, finding fulfillment as a "mother" to many, she found it less important to maintain the competitive spirit needed to build the deaconess institution at a time when the Mennonite church was building hospitals, homes for the aged, and schools.

But Frieda *was* visible in her Mennonite constituency. She used her gift for public speaking and the many opportunities afforded her at that time as a Mennonite woman to give numerous addresses, meditations, and "comments" at funerals, capping services, anniversaries, women's meetings, board meetings. Her eulogy at Sister Catherine Voth's funeral is a masterpiece of affirmation, comfort, and hope. She never preached formal sermons, yet her files are replete with dozens, possibly hundreds, of well-organized Bible study outlines.

An added factor giving her a place in many hearts was her humility. For example, she received an honorary doctoral degree on June 3, 1942 for "long and outstanding services" to the Mennonite Church in connection with Bethel Deaconess Home and Hospital. But when a friend stopped in to congratulate her, instead of sitting comfortably in her office absorbing the praise, she was scrubbing the floor in another room. She modeled an exemplary Christian life for all around her. One day in 1917, when Frieda was recovering from surgery, she sent a sister to her room for a few personal articles. In Frieda's closet she was confronted by a sign which read "Though he slay me, yet will I trust him." Before it stood a little prayer-bench. That was her answer to life's troubles.

Students applauded her for keeping the institution immaculately clean and for responding promptly to all repair needs. The institution's various buildings featured attractive lawns, trees, flowers, and gardens. Frieda took "great delight" in the planning and execution of the hospital expansion and other new buildings.

An oft-repeated anecdote demonstrates both her thoroughness and her guiding hand in the building of First Mennonite Church in Newton. "Work was progressing and two or three feet of brick had been laid. One day Sister Frieda examined the work being done and decided that the brick was the wrong color. It would not look good when the church was finished. She brought the matter up at a church meeting. The result was that several feet of brick were torn down and work began again in a different color."[9]

Richard S. Haury, member of the medical staff in 1945, eulogized her as "a lover of people, and her friendliness and kindness toward everyone won her the admiration and love of those whom she so loyally served and aroused a keen interest in the deaconess work." This latter statement is not entirely accurate, given that the deaconess movement was waning.

Analysis

To comment on Sister Frieda Kaufman as an entrepreneur is to comment on the entire movement, for she symbolized the diaconate among the Mennonites. Although it enjoyed initial success, it never actually took off, instead declining after the mid-1930s. Sister Frieda, the supporting constituency, and the social environment all had a part in the decline of the deaconess movement.

Frieda failed in her high-minded goal for several reasons. Though she had a deeply felt view of the diaconate calling, was willing to work long and hard, and persisted in her goal against severe difficulties, she struggled against assigning work to subordinates as the institution grew. She lacked a working knowledge of the social changes regarding women in church ministry. Her strong mothering instincts and her view of herself as a woman competed subconsciously with the development of the administrative and organizational skills needed to succeed in a male-dominated Mennonite church world.

In a pamphlet describing the diaconate for women, she writes, "A deaconess organization was needed for the sake of efficiency and success and to utilize different abilities," and "because the nature of woman needs the protection and support of a home or a homelike organization." The callings of both wife and deaconess are holy callings, each being full-time and difficult, but suited to different kinds of women, according to Frieda. Thus her appeal was limited to a specific type of woman. She had made a decision of singleness and service at a young age and rarely wavered from that decision. She expected other women to do the same, and this expectation of celibacy surely limited the appeal of the movement.

The deaconess movement might have maintained itself if Sister Frieda had been more aware of women's changing roles in society. A June 22, 1913, letter to the sisters in Cincinnati displays unexpected naivete for a women's leader. "Since we have woman suffrage in Kansas now I will surely have to keep up with the political questions of the day. I did not care for women's suffrage especially but I will surely try to do my duty since it has been laid upon us." Her greatest concern was always for the intangible values that women could contribute to any institution, rather than for their political influence.

Factors in the church also abetted the decline. The Mennonite diaconate movement lacked the authority of tradition possessed by the ordained sisterhood in the Catholic church. It also lacked a critical mass from which to draw candidates. In the early years Mennonites never thoroughly examined the validity of an ordained diaconate for women. Thus the main reason for the demise of the deaconess movement may have been the church's uncritical stance toward it.

In a March 28, 1950 letter to H. J. Andres, Sister Susan Kreutziger of Bethesda Hospital School of Nursing (a Methodist school in Cincinnati) argued a point applicable to Mennonites as well. "As a deaconess, I feel that the church as a whole neglected intelligent analysis and promotion of this work. At the height of its fruitfulness, it seemed so permanently fixed that no one bothered to have it follow the changes that we find in society and the church." She thought it should have had its status reestablished to parallel the status of other professional women—the character of the whole movement should change. Andres felt that women resisted the diaconate because it lacked full conference recognition, the scope of service was too narrow, the garb was not appealing, freedom to marry was not an option. In addition, the pool of candidates was too narrow—it should have been enlarged to married women, widows, and missionaries.[10]

The student nurses generally had great admiration for the sisters. They loved, feared, and respected them, and in later years at times pitied and avoided them, for they represented a way of life the younger women did not want to follow. They recognized that the deaconess movement was dying out. They could not share Sister Frieda's view of singled-minded dedication to the deaconess work. They wanted to marry. And if they had to remain single, they knew there were other ways of finding companionship and fulfillment than in a female institution that would dominate their social and religious life.

As time passed, the age gap widened between the garbed and usually serious sisters, and the less solemn nursing students who, though Christian, did not want the lifestyle they saw modeled, saintly as it appeared. Some students became disillusioned when they discovered that the sisters had faults just like the rest. An image developed of the Bethel sisters as elderly women in long black dresses with a small bonnet perched on their heads who were excellent nurses, instructors, supervisors, laboratory technicians, clerks, secretaries, housekeepers, and cooks—but not much else, despite the initial broad intentions of the movement.

The times themselves worked against the continuation of the deaconess movement. Educational standards rose, colleges and seminaries opened their doors to women, and mission boards asked for more and better preparation for candidates. Traditionally sanctioned feminine credentials like submission and complete dedication were no longer valued as highly as before. As men took over leadership of the deaconess schools, they dropped courses on the history of women and deaconesses, which "had served to develop the students' sense of their uniqueness and identity as Christian workers." And after women's suffrage, the vigor of the women's movement waned.[11]

Such factors combined to bring about the death of a movement which bloomed brightly for a short while and gave women opportunity for a recognized spiritual ministry in the Mennonite church. The deaconess movement forged a corporate identity for women and enabled them to expand their social and religious roles without violating the socially prescribed position of their sex. Sister Frieda Kaufman made a lasting contribution to the church by helping to build institutions and lives that reflected some of the traditional strengths of Mennonite women.

8

Bill Dyck:
A Little More Room to Operate

By Ted Loewen

If Sister Frieda Kaufman expressed her entrepreneurial skills from within church institutions, Bill Dyck (1934-1993) operated from the margins. If Kaufman's activities were visible to all, Dyck's were veiled in mystery, a result of his involvement in the world of real estate investment. Dyck's inquisitive, independent spirit led him beyond his Manitoba roots into the worlds of education, the professions, and high finance. If the tensions experienced by Kaufman were due in part to the internal quandaries of growing institutions, Dyck experienced barriers and/or tensions typical for entrepreneurs who, while maintaining a strong Christian faith, choose a career path and lifestyle beyond the ambit of the church.

BILL DYCK was driving down an interstate highway on a Saturday afternoon in the late 1970s near Dallas, Texas. He was preoccupied with thoughts of business. He had flown from California, rented a car, and was looking at real estate, including an investment in the Dallas area. A carload of people caught his eye. Two men in the front seat were talking intently. Four adults and a number of children were all crowded into an old Jeep Wagoneer. They were an interesting entourage—one black man, a white man, two white women, a number of children. Provisions were clearly meager. All their worldly possessions were likely with them in the vehicle.

Bill followed the car. When it pulled into a gas station, he followed. Approaching them, he learned they were going to southern Texas. Things would be better there. They had not been able to find jobs as hoped in the Pacific Northwest but were having trouble making this move. They were out of money, did not have much gas left, and clearly had not cleaned up or had a good night's sleep in a while.

Bill filled up their tank with gas and told them to follow him. He knew where they could stay for the night. He drove back toward Dallas followed by the Jeep and took them to the motel where he was staying. He checked them in on his tab, gave them time to clean up, and took them out to dinner. The next morning he went with them to the morning church service at a nearby Baptist Church. When they left to go south later in the day, he gave them the $200 he had on him. They told him they thought they had met an angel. How else could this be explained?[1]

William E. ("Bill") Dyck was a Mennonite Brethren entrepreneur who lived in Fresno, California.[2] He passed away in 1993. He worked as a certified public accountant, a dentist, and eventually became simply a businessman—or more precisely, a real estate speculator and developer. He was also a Mennonite philanthropist with strong interests in Mennonite institutions. Dyck's real estate activities were what took him to Texas, where he met the Jeep Wagoneer travelers on their way south. He had bought development property near Dallas, about 125 acres that he would later develop and break down into five-acre parcels. The smaller pieces would be sold to the next wave of land speculators. He likely did not know it then, but his work was in its early stages. It would be another seven years before the job was complete and returns realized—just in time to rescue him from the recession of the early 1980s.

Bill Dyck's career took him beyond the normal confines of Mennonite life at the time, and his business success often burdened him with an air of detachment and mystery. As this chapter will show, however, he was simply a man who needed a little more room to operate, an expansive individual who nurtured a strong Christian faith, yet perhaps felt most comfortable on the periphery of Mennonite life.

Background and Youth

Bill was in many ways a product of his immigrant Russian Mennonite past. He understood and appreciated his ethnic and spiritual heritage and looked to family members of past generations for inspiration. He was born July 22, 1934, on the plains of Manitoba, Canada, the firstborn boy of William W. and Anna (Reimer) Dyck.

Life was full but not easy during those Depression years, particularly for most of the recent immigrants to the Canadian plains. William and Anna were first-generation Canadians. Theirs was a heritage of displaced people. They had experienced and fled from the anguish of the Bolshevik revolution in Russia. Their material possessions were confiscated in Russia and their families torn apart. Siblings disappeared into the morass of communist Russia in the 1920s and '30s, hidden from view behind the iron curtain. Their fate would not be known, if at all, until many years later.

William escaped communist Russia in 1924, three years before his future wife, Anna. His father, Wilhelm I. Dyck, was a successful businessman in czarist Russia, a heritage remembered years later by his entrepreneurial grandson in Canada.[3] Wilhelm involved his children in his business, which was primarily farm implement manufacturing and flour milling. His flourishing businesses expanded to new regions. His children became managers of the new plants. But the whole social order changed when Vladimir Lenin and the communists gained control of Russia.

Wilhelm Dyck had treated his employees fairly and they thought highly of him. But when the revolution came, because he was a capitalist and a wealthy man, Wilhelm became a target of the new order, was taken at night from his home, and imprisoned. His wife, Emilie, slipped past the guards the next day and pleaded with the officers to release him. The officer said he would release Wilhelm for a substantial sum of money, plus over 100 signatures from his workers attesting to him being a good employer and someone they wanted back. Emilie was able to meet both conditions and got Wilhelm released. The family fled to the Kuban, a settlement in southern Russia, managing to survive there for six more years before emigrating to North America in 1924.[4]

The Wilhelm Dyck clan left Russia with little more than the clothes on their backs.[5] They made their way along with other Russian Mennonite emigrants to the plains of Canada. Wilhelm and Emilie's son William was twenty-one when he arrived at his new home. He found work as he could. Making a living was a struggle and involved several moves before he eventually settled down on a farm near Niverville, Manitoba.

When Bill was born, his parents had been in Canada for less than ten years, and spoke little English, finding it hard to switch from their native German. They never would learn much of their new country's language, an experience they shared with many of their friends and neighbors who also fled Russia.

Anna's experiences were similar to William's. She too escaped totalitarian Russia as a young adult. Her family had lived in the Kuban for many years and were well-established farmers.[6] She and Bill met in the early 1920s, after William fled to the Kuban. Though they did not get married until 1929 in Manitoba, their commitment to each other dated from those earlier years in Russia.

Niverville was a town of about 900 people in the 1930s and 1940s. William was not only a farmer but a businessman who operated a chicken hatchery and a lumber business.[7] Times were often lean, and the accepted way, perhaps the only way, of doing business was to extend credit. Hence William got to know his neighbors well.[8] As one family member put it, William was as successful as you could be in Niverville at that time, though even then he was not a wealthy man.

William was also a church leader. He was one of the lay pastors of Niverville Mennonite Brethren Church. He shared in a three-man rotation, preaching every third Sunday. Though having received no formal training, he crafted his sermons with care, often with the help of Anna. William prepared over nine hundred sermons during his lifetime, each handwritten with key points highlighted.[9] Anna was the supportive wife of a church and business leader. But besides raising a large family, she also held a summer Bible school for children and taught Sunday school for forty-five years.[10]

The Dyck home was the crossroads of the Mennonite Brethren community in Niverville. Church dignitaries would often stay overnight. The Dycks frequently hosted meetings involving local church leaders and conference visitors. The Dyck children were not barred from such discussions. They could sit in as long as they were discreet and respectful.

Bill Dyck was the oldest son, though third oldest child, of William and Anna. There were six children in all, three boys and three girls.[11] The children were expected to contribute to the family economic life. When a child turned twelve, it was time to go to work. Bill and his brothers worked on the farm and other family businesses as needed.[12]

Bill started school with a class of forty-seven, but there was a high attrition rate, with only four remaining at graduation. The Niverville school was small, but the teachers left a strong impression. Bill liked books and could not get enough new information. Reading materials were scarce in Niverville. It was a small town, and the Depression years were barely over when Bill started school. The school library, the only public library in the community, consisted of a small collection of volumes that likely were mostly donated. English books had little appeal to the German-speaking immigrants, and German books were unavailable.

There were some books in the Dyck home. William read religious books that guided his spiritual life and helped prepare him for his sermons. Anna enjoyed reading novels and cultivated, as time allowed, an interest in the arts. But these were practical times. Making a living and nurturing Christian faith were matters of primary importance in the Dyck household. William considered higher education, if not frivolous, at least not a necessity. Going to college was not encouraged.

Others outside of the Dyck family recognized and encouraged Bill's academic abilities. An aunt gave him ten years worth of *Das Beste*, a sort of German *Reader's Digest*, as a birthday gift one year. He devoured it. He was chosen to be on the school library committee when in the ninth grade. He helped bring the first set of encyclopedias to Niverville, then read them from cover to cover during the next three years. The Dyck house also became the temporary repository of a large collection of books owned by a German relative, and Bill was intrigued by the information and ideas gleaned from those books.

The Niverville Mennonite Brethren Church practiced adult baptism in the Anabaptist tradition. The custom for children growing up in the church was to take catechism in their early teenage years, then be baptized into the fellowship. Bill chose not to follow that path. Though his father was one of the pastors, Bill was not ready to join the fellowship with the rest of his age-group. There were aspects of church life that could be unattractive. The community was small and relatively homogeneous. The outlook was practical and often focused on life's immediate concerns. Perhaps difficult economic times reduced everyone's options. There was at times, at least from the perspective of some young people, too much of a concern about conformity, or for "what would the people think."

Bill was different from his peers. He was a bookworm. He liked the world of ideas and was easily drawn into a bigger world, whether through the *Encyclopedia Britannica, Das Beste*, the stash of books in the attic, or visitors passing through. It was not until later, at age twenty-three, after he had made his break and the issue of conformity to the community had diminished, that Bill returned to Niverville and was baptized into the fellowship.

When Bill graduated from high school, he tried following the practical course encouraged by his parents. He drove truck for his father for a number of months, but it soon became clear to him that he should go back to school. In the fall of 1957, Bill moved to Winnipeg and began taking courses in accounting.[13] The program involved a combination of night classes and apprenticing with an accounting firm by day. During this time, Bill courted and married Velma DeFehr on June 5, 1959. During the summer of 1962 Bill finished his degree.[14]

After finishing his accounting courses, Bill decided he still wanted more education. He went on to complete a bachelor's degree in German literature, focusing on the works of Johann Goethe. He graduated with distinction, supporting himself with an accounting job.

As strong as Bill's academic interests were, he was not content to seclude himself in a room full of books. His interest in business started early. Though the Dyck children were expected to work for the family, there still was time for other interests. In his early teens, Bill bought molds to make toy soldiers and Indians out of metal. He then collected batteries, melted down the lead, and made toys to sell. Before long, he hired friends. Sets of the figurines were even mounted on cardboard and sold to stores for resale. Bill's first venture in real estate was a project he carried out with his father while still in high school. Some real estate that had been home to a mink ranch came on the market in Niverville. His father bought it and Bill removed the wire and other fixtures. The property was then subdivided and sold as lots.

Some interviewees speculated that part of Bill's business motivation came from his association with the DeFehr family. Velma DeFehr is a daughter of Abraham Cornelius DeFehr, a successful Canadian businessman. Velma was studying to be a dentist, and perhaps she influenced Bill to do so as well. Bill began taking classes in the natural sciences, and in 1967 enrolled in dental school at the University of Minnesota, where Velma had already been enrolled for two years.

When Velma graduated, she entered a program in orthodontics at Loma Linda University in Los Angeles, California. Bill transferred into the Loma Linda dentistry program. In 1971, they both completed their degrees and moved to Fresno, California.

Entrepreneurial Activities

Dyck opened his dental practice in Fresno that same year, when Velma also opened her orthodontic practice. From the beginning Bill's professional interests expanded beyond his private practice. He accepted a position with the Department of Indian Affairs when he first came to Fresno and agreed to help them set up a dental clinic near Eureka, California, on the Hoopa Valley Indian Reservation. Later he went on a mission to China to help provide dental assistance to Southeast Asian boat people.

Bill said that his most significant personal accomplishment was work he did for the Salvation Army. The Army operates numerous rehabilitation centers for recovering alcoholics and drug addicts. They have attempted to establish medical clinics in connection with the larger units. But the Salvation Army was having problems successfully linking up dental services to these programs and was looking for advice when Bill was recommended to them.

Bill told the Salvation Army that they should scrap the old system of outdated dental equipment, marginal supplies, and no staff. He recommended instead that they go to a service club like Rotary International, of which Bill was a member in Fresno, and ask them to fund the purchase of equipment. He suggested that volunteer dentists be asked

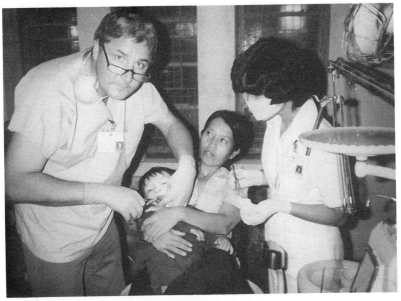

Bill as a dentist on a mission to China.

to provide diagnostic services only at the Salvation Army site. Once the diagnosis was made, other volunteer dentists could be contacted for donation of services in the dentist's private office. The program worked well and has been implemented in four cities. Bill received the "Other Award" for his innovative Salvation Army work.

Bill was well known both in the Mennonite Brethren and larger Fresno communities. His initial focus in Fresno was his dental practice and his real estate ventures a side interest. But as his real estate operations grew, so did their public visibility. He was on many Mennonite Brethren lists of individuals considered to be financially influential and hence possible supporters of projects. He was often perceived to be a wealthy man who generously supported Mennonite institutions and causes.

But there was a mystique about the man and how he made his living. Bill kept a low profile, seeming to avoid addressing the public. One interviewee commented on his readiness to encourage people one-on-one, but his reluctance to speak publicly. Bill's low public profile and accompanying mystique may have been a barrier to being accepted as a church leader. When asked, "What does Bill Dyck do for a living?" interviewees often chuckled, paused, mentioned real estate, or perhaps that he was a dentist, then acknowledged that they really did not know. What Bill did is intangible. He had few employees, in earlier years even operating his real estate ventures without an office.

Bill was mainly in the business of seeing and capitalizing on business opportunities. He was primarily a real estate speculator and to a lesser degree a developer. If he developed property, he often subdivided and improved the land. If he constructed buildings, he generally kept them and leased them out, through a management company with which he contracted for services.

To speculate successfully in land, a speculator must have a good understanding of the economic and political life of a community. He or she must be able to make projections based on evolving patterns. It is often necessary to project population growth. It may be necessary to predict decisions politicians will make about land use. Bill maintained that the key to being successful at this kind of business was not to sell at the right price, but rather to buy at the right price.[15]

The real estate market in the 1970s in the Fresno area was strong. As one California entrepreneur put it, a real estate investor "could do no wrong" during those years. Bill began buying California real estate in the 1960s. In the 1970s his real estate activity continued to expand and diversify. Bill did not limit himself to a particular type of real estate investment. But he primarily bought apartments and the appreciation on those units during the 1970s gave him part of his financial base.

His business continued to expand due to the increased value and equity of his investments, and his ability to attract investors. He formed partnerships and brought new capital that way. If he saw a good investment he would seriously consider the investment, even if it took him in new directions. One time an orange grove was offered to him. The seller was motivated to sell and needed the cash. The price was right, so he ventured into the orange business.

If it was impossible to do wrong in the 1970s, just the opposite was true in the early 1980s. The expansion of the real estate economy and appreciation in values abruptly ended. Inflation was on the rise and interest rates climbed to around 20 percent. Land values declined, sometimes to below the indebtedness on highly leveraged properties. The cash flow generated by sales slowed to a trickle.

Bill at a construction site.

Along with most others aggressively investing in real estate in the early 1980s, Bill found himself in trouble. A large line of credit owed to an institutional lender came due. Bill could pay the interest but not the principal. If the note had been called, Bill likely would have been forced into bankruptcy. Fortunately it was not.

At the same time, Bill began to be pressured and questioned by some of his partners. He ended up restructuring his businesses and separating from outside partners. Bill moved from partnerships to family-owned businesses during this period. A renewed spiritual awakening coincided with his business hardships, and he wanted complete control over his businesses in order to mesh those interests.

Faith and Life

The year 1984 was a watershed in Bill's personal spiritual pilgrimage. He and Velma celebrated their twenty-fifth wedding anniversary that year, and they reflected on what else they wanted to accomplish. At about the same time, Bill sought counsel from spiritual mentors in the larger church fellowship. The previous several years had been difficult ones. A banker's decision stood between him and business failure. He spent significant time in study, prayer, and dialogue and concluded he needed to make a stronger commitment to his faith.

Those who knew Bill well through the 1980s attest to this pilgrimage. Bill's manner of handling financial adversity was to withdraw from social life, perhaps not surprising for a man who valued privacy. The renewed Bill spoke with a new fervor after 1984. There was a perceived change in commitment to church life and enthusiasm for sharing his spiritual convictions. His business card, for example, now made reference to a Bible verse.[16]

Though Bill was considered influential in Mennonite Brethren circles, he did not take prominent leadership roles in the life of his congregation. He was reluctant to serve in official church offices. He served on stewardship committees and, particularly in later years, was active in the life of the congregation by attending church, Bible studies, a pre-worship prayer group, and Sunday school classes. Bill claimed that he was removed from his church's stewardship committee because he was too interested in challenging the giving habits of some parishioners. He acknowledged the limitation of his direct approach by saying he could never be a college president because he would be fired in a week.

His role in church institutions was played out mostly behind the scenes. He had a deep commitment to Christian higher education and generously supported Mennonite Brethren educational institutions. Bill was active in the Mennonite Economic Development Association (MEDA), which has as its mission development projects in various countries.

Through MEDA and in other ways he met many Mennonite entrepreneurs. Some common ideals and principles that he found included the desire to resolve business problems without resorting to litigation, and the desire to temper business activities with an active, accountable faith that practices stewardship. Bill believed that entrepreneurial creativity can solve the nagging problem of many church institutions—adequate funding. He believed there are resources and ideas that can be tapped to raise sufficient funds to endow institutions.

Bill believed Christians are accountable for their lifestyle but acknowledged a personal weakness for "creature comforts." There was some tension with fellow believers over material things. Even so, he

contended that the criticisms sometimes leveled at him were not war-
ranted. Bill drove a late-model (but not new) Cadillac. Bill felt he got a
favorable deal on the vehicle when he bought it from a friend, and that
driving it made good economic sense. But that was not the perception
among some other Mennonites, because he was still driving a luxury
car.

At one point Bill was able to buy ten tickets to the Bracebridge
Dinner, an annual Christmas program held at the Ahwahnee Hotel in
Yosemite National Park. The tickets are sold by lottery and highly
prized. They cost $100 each for a meal and the special Christmas play.
Bill invited a select group of friends from around the country to attend
the event with him. He saw this as an opportunity for several reasons.
He could reestablish contact with friends and gain the chance to share
about his newly enhanced faith. He could perhaps encourage financial
support for church projects. There might be important business contacts. From the outside, the event may have looked extravagant, but
for Bill, it had a significant purpose, well worth the price. How else
could he get that kind of forum with influential and busy people?

Bill did believe there is such a thing as material extravagance.
There must be a purpose to the expenditure, preferably faith or business. And if the financial cost is too high, it may not be justifiable even
if linked to a higher purpose. A used Cadillac is okay, but a new
$85,000 Mercedes is not. At some point pride and arrogance take over
and negate any positive attributes. The Dycks lived in a comfortable
but not ostentatious home in Fresno. It was a ranch-style, middle-class
home. But more recently they began building a home in north Fresno
on a bluff overlooking the San Joaquin River Valley, a highly desirable
location. The lot was bought a number of years before at a much lower
price than its current value, and the house was relatively modest for
the area.

Though Bill maintained a low profile in the life of the congregation, his commitment to active Christian faith as demonstrated by personal evangelism was strong. As one person said, "Bill [was] always
reaching out to people." There are many examples of Bill engaging
people in various ways. Bill had dealings with a Buddhist attorney
from Japan. He found an opening with him for sharing his faith, then
brought him to church.

In another instance, Bill had a piece of development property for sale. A large corporation made an offer. The agent who called to work out terms used crude and offensive language when talking with Bill. Bill called back the potential buyers and said the deal was off because of the impropriety of the agent. The next day the buyers were in his office to apologize, and Bill gave them "a big blast from the Bible." Relationships were smoothed over and the deal later went through.

In recent years, Bill carried around a book called *The Bible from Scratch*, a paperback that gives an overview of the Bible in what could be described as comic-book format. It is easy to read and pick up the main points. Bill kept the books available in case an opportunity arose, and they frequently did.[17]

In early 1991 Bill was diagnosed with multiple myeloma, a cancer of the bone. He underwent cancer treatment and was virtually bedridden for a number of months. But Bill found opportunity even in cancer. He was given an inspirational tape of a speech by theologian Oscar Thompson, Jr., who was suffering from the same disease. The tape advocates approaching life "one day at a time" because there are no certainties in life. All are mortal, even those who do not have cancer. One should live each moment to the fullest, glorifying God.

Bill made 500 copies of the tapes and handed them out to friends and acquaintances, some of whom had cancer and others not. New doors opened. He did not hesitate to share his experience with other cancer patients. On discovering that a businessman who owned a large company with whom Bill had business dealings had the same cancer he did, he wrote a letter. Included in the letter was practical medical information he had learned from his own experience. Also included was a biblical reference. In a week Bill received a handwritten letter back from the multimillionaire businessman, thanking him and inviting him to meet personally with him in southeastern United States (a meeting which later took place). Bill planned to expand this interest by setting up a counseling service for cancer patients and making himself available to nurture others with cancer.

Bill was passionate. He spoke persuasively and usually with conviction. His interests were broad. If Bill had an Achilles heel, it was from the combination of these traits. Some who knew him well say his vision sometimes exceeded his grasp. Projects were envisioned or maybe even started—then not completed.

Bill liked venturing out into uncharted territory, whether in busi-

ness or in his spiritual life. In
an introduction to his father's
printed sermons, Bill wrote of
his father's "three worlds" of
church, family, and business.
He was his father's son in that
sense, because he too emphasized those three areas.

Bill's manner of pursuing
his goals, though, was different from his father's. His father
in many ways exemplified the
accepted, traditional ways of
doing business. Few in Niverville, Manitoba, would have
hesitated to answer the question, "What does William Dyck
do?" The answer was clear;

**Bill Dyck and son William
in ranch costume.**

what William stood for was obvious to all. William seemingly was a
leader people gladly followed. They knew who he was and where he
was going. His friends and parishioners were comfortable with his vision.

But his world, the world of the immigrant during the Great Depression, was perhaps too confined and practical for his son Bill. Bill's
world was one of ideas requiring exploration. The exploration needed
to take place beyond the confines of a small, rural community. Ironically, Bill managed to fulfill his intellectual yearnings while also
achieving the economic success his father had wanted for him—a success his father had felt precluded advanced education.

If William was the public leader, Bill was the more private prophetic voice who shared many of his father's basic convictions. If people understood and instinctively followed William, Bill's more private
voice was carefully listened to but weighed against its prophetic nature and its somewhat mysterious source. Wealth alone creates barriers, but even more so if the wealth comes from something as intangible as investment activity.

Bill's faith commitment remained firm. He constantly looked for
opportunities to practice and express his faith. He was at least as in-

trigued with his spiritual forefathers as with the general world of ideas. Bill was influenced by the lessons he learned at home from both of his parents. He gained deep understanding of and appreciation for his faith community. While he chafed at times under the constraints his community put on him, he internalized the basic message of hope through Christ.

Bill did not lead a "normal" life. His questioning and creative nature took him in unusual directions. That nature also shaped his relationship with his own faith community. His role was that of the loyal parishioner, who prods and challenges the larger group, usually from the periphery, where there is a little more room to operate.

9

Jay Lehman:
Successful Alternatives

By Celia Lehman

Jay Lehman (b. 1929), like many of the figures profiled in this collection, has pursued multiple career tracks in his lifetime. In so doing he has answered both the call of the church—serving for a number of years as a relief worker in Africa—and the demands of the world of commerce. In the end both activities have been brought together in a truly unique business enterprise. Lehman's career illustrates the degree to which faith values of the Mennonite community, and the experience of service for the church, can temper and shape entrepreneurial activity as well as give rise to interesting and "successful"—in a wholistic sense—forms of "business."

WHAT IS IT that brings folks from every walk of life, from every state of the union, and from well over 100 nations of the world, into a small town to visit a hardware store? "Perhaps," as one observer puts it, "it's the fact that there isn't another place in the U.S. where anyone who operates without electricity can buy as many different supplies under one roof as they can at Lehman Hardware in Kidron [Ohio]."[1]

In 1991 Jay Lehman stated, "Our biggest day of the year so far was the day after Thanksgiving [1990]. We sold 3,700 items. Just over 1,000 customers bought something that day. We have occasionally tried to take 'people counts' on busy days, and we know we've had at least 240 customers in here at one time. It can get pretty hectic."[2]

Lehman Hardware is owned and operated by Jay Lehman, his brother Dave, and Jay's son Galen. The store is stocked with non-electric household items for doing all manner of chores without electricity. One showroom has no less than 100 wood- and coal-burning stoves, including one that burns corn. There are potbellied stoves with claw feet, ornate old-fashioned wood stoves, and gas and kerosene stoves. There are also thousands of other items, including a Maytag wringer washer with a gasoline engine, which with a change of attachments can stuff sausages or churn butter.

There are carrot juicers, cookie cutters, washboards, and cooper's tools. There are cast-iron skillets, books about country living, milk pasteurizers, and implements with which to make maple-syrup; mauls for splitting wood, children's sleds, dough makers, cherry pitters, and pea shellers. There are grinders for meat and coffee, butter churns, cream separators, and ice-cream makers; oil and gas lamps, heavy-duty children's toys, tubs, basins, and woodworking tools. The list goes on and on.

Above the ground floor of the 15,000 square foot store are displayed many old stoves and other antiques—not for sale, merely for display. "Lots of people have told us we ought to charge admission to come in here and look around," Jay says. "They tell me it's more interesting than a museum."[3] One of the store's fifteen employees notes, "People like the old-fashioned items. They are interested in going back to what they once knew."[4] Customers come by the busloads to shop and browse in what has been called "a throwback in time," where one can get "back to basics" with "old-timey gadgets," and see a business which "ignores progress, [yet] prospers."[5]

But nostalgia is clearly only one factor in the store's success. Many missionaries and service workers with assignments in less developed areas of the world come to Lehman's where Jay, who has himself served in Africa as a relief worker, personally helps them find what they need. People who for one reason or another don't want to use electricity flock to the store. There is a growing market of people with vacation homes or year-round residences that are off the electric-utility grid, as well as recreational-vehicle owners. There is an obvious ability to sell. A visitor to the store was recently heard to declare, "Those Lehman brothers could sell a refrigerator to an Eskimo!"

The store's success in selling alternative products is interwoven with Jay's earlier choice to take the alternative career path of mission/service worker in Europe, Africa, and the United States. Jay's career is an interesting example of how an unconventional lifestyle, when coupled with entrepreneurial talents, can give rise to unexpected business success. He is a relatively simple, commonsense sort of person who has managed to have his cake and eat it too by serving as a relief worker who has traveled the world, yet transforming that experience into a successful business enterprise. The story of his life is indeed one of successful alternatives.

Formative Years

Jay E. Lehman is a descendant of hardworking Swiss Mennonites who immigrated to Wayne County, Ohio, in 1819. He was born in 1929 near Kidron, the second of six children. The Ezra Lehman farm is a mile north of Kidron, and the family's Mennonite church sits between downtown Kidron and the Lehman farm. Jay quit high school when he was sixteen, though he was ranked in the top ten in his class. "I wanted to get on with my life," he says. He thus has relatively little formal education but Jay is by no means uneducated. He is well-read, informed, and displays a wisdom he would call "common sense."

Jay stayed home on the farm and worked with his dad. Then in 1944 he took a job as an auto mechanic with Eddie Lehman, who owned a building on the square of downtown Kidron. Little did Jay dream that this would someday be the location for Lehman Hardware.

His work as a mechanic was the first in a series of experiences that would help launch him into business. Jay worked as a welder at a garage in Orrville, then as a mechanic for Cottage Creamery. "He never was afraid to use his hands. He did whatever needed to be done. He figured it out and took the responsibility to do it," says his wife, Ella

Mae. Jay and Ella Mae met when she came to teach at the Sonnenberg Christian Day School, near Kidron. Her brother Larry lived in the community; it was through him that Jay came to be acquainted with the brunet from upper New York state.

In 1951 Jay, then known by his nickname "Junior," went to Germany to serve in the first PAX unit, an alternative service program designed to provide European relief after World War II, mainly by building houses. At first Jay transported blocks made by the men to the building sites. The last two years of the three-and-one-half-year assignment were spent fixing the transport trucks. Because he could fix anything and was able to make do with whatever was available, he was chosen to maintain the forty army surplus transport trucks used to deliver food and supplies all over Europe. During this time Jay was drawn out of the rather small world of his own Mennonite community, not least through interaction with widely known Mennonite leaders.

When Jay returned home in 1955, he decided to purchase the hardware store formerly owned by A. B. Sommer, on the square in Kidron. Jay notes that "I borrowed every penny to get started." Jay and Ella Mae were married.

The story might have ended there, but it wasn't long before Jay and Ella Mae entered into discussions with Orie O. Miller, who had spoken at their church, about further service work with the Mennonite Central Committee (MCC). Jay and Orie, a prominent Mennonite leader, had gotten to know each other well while in Europe. Leaving the hardware store in the hands of his brother Dave and their father, Jay and Ella Mae moved into the second phase of their career together.

A Decade of Service

For three-and-a-half years Jay, Ella Mae, and their young son Galen resided in the Republic of Congo (now Zaire), where they had a dual assignment. They were responsible to renovate the mission guest house in Leopoldville (now Kinshasa) and to make travel arrangements and provide support services for missionaries and service workers of all denominations traveling through the Congo. According to Jay, "It was a tremendous contact. They all came through the capital city, so we learned to know all Protestant denominations. We booked passages for everyone, first the men and later the women who came."

The Menno Travel Service (MTS) in the Congo was the first of three travel agencies Jay started. To run this self-taught business, he had to calculate fares and find the most economical ways to travel. Jay worked conscientiously. Word spread, and mission guests from all over the world began using MTS because it was known to provide knowledgeable service for a good price. The Lehmans were eventually asked to move to Nairobi, Kenya, to run an MTS travel office there. By this time two more children had appeared, Glenda and Kevin.

During the next three years the Lehmans built up the MTS rapport with the same success as before. Kenya became a favored place in which to hold conventions, board meetings, and the like for a number of denominations. Even after leaving Kenya, Jay traveled back to Nairobi to help in short-term assignments with MTS, including crisis situations.

He recalls the time he had booked hotel rooms for several thousand Pentecostals. Government officials suddenly requisitioned the rooms for the same weekend, expecting MTS to give them priority. Jay became the person called in to clear up the chaos, but this put him into a bind. Government officials took away his passport and work permit, and a few hectic days went by before his papers were returned.

Many missionaries began wondering whether there shouldn't be an MTS office in New York City, the headquarters for a number of North American mission boards. Thus the Lehmans opened their third MTS office in New York City, where they resided for the next three-and-a-half years. There their fourth and last child, Wendy, was born.

"People respect Jay," says his wife. "He doesn't play games or wear masks. It doesn't matter whether the person is an Amish, African, airline official, stove salesman, or mission or business executive—he's himself and they like that. He treats people with respect, and they can say what they think without being threatened."

Back in Business

Through the years the Lehmans gained good contacts. They had visited hundreds of missionaries and other service workers, and they would often be asked about where to get a generator or gas refrigera-

Jay Lehman displays his merchandise.

Jay describing his business to a visitor.

tor. Jay made note of their requests, determined to supply these needs. In time he began sending out brochures stating that nonelectrical items were available and became the main source for these hard-to-find items. In this way Jay eventually began to transform a "normal" hardware store into the very successful niche enterprise his store has become. When his ten years of service work were finished, he returned to his business and began to build on his contacts and experiences abroad.

One important factor in his success has been that Kidron is near Holmes County, Ohio, which has an Amish population of around 30,000, one of the largest settlements in the world of Amish, who shun most uses of electricity. Jay listened to the Amish, then set about meeting their needs, which helped him to secure the Amish market.

For example, since some Amish prefer all-black stoves, Jay strove to find a company that would make them. He bought obsolete stove parts for the customers who needed them. Once he became familiar with Amish ways, Jay was able to joke and chat with them freely. Sometimes the Lehmans are invited to Amish weddings or to visit in their homes.

An even greater market exists for Lehman's goods among non-Amish people who want special items. People who live on islands, in rain forests, or in other remote places buy goods from Lehman Hardware. According to Jay, the fastest growing part of the store's sales is in mail order. One order—including lanterns, cast iron kettles, and a woodburning stove—went to Hollywood for the movie *Back to the Future III*.

Another factor in the store's success was the oil crisis of the early 1970s. Everyone suddenly wanted a woodburning stove—people watched as fuel prices skyrocketed and feared that they would run out of fuel entirely. At that time the store was already selling woodburning stoves, so people began literally to flock to it. The Lehmans learned of a company that would make special stoves if ordered in lots of seventy. They decided to go ahead. Says Jay, "We bought a truckload at a time, not knowing if we'd get rid of that many. But because everyone wanted a stove we sold them, and the stove business prospered. People came from all over. The sales went 'Boom!' There was little competition at that time. One Saturday we sold fifty stoves."

The early 1970s also saw the beginnings of the ecology move-

Antique-style sign collection.

ment. Appliances and implements that used alternative, natural forms of energy were coming to be seen as important components in an environmentally sustainable lifestyle. Lehman Hardware was there to supply the demand.

Meanwhile Jay and Ella Mae traveled. Once while traveling in Africa they made their way by car from Nairobi to Juba, Sudan, camping as they went. After four days of dusty, rough travel they arrived much in need of a cold drink and a shower. Says Ella Mae, "We didn't more than get settled when I saw Jay on his hands and knees examining the gas refrigerator. He inquired where it had been bought.

"Learning it came from Switzerland, you can guess that the next time we traveled through Switzerland Jay went to find the company. He set up a franchise to sell their product in the United States and he became the sole agent." Today the 7.7 cubic foot natural gas refrigerators are the store's top-selling product. Lehman's is the largest distributor of gas refrigerators in the U.S., selling over 1,300 each year. Woodstoves are the second-highest sellers.

Another factor in the success of the business has been extensive advertising in national publications. The uniqueness of the store has also resulted in a good deal of free advertising via articles written about the enterprise.

Jay explained his first encounter with catalogues. "A lady bought one of our Victoria strainers. She wrote a letter to *Organic Gardening*, explaining how useful it was to process her tomatoes and apples. The magazine sent for a sample strainer to test it and wrote an article about it. Then we sent in an ad which resulted in hundreds of orders. This in turn was followed by hundreds of people coming to see what else they might find. They would pass many stores which could have sold them the same strainer, but they came here because of the advertisement." The brothers sold $50,000 worth of the $22 strainer from that single promotion.

"We started printing brochures, then we printed *Lehman's Non-Electric Good Neighbor Heritage Catalogue*. Now we publish 200,000 catalogues, with each containing 120 pages with pictures and costing two dollars," says Jay. The catalogue lists 400 items out of an inventory of several thousand. A dedicated staff is in place to process the catalogue orders. Galen, Jay's son, is the promotion manager and head of this department. Galen writes the ads, and his mother, Ella Mae, reads them over the local radio station, or they are published in magazines like *Organic Gardening, Harrowsmith*, and *Yankee*.

In 1988 an Amishman approached Jay while he was eating at a local restaurant, with an offer to sell his 160-year-old barn. At first Jay was reluctant. After some thought he made the man an offer. When the deal was made, Jay hired workmen to tear down the twenty-four-by-sixty-foot antique, then reassemble it as an extension to the hardware store, straddling a creek running behind the building. The barn thus became a part of Lehman Hardware and draws attention to the new mini-mall built on the back of the property.

The Olde Millstream Plaza is a two-story, 4,600 square foot mini-mall that leases space to five shops. Hearthside Quilt Shoppe, one store in the mall, specializes in custom-made quilts designed and

Wood and gas-fired cookstoves.

quilted by nearly 100 Amish and Mennonite women in a three-mile radius of Kidron. Another store located in the plaza, The Kidron Oak Connection, features locally crafted furniture. Imported handicrafts from thirty-five developing nations are featured at World Crafts, a store which operates as part of the SELFHELP program sponsored by the Mennonite Central Committee. The Pine Hill Floral and Gift Shop features fresh and silk flowers, Amish dolls, gift baskets, stencils, music, and collectibles. The Olde Corner Cupboard specializes in gourmet foods. Clearly Lehman Hardware has become the flagship in an expanding enterprise.

An Alternative Success

Jay doesn't like to sit in an office—he prefers to walk up to a customer and say, "How can I help you?" When first starting the business, Jay did things by himself. Every evening after work he would deliver washing machines. According to Ella Mae, whom Jay was dating at the time, "This was to my advantage. I never had to worry that Jay was out with someone else. He barely had time to see me!"

A key element in Jay's alternative success has been ability to combine hard work with exceptional customer service. This is due at least in part to the fact that he genuinely likes people. He enjoys helping them and doing favors for them. This doesn't seem like work to him. Pleasing people means more to him than how much money he can make. Had this not been the case, he likely never would have become involved in the alternative appliance business, for it all started with his interest in helping people get the goods they needed, regardless of whether he made any money on them.

As Jay's son Galen puts it, "Whatever success we have, money is not a goal; it's a by-product. We have always given the best we can to help people solve their problems even if at times this means loss to our business. Some people work with money as their driving force; this is not true for us."[6]

Ella Mae recalls that this willingness to help people sometimes has led to strange encounters. One time when they were in Africa a message was radioed to the MTS office that a dog's head was being transported by plane. "Would Jay meet the plane, and take the head to the World Health Organization to be analyzed for rabies? If the dog had rabies, would he be sure to send the proper medicine back on the return flight?" Jay did not consider this an unusual service to perform.

Jay is clearly not status conscious. He is not afraid to get dirty. When customers come into the store they cannot tell that he is the principal owner. He is out on the floor in ordinary clothes, working with the rest. The employees at the store have a high regard for Jay. Whether they are part- or full-time employees, Jay takes the time to train them. There has been a low rate of turnover among his thirty full-time employees. Jay's oldest sister, Pearl, is the secretary, and brother-in-law Glenn Kaufman is a buyer and works in sales. His brother Dave is bookkeeper, handling payroll and scheduling. Recently Jay's youngest son, Kevin, has joined the workforce.

Jay in front of his store, considerably remodeled.

The Lehman family has traveled all over the world. The children were good travelers, and the family made countless friends worldwide. "The guest bed is made up most of the time," says Ella Mae. "I learned from my African friends that I can entertain without a lot of fuss. If people come on short notice they take us as they find us." The lifestyle of the family is comfortable but not lavish. Their brick home is spacious but homey. The car they drive has 100,000 miles on it. Having lived on a meager allowance for many years has given the Lehman's an intimate acquaintance with the simple life.

Jay has served on the Kidron Community Council, the governing body of the town, and on various boards—including Central Christian High School, Mt. Eaton Care Center, and Wayne-United Ministries—which serve the local jail and hospitals. He is on the Menno Travel board both in Pennsylvania and Nairobi and has served on the Kidron Community Historical Society planning committee for a new heritage center.

Jay has encouraged Ella Mae to become involved in church life. She was the first woman ever chosen elder in the Kidron Mennonite Church. She has had seminary training, played an active role in the "Calling and Caring" program of their church, and served on many mission board projects. "I'm thankful he's secure enough to give me freedom to pursue further education and serve the church. His support and encouragement are important to me," says Ella Mae. "I enjoy the energy I get from working with the church and its program." Both Jay and Ella have obviously been committed to the church and its mission, and have contributed to causes supported by the Mennonite church.

A recent Lehman initiative has been to include a letter in correspondence with catalog customers that solicits support for the Mennonite Central Committee (MCC). The letter states that customers' donations to the relief organization will be matched "dollar for dollar" by Lehman Hardware, up to a maximum gift of $10,000. Jay says in the letter, "I believe in the work MCC does. I served under them for ten years. I know, from personal experience, that no other organization is more dedicated to working *with the people* they serve to meet their needs and developing long-term strategies for alleviating oppression, suffering, poverty, conflict, and natural disaster. Please allow us here at Lehman's to double the impact of your giving. . . . " Customers can sense this kind of emphasis when entering the store; there are MCC posters on the walls, and Choice Books, a line of Christian books, are on sale.

In his spare time Jay is a man of many interests. When he comes home from work he often heads for the 5,000 walnut trees in the field beside his house. "There is much more to relaxing than just sitting in a chair," he says. He would rather be trimming the fruit trees, or mowing the grass, or perhaps collecting stamps or playing chess. Reading is another favored sparetime activity. He has appeared on television a number of times and was asked to play the lead role in *Wild Country*, a travel film about Africa. With his flowing white hair and beard, Jay looks every bit the dashing adventurer. In reality, however, Jay is a quiet man, who can become very articulate when he gets interested in a topic. His wry sense of humor is unmistakable.

Jay and Ella Mae are rather reserved when it comes to addressing some of the difficult questions that accompany entrepreneurial success, such as the existence of jealousy or mistrust in the community. It seems unlikely that there are strong feelings of jealousy present among the Lehman's friends and acquaintances. Jay's pastor Bill Detweiler comments, "Jay is a down-to-earth person. He does not put on airs or flaunt his wealth about. I get the impression people rejoice with [Jay] that he is successful. I do not sense any jealousy. He's a common layman, not pretentious."[7]

But there are risks involved with owning an expanding enterprise in a small town. One does hear comments on the street in Kidron such as "I sure hope Kidron doesn't become another tourist trap like Berlin, Ohio, or Lancaster, Pennsylvania." "I wonder what Jay does with all his money?" "Jay uses the word 'Amish' to promote his business."

Son Galen remarks, "Sometimes I think it's almost too big for us —the rate of growth almost gets out of hand. What shall we do to make it slow down? If we see that something will work we go about feverishly to make it work. When you work closely in a business, you see things can be good for the store and do them even if it will make you busier. We can't turn it off." Galen adds, however, that although "some people are bothered by the growth we brought to Kidron . . . they should realize that others are benefiting too."

Jay Lehman did not set out to become rich. He did not aim to become a successful man in the usual sense of the term. He was content to work at a subsistence level in Europe, Africa, and New York City. He put in his best effort in those places, and when he came home he made a deliberate effort to help missionaries and service workers get needed supplies.

He also built up a successful enterprise in the process, by aggressively pursuing markets outside the service field. He has shown the same commitment to his task in whatever situation he found himself. His success in the alternative hardware business must be seen at least in part as a by-product of his success in doing alternative service work. There is a pleasing symmetry to Lehman's entrepreneurial career, one that in many ways crosses the normal boundaries between economics and Christian service. A Christian might say that God uses ordinary people in extraordinary ways when they allow themselves to be used by God.

10

Levi Giesbrecht:
The Mennonite Ethic and the Spirit of Family

By Benjamin W. Redekop

Levi Giesbrecht (b. 1957) is another example of a Mennonite entrepreneur whose success has been informed by communal and religious values. In his case the role of the family as a carrier of values and as a community in itself has been highlighted as an important factor in entrepreneurial behavior. Like most of the figures profiled in this collection, Levi Giesbrecht's experience has been determined mainly by a sense of community which is rooted ultimately in the family as a subset of the faith community. But there are nevertheless clear indications of a personalized approach to religious faith and its expression, complemented by a growing vision of service to a wider community.

ON ONE HAND, Levi Giesbrecht fits the mold of the classic entrepreneur. Through personal initiative, hard work, and risk-taking he has succeeded in carving a niche for his company, Spruceland Millworks

British Columbia, in the volatile British Columbia lumber industry. On the other hand, Levi's life and career remain embedded in a thick tapestry of family and struggle, faith, and history.

Born into a large family of Mennonite colonists in the Paraguayan Chaco, he has been shaped significantly by these forces. His present success, which extends far beyond the narrow confines of an individualist business ethic, can only be understood in the context of this larger tapestry.

Levi's personal history illustrates important aspects of the Mennonite story. These include the role of large families in instilling a sense of community and common purpose; how deprivation and struggle, often brought on by migrations for the sake of a distinctive faith and sense of peoplehood, have nurtured a strong work ethic and desire for material success; and the role of Christian faith in fostering clean living and a sense of security in situations ranging from the uncertainties of pioneer life to the fluctuations of a resource-based economy.

Levi's success can be measured both in terms of typical economic criteria and faithfulness to the legacy already outlined. Thus the wood-cutting business has grown from scratch to $15 million in annual sales in ten years, with little capital outlay. At the same time, it has maintained an honest, open, and caring approach to employees and business associates. And most significantly, Levi has at least partly reconstituted his Mennonite family and communal heritage by opening up the business to three of his brothers and a brother-in-law, allowing them to buy in as equal partners.

Background

Levi's ancestors were part of the later nineteenth-century migration of Mennonites from the Russian colonies to southern Manitoba and Saskatchewan. Withdrawal of Mennonite exemption from all forms of military service, along with increasing Russification pressures in the schools and local governments, caused 18,000 of the Mennonite colonists to emigrate in the 1870s. Roughly 10,000 settled in the United States and 8,000 in Canada.

The Canadian group "consisted primarily of Chortitza people, descendants of those poor and simple pioneers who in the previous century had first left Prussia for Russia."[1] The majority of these settlers were to remain in the East and West Reserves of Southern Manitoba, until circumstances similar to those in Russia brought about the removal of a smaller contingent to the wilderness of the Paraguayan Chaco during the later 1920s.

The issue was control of the schools. During the Great War, provincial governments severely restricted the use of languages other than English in public schools, striving to make them instruments of Anglo-Canadian conformity and nationalism. Meanwhile accreditation of private schools was made difficult, forcing Mennonite children into public schools. These were ominous developments for the German-speaking colonists. As historian Frank Epp put it, "The public school pointed to Anglo-Canadianism rather than German Mennonitism, to urbanization rather than rural life, to militarism rather than pacifism, to ostentation rather than the simple lifestyle they and their ancestors in the faith had always advocated."[2]

The eventual result was the migration of around 6,000 Mennonites from Manitoba and Saskatchewan to Mexico in the early 1920s, while approximately 1,800 went to Paraguay in the latter part of the decade, both countries offering terms of settlement acceptable to the emigrants. The majority of those who migrated to Paraguay were Manitoba Chortitzer, the families of Levi's parents among them.[3]

The economic experience of Canadian Mennonites up to this point had not been entirely unsuccessful, despite difficulties in the early years of settlement, when agricultural conditions were harsh and crude. Economic success and the accompanying growth of an incipient individualism helped bring about the steady disintegration of the closed "block" settlements in the decades after the Mennonites arrived in Canada. Some farmers became rich, such as "Gerhard Braun near Morden, who [having begun] in 1875 with $75, owned 1600 acres of land, twenty-four horses and twenty cows, including purebred stallions and bulls."[4]

Mennonites thus showed considerable ambition for economic success, even to the detriment of closed communities. They did so, however, in the context of large families, which were the working and living units necessary for success under pioneer conditions. Large families were often the primary "communities" for Mennonites—including for the Giesbrechts—functioning as relatively complete economic, social, and religious units.

The early years spent in Paraguay were tough ones for the Giesbrecht family, as they were for most of the Mennonite settlers there. Just to get to the capital of the "Menno" colony, Sommerfeld, required a 320-mile boat trip from the Paraguayan capital, Asunción, up the Paraguay River to Puerto Casado, followed by a ninety-mile train trip, then fifty-five miles through the bush by oxcart, wagon, or truck. The whole trip took four to five days. Once there, the early settlers encountered "terrific struggles," including an outbreak of typhoid which took one-tenth of the first contingent of settlers. Other deprivations included a harsh climate, prohibitive agricultural conditions, a variety of pests and wild animals, malaria, and a lack of good water.[5]

The Giesbrecht family was not to survive the rigors of the Chaco intact. The mother, Levi's grandmother, died in September 1932, in childbirth, and the father passed away four months later in a tragic altercation with Paraguayan soldiers in front of the family residence. The Chaco War between Paraguay and Bolivia had broken out earlier in 1932, and battles were fought near the Mennonite colonies. A contemporary recounts, "For months we could hear the roar of the cannon and the rattle of the machine guns and lived in constant danger of being forced to flee."[6]

The incident leading to Giesbrecht's death began when one of his daughters was abducted by soldiers passing through the village. Giesbrecht and a number of his neighbors rushed into the street to rescue her. The girl was able to break free, and the soldiers angrily brandished weapons. As the crowd scattered, shots were fired; shortly after Giesbrecht was found lying in a pool of blood, dead. Parentless, the children were given over to the families of local friends and relatives.

A photo taken of the family before the shooting evokes the austere circumstances of the time. The faded black-and-white photograph reveals a large, Germanic-looking family, dressed in their Sunday best, assembled on the sun-baked Paraguayan clay ground. Three daughters and five sons surround the seated parents. No one is smiling. The father's large, weathered hands point the head of a boy standing between his legs toward the camera. Although the clothes are not particularly worn or threadbare, everyone looks tired and thin, and shoulders are sloping.

Eventually Levi's father, one of the boys in the picture, married Gertrude Friesen, and the couple struck out on their own. After moving around a bit in the colony, they settled on about fifty acres in the village of Osterwick. Levi was born in 1957, seventh of twelve children. The family was poor and had to struggle for its bread. This of course meant that all available hands, however tender, were expected to work in the fields. Levi's father worked for a time as a schoolteacher, in addition to running the family farm. This put further responsibility on younger family members to contribute. By the time he was seven, Levi was already spending a significant amount of time working alongside other family members, picking cotton and tending a dozen draft horses and a moderate herd of cattle.

Though the Giesbrecht family lived in one of the typical Mennonite *strassendoerfer* (villages laid along one main street), Levi's early memories are dominated by a sense of isolation and of his family as his primary social world. Hard work was an accepted part of belonging to this "little community." Little thought was given to playing when work needed to be done. "We all had to chip in, we were a family unit, we were a team, and, certainly we'd rather go and play; but we were taught very early that one needed to help: if the cotton needed picking, we had to go help pick it; if the plants needed weeding, we had to do that."[7] Not surprisingly, a strong work ethic developed. Levi learned that "if you want something, you're going to have to work for it. There's nothing free out there."

But there is little bitterness present in Levi's recollections. Despite being forced to work, family members were not so much a group of *slaves*, as the original Latin *familia* implied, as a band of *workers*, united in overcoming the struggles of pioneer life. And the slave/worker aspect was balanced by another ancient understanding of family, "an organized and stable community" which shared, in Tertullian's words, "common hope, fear, joy, pain, and suffering."[8] As Levi puts it, "We've always been proud and pleased with the family being united, and sticking together through difficulties . . . may it be whatever difficulty there arose, we were together on things."

As such, the family was a relatively happy one. Its size militated against strong bonding between the parents and individual children, however. Levi learned the alphabet from brothers and sisters and participated in little one-to-one interaction with his parents, who had little time for such things. But they did provide a strong Christian example for their children, instilling a faith still held by all family members.[9]

There were plenty of opportunities for faith to be communicated —desperate circumstances have a way of making faith concrete. For a boy growing up in the Chaco, "Faith in most instances was made real. . . . In those days it was made real very many times; we had real struggles, and we needed to depend on God." The family had few books in its possession, so religious teaching was usually verbal, in response to practical situations. Church was a place to go on Sundays, and for funerals and weddings. Church had a different, lesser sort of religious significance for Levi at this time. The family was the primary religious community.[10]

Return to Canada

Owing to the continuing hard times[11] and positive prospects in Canada, the family moved to Niverville, Manitoba, in 1967. Although Canada offered the chance of a better life, plenty of hard work and struggle was still needed to make ends meet. During the summer, instead of playing or going to camp, the children worked in the beetfields to bring in extra money for the family coffers. The father worked as a construction laborer before starting his own small concrete business. As one would expect, the family pitched in whenever possible here too.

With some encouragement from his parents, Levi quit school at age sixteen and went to work in a factory. "By Paraguayan standards, I had had a good education, and there was work waiting for me." After eight months he took a job in construction and eventually ended up working in his father's business. Until he was eighteen, most of the wages Levi earned were turned over to the family, from which he received an allowance. Levi never did finish high school, although he completed correspondence courses through grade 11.

Life may have continued to be something of a struggle, but family life was not without humor, and sports were a frequent source of relief from work. Levi excelled in both areas—he was known for his sunny disposition and for his abilities on the soccer field and hockey rink. The family felt accepted in the predominantly Mennonite community of Niverville, and experienced success in the modest terms of the area. Working together with family, friends, or relatives could be fun, and a sense of accomplishment accompanied completion of the tasks at hand.

There was of course a strong moral and religious component to all of this. "Clean living" remains the hallmark of the family, as the parents provided a strong example for their children. Things like drinking, smoking, and swearing were clearly taboo. Religious faith found its clearest expression in a strict personal morality. When Levi was in his early teens, he made a personal faith commitment after hearing a traveling evangelist in town. His faith was simple. "I just said 'Lord Jesus, come into my heart and live there, from now on you're going to live there.' " Although it has matured since then, his faith retains this disarming simplicity.

As for the particular relationship between economic practice and religious faith, there seems to have been little consciousness. Faith was and remains bound up in personal relationships, morality, and evangelism. As it evolved in the Paraguayan and Canadian contexts, Russian Mennonite religious life did not make explicit connections between economic and religious life. Possible ties between faith and opposition to acquiring too much wealth, buying and selling for profit, or not sharing were not stressed. Given the tough circumstances of the poor, wandering Chortitzer, such teachings would not always have been particularly relevant. Yet as will become apparent, a form of stewardship and sharing has emerged for Levi from the combination of a strong personal faith and sense of family and community.

In terms of the larger Mennonite picture, movement to Canada brought with it the kind of religious and cultural identity changes Levi's ancestors had been evading for generations. The younger children readily learned English and increasingly saw the Germanic aspects of Mennonitism as "belonging to the past." Levi's parents made efforts to keep the German-language faith alive in their children by commuting to a German-speaking church in Winnipeg.

Eventually, however, the distance and effort involved overrode these concerns, and the family attended an English-speaking church. The Niverville Chortitzer church, with its use of Low German and kneeling during prayer, came to seem more foreign than English Mennonite styles of piety, which had been influenced in varying degrees by North American evangelicalism.

By the time Levi left home, he had been influenced in ways which were to shape his further life and career. He had experienced family as both a "band of workers" united in a common task and as a stable community which shared hopes, fears, joys, and struggles. He had imbibed a strong work ethic as well as a moral character and strong faith that did not put restrictions on economic activity.

All these factors shaped his approach to his business activities and contributed to his success. Perhaps most importantly for his later entrepreneurial activity, Levi took with him a desire to get ahead. "Probably the biggest motivating factor was . . . that since we came from a poor situation, to get ahead. And to say, 'Look, I don't always want to be poor, like my parents were poor.' It was always a struggle; we always had enough food and everything, but it was a struggle to make ends meet, and to get past that poverty line, and I didn't want that."

"Somewhere in those years," he adds, "I would have said to myself, 'I want to get past that stage,' and I would have become ambitious enough to think that I might take some gambles and some risks. But I'm going to work, and of course I already had the work ethic, so I didn't need to be persuaded to work harder; it was a decision that I didn't want to be as poor as my family."

In 1976 Levi moved to British Columbia to attend Columbia Bible College (CBC—formerly Columbia Bible Institute) in Clearbrook. There he gained further educational experience. He also became known as a fun-loving and popular character, whom one might expect to see in the tops of trees or walking on his hands across campus. His natural athletic abilities were evident on the soccer field or on the ski slopes, where Levi was a "hot-dogger."[12] At CBI Levi also met his future wife, Lorel Dueck.

After graduating from CBI in 1977, Levi took a trip around the world with a friend and a backpack, on an airline promotion called "Around the World in Eighty Days with Pan Am Airlines." The world suddenly seemed a very big place to someone who had spent most of his first twenty years in relatively isolated communities.

After the trip Levi made a decision to stay in British Columbia. He began working with his brother Martin in house construction while his fiancée did further studies in the lower mainland. They were married in 1981. It was becoming increasingly clear to Levi at this time that he preferred being self-employed in a family context. "I already had the initiative or the ambition to work for myself or with other members of the family, and not for someone else." Working for someone else meant limiting one's input and control, and sacrificing the sense of contributing to a family unit, which had become an important part of Levi's personal makeup.

Starting a New Company

In the fall of 1983, as the British Columbia economy climbed out of recession, an opportunity for going into business arose. A friend from Niverville days happened to be passing through, and conversation turned to work. Ben Sawatsky told of the enterprise he had started the year before in Edmonton, in which he bought low-grade lumber and cut it into components, then shipped it to various markets in the United States.

Levi was interested in doing something similar in British Columbia, in partnership with Sawatsky. They commissioned a feasibility, study, with positive results. By January 1984 they had started Spruceland Millworks British Columbia, using the same name as Sawatsky's Edmonton company. With each partner investing $7,000, a plant on three-fourths of an acre was leased in Richmond (a suburb of Vancouver) and some old equipment acquired. Two employees were hired. The fledgling company received thirty-day terms on their first load of lumber, which was cut up and shipped south. The processed lumber fetched a price double what they had paid for it, enabling the liquidation of their bank loans and the financing of further operations. The pattern has continued to this day—the business has essentially been able to finance its own growth. The original intent of the partners had been to keep the overhead down to a minimum, upgrading machinery, and adding employees as the business could afford it. At first they rented a forklift, for example, and bought older cutting equipment.

The actual operation of the company is simple. Low-grade lumber is bought from lumber mills in northern British Columbia, upgraded by having defects cut out, and cut to specific sizes, such as for vegetable produce pallets in California. This California pallet market accounts for half of Spruceland's business. Other uses include home-improvement pieces sold by retail outlets, and various construction and shipping/packaging applications. Currently 80 percent of business involves exports to the United States. An additional 10 percent of products are shipped offshore. The remaining business is local.

The company grew quickly. By the end of the first year it had upgraded its equipment and added a night shift, employing a total of eight people. Growth was steady for the rest of the decade, so that by 1991 the business had been moved to a four-acre plant in Surrey, achieving $6 million in annual sales. There were now thirty-five full time employees, including management, which by then included four Giesbrecht brothers and one brother-in-law, all 20 percent owners. By 1994 sales reached $15 million. Ben Sawatsky, whose own business had been expanding at an even faster rate, sold Levi his share of the business a few years after it was started. His intention had always been more to help Levi get started than to stay with the business for a long time.

Before looking closer at this company and the related personal and faith dynamics for Levi and his wider family/community, it is necessary briefly to describe the economic environment in which such a thriving enterprise was possible. The British Columbia lumber industry has been and remains the most important industry in the province, accounting for around half of its exports.[13] Since until recently the softwood lumber trade between Canada and the United States has been almost unrestricted,[14] and British Columbia has had such large reserves of timber, the province has become the largest single source of softwood lumber exports to the U.S.[15] Combine a large (if declining) resource base with a big export market, and there are bound to be lucrative opportunities, especially for those able to fill gaps left by the huge producers.

Spruceland has exploited the gaps. As softwood lumber production has increased in the past few decades, the number of operating sawmills has declined. The industry has moved toward larger, consolidated companies like Fletcher Challenge and Macmillan Bloedel, which are more efficient, vertically integrated, and capital-intensive. At the same time, spaces have remained for smaller firms which can respond quickly to the often volatile market changes and concentrate on specialty items, as Spruceland does. And the prevailing mode of trading lumber favors an open market. "Since softwood lumber is usually traded in [train] carload or truckload quantities, the market is open to almost any producer regardless of size."[16]

In addition, there has been in recent years an increase in production of lower grades of lumber, the kind Spruceland buys and sells, due to the decline of old-growth stands and increased dependence on smaller and less mature second-growth timber.[17] Finally and most importantly, the British Columbia lumber industry experienced stable growth 1982-90, coinciding almost exactly with the period in which Spruceland began and grew. Lumber demand from the U.S. market increased, after shrinking in the late 1970s and early 1980s, as the North American economy as a whole enjoyed a period of relative prosperity.[18] Figures compiled by Statistics Canada indicate that 1983-1989 lumber exports from British Columbia to the United States increased by 54 percent and to Japan by 75 percent. There was an overall growth in production levels of 50 percent.[19] Clearly, Levi entered the industry at a propitious time and in an appropriate manner.

However, the existence of positive conditions for economic success only provide the necessary backdrop for our story. They do not preclude the importance of the various historical, social, and religious factors sketched thus far in shaping Levi's life and career. It is one thing for favorable conditions to be present; it is quite another for an individual to take advantage of them, transforming the outcome according to his or her own abilities, desires, and expectations.

A Family Business

Levi has taken advantage of circumstances in a number of ways, most significantly by making Spruceland truly a family business. During the early years, when Levi was principal partner in the business, the pressures were hard to bear alone. The business was growing quickly; it demanded close supervision and long days of hard work. Levi and Lorel were becoming more involved in their church, Sherbrooke Mennonite Church in Vancouver, while also starting a family with the birth of daughter Adriana and later son David. Their church involvement included the roles of deacon, Sunday school teacher, youth group sponsor, singing in the choir. Lorel was church pianist.

It was a time of learning limits, as Levi now admits. He was healthy, independently employed, and felt called to accept the responsibilities presented him. Whereas most people would probably focus on getting a new business on its feet, Levi became simultaneous-

Levi and partners.

ly occupied with a new business, church responsibilities, and a grow-ing family. And they were often ranked in that order of priority. "The day simply couldn't be long enough," especially since there seemed to be no end to the potential for growth in the business and all decisions and problems were directed to Levi.

At some point the pressures became too intense. A period of "burnout" set in and lasted about two years. "It became after a while a very heavy burden, very stressful, trying to keep up with the demands of it all." It was also becoming clear that for the business to grow fur-ther, Levi would need management help.

Thus during 1987-88 Levi's brothers Vic, Martin, and Tony, and brother-in-law Hartwig Neufeld, bought into the company as equal partners, with Levi remaining president of the company. In some cases financing of the buyouts was done through the company, in oth-ers it was done privately, according to circumstances and needs. In all cases, the desire for capital input was clearly not the point. "I had to that point done relatively well—we'd made some good money al-ready, and really financing was not the main issue. It was not as if I was here trying to make some money on the situation." The primary goals were to relieve pressure on Levi, allow the company to grow, and give family members opportunity to be involved in a successful enterprise. Levi knew and trusted them and felt comfortable having them involved. Given his background, such a move could only have seemed natural.

But why relinquish control to such a large degree? Here too the sense of a family unit working equally toward a common goal is present. "I could have easily kept a larger share of equity in the company. I purposely did not so that I would be on an even playing field with the rest, and I would not feel that I could make maneuvers that would be advantageous to me at the expense of someone else, just because I had the authority to do so," Levi explains.

"I deliberately set up equality so the input would be valued equally. My lawyer at the time said that what I was doing was very courageous, but added that businesswise, it may not have been that wise."

Being "younger brother" to some of his partners also played a role, Levi admits. It didn't seem right for the little brother to be the "big boss" always telling the older ones what to do.

A desire to share also played a part—brother Vic thinks that "perhaps Levi didn't want to be seen as greedy." Levi concurs, saying that "I came to a point in time where I said that if I keep piling [money] up it makes me feel a little bit greedy or that I'm making profits too important." This in turn was tied to his faith, though not as a result of any particular teaching of the church. "I think it was more of an inner conviction that just came to me, like 'what is it all for?' It's not pursuit of money, and I just wanted to prove to myself that my job was not only the pursuit of profits, that it was more than that, it also had to do with helping out people, and letting God be in control of my life and my work."

The new partnership has worked well. There have been minor conflicts, but in general each person has been able to contribute according to strengths. One person focuses on mechanical problems, another on shipping/receiving, another on personnel, and so forth. Levi does the buying and selling and basically steers the company.

His sister Frieda Giesbrecht has worked for a number of years with the company as secretary. Although having five bosses is sometimes not easy, she feels that the atmosphere is relaxed, and she is free to speak her mind. She believes that a strong Christian family background undergirds the strength and harmony of the company. In addition, the family has always worked together. "We know each other really well, and what to expect from each other—it doesn't even have to be put into words sometimes."[20]

Levi has similar feelings. "People sometimes wonder at how we can work together as a family, in such a daily way, but it has worked out well. We have our differences, but we've always worked them out and are determined to all have the same goal. And generally we've been so busy we haven't had too much time to gripe."

There is no doubt as to the latter assertion. The plant site is a hub of activity. Trucks load and unload. Pallets of wood are stacked or cut. Various woodcutting machines whine in the shop. Phones ring in the modest portable offices. To keep things running smoothly, the five partners go out every morning for coffee and discuss the day's business. The "boardroom," which is also Levi's office, looks rather neglected. The paneling is peeling in places, a few battered chairs are scattered about a large, empty table, and a lonely looking couch sits off in a corner. This is clearly a "hands-on" business.

Faith and Business

Spruceland Millworks is also a place for "hands-on" faith, offering many practical ways for the Giesbrechts to make their faith real, as it was on the Paraguayan frontier. Vic feels that although there are sometimes situations in which employee-employer relations are not entirely satisfactory, Spruceland workers are treated "a cut above" the average—each employee is not just dealt with as a worker, but as someone "loved by the Lord."

Often Levi or other brothers counseled employees, in a few instances even taking them briefly into their homes. Some have had drinking or marital problems, and one made a faith commitment under Levi's guidance. The company's hiring policy has been to hire anyone who wants to work, regardless of experience or background. This gives some individuals a chance they might not have receive elsewhere.

Levi is not quick to talk about his faith, preferring to let his example speak for him, but does not hesitate to share beliefs when appropriate. At company functions the Giesbrechts do not restrict consumption of alcohol but do not themselves imbibe. At the Christmas banquet one brother will usually make a short statement with just a touch of sensitive religious content. In recent years some employees have come to the company through church connections. Thus the company as a whole has become a more thoroughly "Christian" enterprise. Besides reflecting mutual support among the faith community, this has a pragmatic end as well. Frieda maintains that things "go a lot easier" with such workers. "You know they're going to be reliable and hard workers."

Most production employees are paid by piecework and receive occasional production bonuses for work well done. The company tried a profit-sharing program for a while, but the transiency of the workforce militated against this kind of long-term approach. Levi believes that paying according to piecework and giving bonuses offer incentives to work hard, and simultaneously allow the company to share profits when times are good. He thinks that in general employees are "well-rewarded for their work." Although he admits that perspective varies according to position, he tries to look at all employees as fellow workers, rather than subordinates. Firings have taken place only after repeated failures of employees to perform duties properly. Even then some fired workers have later been rehired.[21]

The view from the employee end is, as one might expect, varied but largely positive. Some employees feel the work itself is not that exciting—it tends to be manual, repetitive, and tiring. The pay is good. However, it is at times lower than elsewhere due to slowdowns in business, and this has troubled some workers. But as one supervisor relates, management has consistently tried to keep everyone working, even if at a lower rate and when the company is making no profits, rather than resorting to layoffs.

Most employees do sense they are treated fairly and honestly, to the best of the partners' abilities. And most are happy to be with the company. As one longer-term employee states, "I couldn't find a better place to work—they're extremely generous in every way. . . . For me, they're not like my bosses—they've become like friends." The brothers provide a good example for the workers, and problems are handled with class and dignity. Others concur that worker-management problems, when they arise, are generally solved in a satisfactory way.[22]

The company as a whole does make some corporate donations, but also frees individual partners to decide where donations should be made. It currently supports missionaries in Brazil and India and will sometimes make an instant donation to a cause everyone agrees on. Levi and the others prefer "Spirit-led" giving to a more structured approach. In addition to opening them to the Spirit's leading, this orientation allows for careful analysis of each situation before support is promised. And at this point none of the partners has grown tremendously wealthy. Profits have been reinvested in the company, until recently leaving all partners but Levi with mortgages on their homes. "It's not like we've got dollar bills hanging out of our pockets," says Levi. "But we are actively pursuing possibilities in the area of corporate donations. Down the road, if we continue to be successful, we'll certainly be looking to expand our corporate giving."

Since making these statements in 1990, Levi has continued to explore new charitable opportunities. In early 1994, he and former partner Ben Sawatsky opened a woodcutting operation in northern Alberta specializing in finger-joint wood products. In this process offsize pieces of wood are joined to make sturdy, larger pieces for a wide range of applications. The partners in this enterprise are committed to donating half of all profits to development projects in developing countries. The plant grew quickly to thirty employees and by early 1995 began turning a healthy profit. Levi traveled to Rwanda at that time to help set up an orphanage in conjunction with International Child Care Fund.

Since opening the company to family members, the pressure on Levi has decreased and smoother sailing prevailed. He also cut back somewhat on his church involvement, declining to reassume the post of deacon after the couple's three-year term was over. Lorel's activity as pianist has been curtailed as well. Levi's family has received greater priority, completing the series of adjustments necessary since his earlier experience of burnout. There was some pressure to remain heavily involved with their church, but "most people are fairly understanding as to what it means to raise a family and run a business—that's fairly demanding. The church leadership did not impress on us that we were making a move that was unreasonable at all." The recent addition of twins, Kerrin and Candance, has added weight to the concern to spend more time with family.

The couple's Vancouver pastor has high praise for Levi and does not know of any particular tensions in the congregation related to his business success. This may be due in part to the fact that the Russian Mennonites who have settled in the area have become relatively affluent and retain few strictures against accumulation of wealth. Levi's admittedly "upper-middle-class" lifestyle isn't out of keeping with prevailing standards. Some of his friends from Bible school days do occasionally comment on the Giesbrecht lifestyle, such as evidenced in their somewhat lavish new home in Surrey, for example. "Having come from a very meager background, I don't have a real problem enjoying a fine home," says Levi.

On the other hand, Levi does not consider himself rich and feels that wealth is not the primary goal of his entrepreneurial activities. At least as important to him is making use of opportunities which arise and challenge his abilities. And new business ventures offer the chance to provide work for others in a healthy Christian atmosphere, thereby opening the way for a positive effect on their lives. The new joint venture in Alberta obviously goes even farther than this in its impact on others.

Levi's pastor describes him as a "sincere, caring, charitable person" with real integrity. When someone in the congregation needs scrap wood, Levi is always eager to provide any he may have. Levi is strongly committed to his family, which ranks first in priority, followed by church and business. "Levi's ministry is in relating to business associates as well as in the church setting," says the pastor, who feels that Levi has become able to balance his commitments well. But there have been struggles—the pastor witnessed the period of burnout already mentioned, when Levi seemed to be at a point of "mental exhaustion," brought on primarily by trying to do too many different things. "Levi like his father is something of a dreamer, and in this case I think he took on more than he could handle."

Then there is the question of church loyalty. Since the company has moved from Richmond to more distant Surrey in the Fraser valley (largely for reasons of space and operating costs), Levi and other members of his family have also moved in that direction. They have begun to attend other Mennonite churches. Previously most of them attended the Sherbrooke Mennonite Church in Vancouver. While there does not seem to have been any particular problem with this, the pastor feels some discomfort at how "church loyalty is undermined by the transiency of our whole business ethic." He worries that the search for lower operating costs or better business climes often become the determining factor in church membership. He is not bitter, however, recognizing that there are other reasons for the family's movement towards the Fraser valley, and that such moves are simply part of the prevailing socioeconomic system.[23]

Clearly, faith is for Levi not tied solely to church involvement but is a personal experience which radiates out through family and business to the larger community, including the church. This more personal faith reflects both the pietistic elements in the Mennonite tradition as well as the individualistic currents of North American evangelicalism. It could also reflect something of a reaction to the highly traditional and ritualized church life Levi experienced as he was growing up. In any case, outside of church involvements Levi's faith is lived most concretely in the context of family and business, where decisions and relationships are a constant reality requiring right action. His faith stands, along with family, as a source of support and relief from what can be a hectic and volatile business climate.

A Faith "Made Real"

It is apparent from discussions with Levi that his God is involved in all his decisions and actions throughout the day through meditation and prayer. Through experience he has learned to turn problems over to a higher power rather than sit and agonize over them. "Basically I have learned to wait on the Lord and let him take care of things. I learned to praise and thank him a lot more. There were many times I didn't even have to ask him for things, and they just fell into place. He just took control. So I learned that many times I just needed to be thankful and watch him work. . . . If my faith hadn't been what it was, things could have turned out very differently, in terms of where the business is today and the ability to deal with problems. When you're in a business of this nature, you're always dealing with problems."

A business associate and fellow Christian feels strongly that Levi and the company do display a deeply Christian character. As businessmen, he and Levi make decisions based on the market. In the final analysis, however, they try to work together to make decisions which they feel serve "the Lord's will." The associate says that "getting on the phone with Levi is the high point of my day—our relationship is very encouraging and mutually uplifting." There is an implicit trust in the relationship, with an awareness present that both individuals place honest Christian dealings above moneymaking. The associate expresses appreciation for Levi's heritage, which Levi has occasionally shared with him. Being a "born-again" Christian from a non-Christian background, he takes delight in hearing stories of the life, faith, and struggles of Levi's Mennonite ancestors.[24]

Other business associates corroborate this positive assessment. One hauler, who operates trucks that deliver wood to California for Spruceland, maintains, "You won't find a better bunch of people to work with." He has a high opinion of both Levi and the other partners, noting, "They are the hardest-working people I know." Payment is always made up front, and Levi's word is trusted. "When he tells you something, he does it."[25] Anyone conversant with Mennonite history will recognize the traditional "Mennonite terms" of business here. Contracts were normally sealed on a handshake and absolute honesty was a given.

Another hauler gives a similar report. Shipments are always ready and waiting, payment is on time (a rarity in the business, he finds), and he experiences respect and kindness. "They always treat me nicer [than other firms], and they're always fair. They're always happy and in a good mood, I don't know why. . . . They work hard, very hard—they just don't give up. I've really got to hand it to them. I guess that being part-owners really makes a difference." All in all, he is impressed with the organization, attitudes, and work ethic of the partners; he is particularly pleased with the personal interest Levi has taken in him and the way the company has "taken care of" him.[26]

In the cynical business climate of the past decades, such accolades may seem out of place—surely there must be blemishes in the Spruceland record. As should be clear, there have been, in the form of struggles with commitments and priorities. But it seems clear that Levi has fashioned a company and way of doing business which are true to his faith and heritage *and* are commercially viable. Indeed, one could argue that many of the attributes which make this company special are also good for business.

Criticisms might best be made in the form of challenges. Could the company do more profit-sharing? Could Levi become more articulate about stewardship concerns? Included in stewardship might be greater awareness of environmental issues. Spruceland currently donates waste wood to a local Mennonite craftsman who creates articles (such as building-block sets) for sale at Mennonite Central Committee stores (MCC—a relief organization);[27] could more be done to make positive use of all waste wood? One foreman faults management for sometimes being *too easy* on employees, allowing them to develop "bad habits" which will not serve them well if they move to less-tolerant organizations. Should management explore ways to "go the extra mile" with workers while instilling in them a deeper sense of personal responsibility and discipline?

These are obviously rather minor critiques, if important challenges. And one can be sure that Levi Giesbrecht is not afraid of challenges, including those that involve risk. "People should be out there taking risks—take them for the Lord, or whatever. . . . I'm not saying great big things—people should be crossing the border of their comfort zone, wherever it is. . . . Don't be afraid to do something where some extra courage is required. Those difficult times are really important, and I see those as real stepping-stones. Difficulties come your way, and they truly do strengthen your faith and make you get rid of some of the chaff of your life."

Levi has indeed been changed by his entrepreneurial experience, having gone in less than a decade from being a relatively carefree construction worker to responsible company president, family man, and churchman. "He's come a long way, in terms of business and personal growth" says brother Vic. Levi has learned to be diplomatic, a trait Vic feels can make or break a business. He has apparently learned from mistakes: "As time progresses, he has matured and hasn't stood still."

In summary, Levi's story reveals an approach different than the Weberian "Protestant ethic" of work and accumulation, with its staunchly individualistic and acquisitive connotations. Such traits are present in Levi's experience, but they have been shaped and tempered by the larger forces of family and struggle, faith and history.

Levi's entrepreneurial effort has involved a reconstitution of one form of traditional Mennonite socioeconomic life, which can be summed up in the phrase, "The Mennonite ethic and the spirit of family," a modification of Weber's, "The Protestant ethic and the spirit of capitalism." The Mennonite ethic refers to the combination of a strong faith, work ethic, moral character, desire for material prosperity, and family/communal life which has emerged from the Mennonite experience. That Levi Giesbrecht has been able to transform this ethic to fit contemporary circumstances is his real success. As on the Paraguayan frontier, faith here has been made real.

11

Merle Good and Phyllis Pellman Good:
"Sort of a Business, Sort of the Church, Sort of the Arts"

BY PHIL JOHNSON RUTH

As the title indicates, Merle Good (b. 1946) and Phyllis Pellman Good (b. 1948) have straddled three normally distinct worlds. Their story is a fascinating account of how two creative and enterprising individuals have tried to strike a wholesome balance between these worlds. The Goods, like Alta Schrock, are relatively unique in their addition of both a communal/religious and an aesthetic component to the entrepreneurial mix. The sparks that fly from doing this illuminate not only the potentially tense relationship between business and the faith community, but also that between the arts and these entities as well.

IN CHOOSING to live and work in a dynamic matrix of Christian conviction, artistic vision, and commercial viability, Merle and Phyllis Good have sometimes found themselves at the center of controversy.

Perhaps the only point on which their many supporters and occasional critics can agree is that this husband-wife team has exhibited remarkable energy and entrepreneurial spirit through the years.

Fortunately for those who have tried to understand and appreciate the forces at work behind the Goods' multifaceted "mission," Merle and Phyllis have not relied solely on their acts speaking for themselves. When pressed they have tried to share—with characteristic eloquence—the meaning of their unconventional pilgrimage.[1]

It can be difficult at first glance to recognize a common denominator among the Goods many ventures. Visitors to the tourist mecca of Intercourse, Pennsylvania, find a collection of museums, galleries, and stores with names such as The People's Place, The People's Place Gallery, The People's Place Quilt Museum, The Old Country Store, Old Road Furniture Company, Crafts of the World, the Village Pottery, and the Village Pantry. Those who step into The People's Place Bookshop can browse through scores of publications bearing a Good Books imprint, as well as a magazine known as *Festival Quarterly*. What few visitors realize is that each of these entities is a component of Good Enterprises, Ltd., a for-profit company created almost twenty-five years ago around the Goods' extraordinary combination of skills, vision, and initiative.

Childhood Years

No one could have predicted while Merle and Phyllis were children that they would one day have their fingers in so many pies. Both came from down-to-earth families, with centuries of farming in their blood. Like his six brothers, Merle seemed destined to make his living from the land, as had the eight previous generations of both his paternal and maternal forebears. He was born Ira Merle Good on February 10, 1946, and was raised on a farm near Lititz, Pennsylvania, eight miles north of Lancaster. His parents, Ira M. and Ruth (Weaver) Good, welcomed Merle as the fourth child in what would become a brood of seven children—all boys.

In his father, who had grown up at a busy farm and mill, Merle saw a model of diligent husbandry and faithful service to the Mennonite church. Ira's abilities as a church leader had been recognized early in life. Barely twenty-six years old, he had been among those placed in "the lot" when Weaverland Mennonite Church needed a new minister. The lot passed over him at that time but fell on him a few decades later at Hammer Creek Mennonite Church.

Merle remembers his father's 1955 ordination with great fondness. Unlike some of his brothers, Merle took off from school to attend the service and was glad he did. The joyful solemnity of the occasion helped to confirm in his nine-year-old mind what he has since described as a longstanding "affection for the church, its workings, and its special moments." An expression of this esteem surfaced later as Merle spent time carefully reading through the Lancaster Mennonite Conference reports his father brought home from the semi-annual meetings.

Ira Good's faithfulness was not reserved for his ministerial functions. He was just as much a Christian at home, in everyday situations. "He was always the first one up," Merle says of his father, who took some pleasure in signing his name "I. M. Good." "He'd get up so he could read the Bible a half-hour before he went out to work in the barn. It might have been four-thirty or five. Then, only when he'd been working in the barn a while, would he call us boys."

Any day could bring a lesson in real-life ethics. "One of Dad's rules was, if you borrow a piece of equipment, you take it back in better condition than you got it. If it breaks or anything, then you buy a new part and put it on," Merle says. "We had some neighbors who did the opposite to us. They'd borrow something and it would come back half-broken. We'd say, 'What in the world?' But we wouldn't get even with them when we borrowed one of their things."

Then there were the larger lessons of life. Merle remembers that Ira taught his children "that we always give thanks regardless of whether it's been a good harvest or a bad one. And we don't blaspheme by suggesting that the size of the harvest indicates how much God cares for us. We plant the crops, we water, we till, we cultivate, we gather in. And regardless of the measure of the harvest—in good times and bad—we learn how to be content, we reach out to others, we discover how much is enough, and we *always, always* give thanks."

Though he lived in a small world, Ira displayed inquisitiveness that might have surprised the casual observer of his religious orthodoxy, eighth-grade education, and provincial outlook. Merle attributes his father's "interest in ideas and how things work" to Ira's having been raised at a mill, which was the social center and information clearinghouse of its day. Symbolic of Ira's desire to learn was the family's *World Book Encyclopedia* set, which ranked in authority and frequency of use in the Good household only lower than the Bible. It was not unusual during mealtimes for questions to come up that could only be resolved by consulting the resident resource, preceded by shouts of "Get the World Book!"

Merle's mother, Ruth, fostered healthy curiosity in the Good household. From her Weaver ancestors she inherited an unabashed yen to know details. "It isn't that she's nosy," Merle explains. "She's just curious, and she's not afraid to appear vulnerable in her desire to know. 'I'd like to learn about that,' she'll say. 'Why do you tuck yours under rather than over? Oh, is that right? Well, I should learn to do it that way.'" Adds Phyllis, "She isn't being critical or messing in. There's a compliment in her asking."

Healthy curiosity was one thing. Formal education was another. "Look at some of these people who went away and got their doctor's degrees," Merle remembers his father observing. "You listen to them talk, and they don't seem any wiser. They know facts, but are they wiser about how to raise their children, how to relate in the church, how to relate to their neighbors? I've seen people who don't have even an eighth-grade education live more faithful lives." But his view was more cautionary than proscriptive. It wasn't that one couldn't be highly educated *and* a good Christian, only that the attempt was fraught with risks, and the odds were not in the church's favor. Whether or not his fears were well-founded, they were at least not borne out in his own children. Though one boy after another went off to college—and some even went on to earn graduate degrees—each remained in the church, and all have opted for service-related careers.

Although Merle's curiosity was cultivated by both of his parents, he believes he owes much of his entrepreneurial temperament to his mother, whose Weaver relatives owned several large businesses. Like a lot of farm boys, Merle found ways to raise some spending money—by trapping muskrats, mostly—but he first became aware of a knack for "marketing" when he was about ten.

"Our class," he remembers, "was selling the greatest invention of the Western World—the 'Rubberscrubber.' It was a square of sponge for washing dishes, with one side rough to serve as a pot scratcher. I adapted a cereal box for the back of my bike and rode from our farm all over the farming country. The nearest farms were about a half-mile away. And I became top salesman in my class!

"The money was to be used for a class field trip to the zoo, only at the last minute the class voted to go to the *circus*. And being from a conservative Mennonite home where we believed the circus was worldly, my parents said I could not go. It was one of my first crises between enterprise and conscience."

Many more crises would follow, as the "enterprising energy" he inherited from his mother wrestled with the "people priorities" established by his father. If the Weaver motto was, "Why wasn't this done yesterday?" the Goods' might have been, "If it isn't done today, we'll do it tomorrow."

Ira's preference for human relationships over commerce was dramatically expressed on one occasion that still reverberates in Merle's psyche. As he tells it, "The neighboring farm came up for sale. Dad had the money to buy it, and it would have made financial sense to do it, but he decided not to. He said, 'If we buy that, we won't have time to visit as many people.' His decision not to buy was one of the crucial influences in my teenage years."

Fifteen miles southwest of the Good farm, just outside the town of Millersville ("still Lancaster County, but a totally different world," muses Merle), lived the family of Richard and Betty (Neff) Pellman. To the Pellmans was born a first child, Phyllis, on December 18, 1948. The family was later joined by a second and last child, Kenny.

A native of central Pennsylvania's Juniata County, Richard had moved to Lancaster County as a young adult. He set up housekeeping with Betty on a farm west of East Petersburg. Eventually the family moved to a piece of Millersville property bought from Betty's father. In the ensuing years, Richard became a salesman for Turkey Hill Dairy and worked his way up to sales manager. After an era devoted to homemaking and child-rearing, Betty found work as a bookkeeper at Millersville University.

Though the Pellmans and the Goods belonged to churches in the same conference (Lancaster Mennonite), Phyllis and her future husband grew up under markedly different circumstances. For one thing, formal education was esteemed in the Pellman household. Both of Phyllis's paternal grandparents were college graduates and teachers.

Richard and Betty would probably have followed suit if economic hard times hadn't pushed them prematurely into the labor force. Even so, each had managed to finish high school.

Not surprisingly, they gave their firstborn encouragement to grab the ring that had been out of their reach. "I didn't feel pushed into it in a way that was detrimental," says Phyllis about her longstanding inclination toward academics. "They never attempted to tell me what to do. Their encouragement was always in line with my abilities."

Phyllis had a robust appetite for reading, which Betty helped her satisfy through regular trips to the library. A self-described "fairly timid, introverted person," Phyllis was most comfortable curled up with a good book. This was not a reflection of deficient self-esteem, however. She felt loved and supported. There was never any suggestion that her potential was limited by the fact that she was female. Part of her security she attributes to having her Neff grandparents living next door. Phyllis and Kenny were the Neffs' only grandchildren. They thus had lots of love and attention lavished on them, making Phyllis feel that she lived in "a small, affirming world."

She enjoyed the protectiveness represented by Neff relations, but Phyllis's ambitions sprang more from the influence of Pellman aunts and uncles. "They were the people I really admired and thought I would be like," she reflects. "They became my most important role models. There was a settlement of them in Harrisonburg [Va.], and we would visit them. I was always attending college functions with them. Several of my other aunts and uncles moved around, often because they were on faculties, and I have very clear memories of visiting them." For much of her youth, Phyllis and her family assumed she would follow Pellman relatives into teaching, likely English.

More generally, Phyllis was encouraged by her parents to succeed through hard work, fair dealings, and religious faith. She was expected to do well yet not get "too big for her britches." "I had a strong sense of what a Pellman should do, which was mixed in with what a Christian should do." Through stories told around the supper table, she learned from her sales manager father how to deal respectfully with people in the business world, when to let employees go, how to handle old accounts. At the same time she gained appreciation for the Mennonite church—her primary arena of activity outside of school. In her congregation her father was Sunday school superintendent and her mother librarian. From them she learned the importance of tithing, supporting all church-related activities, and more.

Phyllis counts herself fortunate not to have developed bitterness toward the church, as did some peers. For this she gives credit to her parents, who could have easily allowed this to happen, particularly when Phyllis was around age thirteen. The Pellmans' congregation and larger conference of churches were experiencing serious difficulties and tensions, with the result that the Pellmans' transferred their membership to another congregation.

"Thankfully, my parents' love of the church superseded the turmoil of the time," she affirms. "Instead of insisting on keeping score, reciting all the wrongs, and entertaining themselves and their friends with tales of the regrettable behavior of some leaders, they shifted their support to our new congregation without losing a beat. I never sensed a slack in our involvement in church activity."[2]

Expanding Worlds

Up in Lititz, Merle Good was also maintaining his appreciation for the church in the face of a different sort of conflict. He found himself with an inexplicable and growing desire to write poems. "I would see something, or feel something," he now says, "and I wanted to share it with somebody and say, 'Don't you see that? Don't you feel that? That sadness, or that delight, or that paradox?' "

Through a pen-pal connection with "Aunt Beth," a fixture of the Mennonite children's publication *Words of Cheer*, Merle submitted and saw published his first piece, a four-line poem entitled "Snow." The year was 1957; he was eleven.

This inclination to write was not something Merle's family and church understood or were inclined to foster. As Merle began submitting poems, articles, and short stories by the dozens, the rest of his family scoffed at his pretensions. They teased him when a poem was accepted and a dollar payment arrived in the mail. Despite his obvious ability with a tractor, they hooted at his habit of keeping pencil and paper handy while working in the fields.

A myth developed that Merle didn't like to work, though he claims it was more a matter of his mind being elsewhere. His mother even made him pay for his own envelopes and stamps when he mailed off his writings, reasoning that if he was going to earn money through writing, he might as well be responsible for his expenses. To her credit, Merle realizes now, "She would have encouraged me more if I had exercised less confidence. But it was like, all at once I'm turning out hundreds of pieces. It was too much, too fast." He sent off articles almost weekly, and at any given time he might have had half-a-dozen manuscripts making the rounds, not just of Mennonite publishers, but of other denominational and nondenominational houses.

Until his family and neighbors could catch up with him, Merle accepted encouragement from more far-flung sources. He attended public school through his first nine grades, and his teachers there showed more appreciation for his talents.

He also developed a camaraderie with editors at the Mennonite Publishing House in Scottdale, Pennsylvania. "I have files of letters that people like Paul Schrock, Paul Erb, Urie Bender, and Willard Roth wrote me through the years," he reports. "They'd send me a two-page letter when they rejected a poem! That's unheard of. What they did for me I try to pass on in many ways. If I hadn't gotten that attention from Scottdale, I might easily have focused on secular markets, because I didn't feel there was any place in the church for me."

With the help of others, Merle's family eventually came to acknowledge his gift. "When I was fifteen or sixteen," he recalls, "people like [Mennonite scholar] J. C. Wenger would come to our community. He knew me because he had read my stuff in the *Gospel Herald* (a Mennonite periodical). He'd go out of his way to say hello to me and talk to me and say he liked my latest piece. Well, my dad liked J. C. Wenger, so he took notice. It wasn't too long before some of my uncles were saying, 'Hey, I saw Merle's piece in *Gospel Herald!*' "

Merle felt further confirmed in his literary pursuits when, as a sixteen-year-old, he made a trip to Peoria, Illinois, to attend a Mennonite Youth Fellowship assembly. There, among what he then regarded as "worldly Mennonites," he met people who recognized him solely on the basis of his bylines. Flush with this experience, Merle began making noises to his parents about finishing high school and perhaps going on to college. This represented a grand departure from the family pattern, which saw its young men quit school after tenth grade, work on the home farm until the age of twenty, then get their high school equivalency degrees before moving on with their adult lives.

Merle's desire to stay in school through his junior and senior years threw a wrench into this traditional schedule. "I argued with my dad all through the milking during my sophomore year," recalls Merle. "I was the ninth generation on my mother's side, ninth on my father's, to live and farm in a thirteen-mile radius of the ancestral farms in Lancaster County. You could practically hear everyone saying, 'What are these young people up to?' "

Eventually a compromise was struck. Merle would be allowed to finish high school if he agreed to stay on the farm and work an extra year, until his twenty-first birthday. On the heels of his graduation in the spring of 1964, Lancaster Mennonite Conference asked Merle to serve as director of its Youth Service Committee. When he accepted the two-year, half-time position, he became the first salaried youth director in the Mennonite church. As the summer unfolded, he settled into a routine of working half-time on his parents' farm and half-time at the Lancaster Mennonite Conference's offices in Salunga, roughly seventeen miles to the southwest.

Then national politics intervened. Merle learned on a Thursday in late August that he had lost his farm draft deferment by virtue of his church work. By the following Tuesday he was enrolled at Eastern Mennonite College (EMC), in Harrisonburg, Virginia, and was newly protected by a student deferment. Though he carried a full load at EMC, he maintained his position with the conference back home in Lancaster. During the school year he did what he could through the mail. With the arrival of summer vacation he picked up where he had left off in Salunga.

Merle's eyes were opened as never before during his freshman year at EMC. Not only did he experience his first major theatrical production—T. S. Eliot's *Murder in the Cathedral*—he received the lead role. He dipped into classic literature. He watched television for the first time. "My whole world changed," he maintains. "But I never felt that the cord to my previous life was broken. Many of the people from the world I had come from probably thought I rejected them or cut my ties with them, but I never felt I had. I didn't feel there was a 'before' and an 'after.' I felt what I was doing in this generation was similar to what my dad had done in his."

To be closer to his youth ministry work, Merle enrolled for his sophomore year—1966-67—at Millersville University. There he bumped again into his former schoolmate, Phyllis Pellman, who had graduated from Lancaster Mennonite High School that spring and was heading toward a career in academia. She had deviated only slightly from her longstanding goal to become an English teacher. "I entered college as a sociology major," she explains, "because I was questioning and quarreling with my identity, and I wanted to be sure I chose what I was doing rather than having it foisted on me."

She and Merle had a year at Millersville to get to know each other. The following year Merle was back at EMC while Phyllis stayed for her sophomore year at Millersville. The connection had been made however, and by Merle's final year at EMC—1968-69—Phyllis had joined him in Harrisonburg.

The summer of 1967 had been pivotal for Merle. For nine weeks he traveled through Europe on a sociology tour, experiencing foreign cultures and reflecting in new ways on his own. Along the way, in London, he attended his first Broadway-style play, *A Midsummer Night's Dream*. Back home he stewed over musicals such as *Plain and Fancy* and the less successful *By Hex*, which were helping put Lancaster County squarely on the tourist map.

Irritated by the premise behind such garishly commercial productions—"They implied that to really be free, you have to leave your people"—Merle resolved to mount a more authentic and home-grown alternative. He wanted to reach not only for his own people but also the two million visitors pouring into Lancaster County every year, mainly because of the large indigenous population of Amish and Mennonites. "We really ought to tell our own story," was how he put it then.

Theatrical Pursuits

After his junior year at EMC in spring 1968, Merle organized a summer theater in Lancaster. He admits now he had the cart a bit before the horse. "I got the backing and we rented a place—the Guernsey Sales Pavilion—and announced that we were going to put on a play before I had actually written the piece."

Simply getting the backing had taken a lot of his time and energy, but it gave him an education he would never forget. As Merle relates it, "I got this idea we should present a play. I loved to write, and although drama was rather controversial here in Lancaster, I felt a play would communicate. But we needed money for twenty-seven performances throughout the summer. We needed backing.

"Someone suggested I should go see Orie Miller, a Mennonite businessman who gave his life to the church, although he didn't appreciate the arts very much. He was then in his seventies, retired here in Akron [Pa.]. First he questioned me for about a half-hour about what I as a young person thought the Mennonite church would be like twenty-five years from then. I chuckled—and he waited. Finally I told him what I thought, not knowing if that would lead to his saying 'No' to my request.

"To make a long story short, he made me write out a proposal—a prospectus, he called it. He made me develop a budget which listed expenses of $18,000 for rent, cast and crew, advertising. At our second meeting he said, 'I don't go to plays, I don't have TV, I seldom listen to the radio. I don't know what all the fuss is about, but I've checked around and some people seem to think this might be a good thing.

" 'Now you're a young man, and I don't want you strapped with debt the rest of your life. So we're going to set this up so that if the play's a flop, you won't be in debt. But to do that, we'll have to see if others believe in this as much as you do. For the top $6,000 of the $18,000, you'll have to find persons who will pledge to cover that out of their pocket if this fails. It's an outright gift. And I'll make the first pledge for $250.

" 'Also, I want you to ask [a well-known Mennonite businessman] to be your treasurer. And if you do those two things—get the pledges and line up a treasurer—then I'll sign a note at the bank for the bottom $12,000 of the budget.'

"Orie went to the bank and signed the note. He came to see our play *Strangers at the Mill* once and said he didn't know what all the fuss was about. And our receipts were a bit higher than our expenses, so we never needed the pledges. But when Mr. Barry, the banker, told me about Orie's coming to the bank, his eyes filled with tears. 'I've never met such a man,' he said. 'He's a true Christian.' Orie took a big risk for me, and that is certainly one of the reasons I'm still in the church."

Strangers at the Mill, Merle's self-described "loosely-structured musical," ran for nine weekends in the summer of 1968 (performances were held on Friday evenings, Saturday afternoons, and Saturday evenings). Despite being staged in a barn lacking air conditioning, the play drew ever larger audiences throughout its run. "People were driving in from Ohio, from everywhere," Merle recalls. "It was one of those phenomenons. The word-of-mouth was incredible. This kind of thing just hadn't been done before." Part of its success Merle attributes to lead player Paul Lehman, whom he characterizes as "a natural performer and singer."

Phyllis was not involved in this first Festival Players production, but she was on board the following spring when they decided to expand to a two-play format and offer weeknight performances. It was a heady time. Says Phyllis, "We were determined that this theater should operate with artistic integrity—*and* as a business. We wanted to create a writing laboratory as well as a business workshop. We wanted freedom. We had seen artistic types leave the church, and that disappointed us. We wanted to do churchly business, yet not in the official church."

The 1969 season featured a revised version of *Strangers at the Mill* and a play newly written by Merle, *Who Burned the Barn Down?* The controversy with which he and the Festival Players had flirted a year earlier now erupted into full conflict. According to Merle, "We were running our summer theater for a second year, which alone was controversial. On top of that we were presenting a play I had written, set in the American Civil War, which did not take a traditional Mennonite approach to war and peace.

"So we had a dicey situation. The local newspapers did a preview story about the play and splashed a rather arrogant-looking picture of me across a prominent page of Friday's paper, topped off with the headline 'Message Theater.' While I cringed at the characterization of the play, folks at my home church were chagrined by the word 'theater.' "

The result was a strongly negative local Mennonite reaction. "I remember feeling hurt but not angry. I understood. It was too big a jump in too short a time. They had no other choice. And yet it hurt. I also felt sorry for my parents."[3]

In the midst of the controversial 1969 season, Merle and Phyllis were married, recognizing that they really "got a charge out of working with each other." Now that he had graduated from college, Merle was facing the draft again. He considered law school but he leaned more toward enrolling in seminary. Ultimately the latter won out. He settled on New York's Union Theological Seminary. Phyllis still had a year to go on an undergraduate degree in English, so she enrolled in New York University's Washington Square College.

The Goods would make their home in New York City for the next three years. Merle worked on completing a master of divinity degree at Union. Phyllis satisfied requirements for a B.A. in English before acquiring a master's degree in English from the New York University Graduate School of Arts and Sciences.

These were tumultuous years for the Goods, as they were for many people in the Western world. Assumptions and ambitions were questioned; issues of culture and patriotism were hotly debated. With two seasons of summer theater under their belts—and more planned —the Goods found themselves needing to clarify their thinking on the relationship between faith, business, and the arts. Merle had been struggling with what he regarded as "the excesses of capitalism" since his first years in college, but now the issue was forced with renewed urgency. How best could he and Phyllis use their God-given talents and energy not only to make a living, but to make a life? As he put it, "I knew I had an enterprising spirit. Was that something to confess as a sin, or was that something to offer to God for kingdom purposes?"

The debate eventually centered on whether the Goods should form around themselves and their projects a nonprofit, church-oriented foundation, or adopt a more traditional business model. On the one hand they were fearful of losing their initiative and prophetic edge by submitting themselves to a church bureaucracy and "being nudged toward the 'principality and power' category." On the other hand they were leery of what Merle has described as "a greedy, vicious economic system designed to destroy people for the growth of capital."

Eventually a discussion with a friend, Dale Weaver, helped resolve the issue for the Goods. Over dinner Weaver "listened to our concerns that traditional capitalism—and business as we know it in North America—would corrupt our intent, our vision, and our spirit. And [he] asked, 'What doesn't corrupt? What can you do with your life where your ideals will not be in danger of compromise or corruption?' At another point he said, 'Look at Walt Disney; anything is pos-

Merle speaking to members of the community.

sible'. . . . It was one of those formative moments where life questions seem to fall in place. And we adopted the term 'benevolent capitalism.' "

Good Enterprises, Ltd.

Thus in 1970 the Goods formed a private corporation called Good Enterprises, Ltd. The initial investment was small but in time has grown considerably. Almost every venture the Goods have pursued since then has fallen under the umbrella of Good Enterprises. Any money earned in the intervening years—whether through dramatic productions, writing, or speaking engagements—has gone into the company. They have received, in turn, regular paychecks.

They have taken seriously Orie Miller's advice. He told them not to go the popular route and own 51 percent of the stock; owning only about 20 percent was best. "That way you will always clearly need other people," Merle remembers Miller saying. "If you own 51 percent, then other stockholders know their votes aren't essential, and they'll be much less supportive."

The Goods expanded the summer theater yet again in 1970, electing to run daytime features in addition to weeknight and weekend performances. They wanted to make better use of their time and the rented space, and they hoped to earn more money so they could "run something" at the Guernsey Barn permanently. That something turned out to be the Dutch Family Festival. In addition to standard theater, the Festival offered a daytime presentation called *So This Is Lancaster* followed by *Pageant of the Plain People*. The first production made use of seven screens, with actors positioned between screens in a three-quarter-round configuration. Audience members sat on hay bales so they could swivel to follow the action, then turn to face the main stage when the *Pageant* unfolded. Before or after the presentations, patrons could enjoy craft demonstrations and traditional Pennsylvania Dutch foods.

In 1970 Merle also had his first novel published. When *Happy as the Grass Was Green* appeared it received much attention and some complimentary reviews. It was a novel in every sense of the word, breaking new literary ground for Lancaster Conference Mennonites. "I remember one of my brothers called me long-distance," says Merle. "He had just finished reading the book, and he felt like he had just read about his life. Not that he recognized anyone from our family . . . but . . . it was really from our world, and he was very moved by it."

Another person moved by the coming-of-age story was a Lancaster Conference bishop who had recently worked with a motion picture director-producer team from California to supply the Lancaster Mennonite Information Center with a documentary film. The bishop handed Merle's novel to the Californians and suggested they think about turning it into a movie. Though neither of the men had ever tackled a feature film—the director's experience was limited to acting on Broadway and a handful of films—they were intrigued by the book and its screenplay possibilities. The producer, Burt Martin, subsequently paid the Goods a visit in New York.

Thus began the sequence of events that would result in the movie, *Hazel's People*. A proposal was drawn up, Merle began pooling investment money, and preproduction commenced. It was a demanding job, and it wasn't the only entree on the Goods' plate, by any means. Having each completed their masters degrees in the spring of 1972, Merle and Phyllis moved back to Lancaster for another season of summer theater and to begin preparing to teach at Lancaster Mennonite High School in the fall. Somehow Merle also managed to turn out a musical "pageant play" commissioned for the 1972 Mennonite World Conference to be held in Curitiba, Brazil. "It was sort of nuts," Phyllis says of this time in their lives, but it was also exciting.

When *Hazel's People* was shot in the spring of 1973, Merle took five weeks off from teaching to be on the set. Phyllis managed to keep up with school commitments while also creating the film's costumes. In weeks the movie was finished and burst onto the scene with a June premiere at Lancaster's Fulton Opera house. In ten days 20,000 folks had viewed it. "The response was electrifying," Merle recalls. "There are certain moments that are just fantastic, when you know you've got the right piece for just the right moment."

The sensation was similar to what he and Phyllis had experienced at the Mennonite World Conference a year earlier. There, in Brazil, Merle's play *These People Mine* had so moved its audience that Mennonite leaders from all over North America had asked him to bring the play into their communities. So it was that in the summer of 1973—as *Hazel's People* was setting attendance records in Lancaster and the Dutch Family Festival was in full swing—Merle and Phyllis traveled with a theater troupe throughout the United States and Canada.

As they visited Mennonite communities from Kansas to Winnipeg and back through Ontario, the Goods met many creative people who were both excited by the artistic flowering they observed on the American east coast and frustrated by their own feelings of isolation. They were sharing many questions, Phyllis remembers, " 'How can we stay more connected with all of these things going on? How can we encourage each other? Why can't we read about this stuff? You're doing all these creative things. Could there be a way to have this stuff more widely enjoyed? And how should we decide what movies we should see? Could we have a newsletter or something?' "

In response to this demand, Good Enterprises published its first issue of *Festival Quarterly* the following February. As noted on its editorial page, the magazine was "dedicated to exploring the culture, faith and arts of various Mennonite groups worldwide, believing that faith and the arts are as inseparable as [our faith] is inseparable from how we live." Subscriptions were free for the journal's first two years, boosting circulation to 30,000 (largest of any Mennonite periodical).

Though the Goods sold advertising space and many books through the magazine's informal book club, *Festival Quarterly* lost money for Good Enterprises and has continued to do so. Making money was never the point, however; indeed after readers helped to lift it out of a serious financial slump in 1988, Merle promised that "if *FQ* ever starts to show a profit, we will roll back the subscription price accordingly."

After the 1973-74 school year, Phyllis and Merle left their teaching jobs at the high school. "We just couldn't do it all anymore," explains Phyllis. Merle adds, "We either had to quit teaching or give up our projects, which were just growing and generating such enthusiasm. They were new and seemed to be needed. We were speaking a lot and going places. We didn't have children."

For the next two years the Goods ran the Festival, published *Festival Quarterly*, and wrote—activities that didn't bring in much money. Attendance at the Festival rose and fell but mostly rose, while audiences grew more sophisticated. Merle wrote new plays each season and turned out two novels (unpublished).

Though they found this work rewarding, the Goods were ready for change by 1976. "We wanted to get a little more stability, more regularity, more of a routine in our lives," reports Phyllis. "We were tired of tearing down and packing up the Festival all the time. We wanted to go to a year-round base, and we needed a permanent location."

They found such a venue through John Rutt, a member of their board of directors, who owned a house in Intercourse, Pennsylvania. With tourism on the rise, Rutt was concerned for the safety of his children, as upwards of sixty buses per day steamed past the yard in which they played. In June of 1976 Merle and Phyllis bought his property and put out a shingle for something called The People's Place.

Initially this museum and visitors' center relied heavily on the Goods' collection of Aaron Zook carvings depicting Amish life, along with a documentary on the Amish produced by Mennonite writer and historian John Ruth. In time Merle and Phyllis put together their own documentary and created an exhibit known as Amish World.

Meanwhile they continued running the theater, which was enjoying some of its most successful seasons. Despite this success, the Goods pulled the plug on the Festival following the 1977 season. In February of that year, Phyllis had given birth to their first child, Kate, and the demands of running the Festival did not square with child-rearing. "Theater is extremely exhausting," reports Merle. "You can be there till ten or ten-thirty at night. If you want to keep up the quality of the show, directors and producers have to be on hand." Phyllis adds, "We needed to become even more regular in our living, both in terms of schedule and reliability of salary."

This need grew stronger again as they welcomed their second

Merle and Phyllis in front of their historic Old Country Store.

child, Rebecca, into the world in July 1979. As the Goods' vision of what they could do with their opportunities in Intercourse grew more sharply focused, they began to make use of neighboring sites. In fall 1977 the building next door became available and so Good Enterprises took out its first lease on what today houses The People's Place Gallery. One day in June 1978 a "For Rent" sign appeared in a window of the historic country store across the street from The People's Place. Merle went over to investigate, and Good Enterprises ended up renting a room in the store and using that space to display quilts. By the end of 1979, the entire facility—except for a room housing an antique shop—was leased to the Goods.

With the Festival defunct, Merle was without a venue for his writing. At the same time, Phyllis was having to cut back on the amount of time she spent at the office in Intercourse, now that she was primary caregiver for two little girls. Neither she nor Merle wanted her to become "number two" to Merle's "number one." How could she continue to be heavily involved with Good Enterprises from their home in Lancaster city, which had been outfitted with a third-floor office?

What new forum could be found for Merle's creative expression?

The Goods' thoughts turned toward publishing, which had seemed only a remote possibility when they opened The People's Place three years earlier. Since that time, however, they had become aware of a shortage of literature dealing with Mennonite and Amish subjects. Maybe they should start up a publishing company that specialized in such educational materials.

The Goods had already floated a few of their ideas for producing informative books past the editors of the Mennonite Church's publishing company, Herald Press, but had received no nibbles. They had taken this to mean that they were free to publish materials on their own; they would not be competing with their own church's publishing organization. This freedom to proceed—along with Merle's desire to write and Phyllis's need for editorial work she could perform at the home office—resulted in the publication of two booklets in 1979— *Twenty Most Asked Questions About the Amish and Mennonites*, co-written by Merle and Phyllis, and *A Quiet and Peaceable Life* by John Ruth. Both bore Good Enterprises's newly created publishing imprint: Good Books.

As this venture was getting off the ground, Phyllis's brother Kenny became a full-time member of The People's Place staff (he had worked there several summers since its inception). His wife, Rachel, who had been part of the *Hazel's People* cast, came on board as well. She worked across the street at the Goods' expanding retail facility, The Old Country Store. The sale of quilts and handicrafts had been part of Good Enterprises since the days of the Dutch Family Festival. As tourism increased, demand for such products continued to grow, prompting the Goods to expand their retail operations.

"It was tied in very much with wanting to encourage creative people," Merle explains, "to help them find a market for their work." Adds Phyllis, "A lot of them weren't looking to have people drive in their lanes and buy merchandise out of their living rooms, but they were happy to have a place like The Old Country Store to put their work up for sale." This mission to connect artists and artisans with customers led the Goods in 1984 to purchase the block of buildings housing The Old Country Store, and to establish there a pottery gallery and furniture store, along with a suite of offices.

For Good Books 1984 was also a year of expansion. Says Merle,

"We decided to get a little more serious about publishing, to launch a broader line of books and become more of a publisher for the general market." Adds Phyllis, "We were concerned that some of the best creative writing by Mennonite-related authors was not finding its way into the marketplace."

Hoping to attract the attention of national retail chains such as Waldenbooks, Good Books released what Merle describes as "our first novel," Sara Stambaugh's *I Hear the Reaper's Song*. The glossy four-color *World of Amish Quilts* and *From Amish and Mennonite Kitchens* and others were published in 1984. Thus began an era in which Good Books published upward of twenty books per year (with a current booklist of nearly two hundred active titles).

If Good Books continues to grow, it will be in numbers of books sold rather than titles issued. "We want to sell more books but also keep a small staff," says Merle. "If we hire more people and try to publish more books, we'll just end up supervising the supervisors. We want to have our hands on each book, its tone, its jacket, and so forth." Phyllis emphatically concurs. "I doubt we would ever alter from that, because that's where our passion lies. Why grow and spoil it?"

"Sort of a Business, Sort of the Church, Sort of the Arts"

As Good Enterprises approached its twenty-fifth anniversary in 1995, Merle and Phyllis paused at what they saw as the midpoint of their conjoined careers to reflect on the meaning of their work. There had been frustrations and anxiety. Said Phyllis, "A sadness that we've faced in recent years is that one of our reasons for getting into business—to give Merle time to write—may have been squelched by the difficulties of managing everything. He's often too busy to write."

Merle agrees. "The bad news is that we sort of saw ourselves as writers who wanted to develop a little bit of a permanent base," he says, "and we wanted to involve others as we did it. Part of the *good* news is that we have enough people interested in the variety of things that we're doing to support us—buying books, art, furniture, quilts. And I like working with Phyllis very much, even more than I like writing. If I had to choose between working for an advertising agency— and having a lot more financial independence—without Phyllis, or toughing it out together, I would choose the route we have taken."

There have been no maps to consult on this remarkable journey. The Goods have tried to make their way in consultation with "a cloud of witnesses," as Phyllis calls them, not least of whom are the two-score members of their staff. "We've made conscious attempts to surround ourselves with strong persons who can speak the truth to us," Merle declares—"members of our board and staff, our small group, family members, persons from our church and neighborhood."

"You try to live in full view of these folks," adds Phyllis. "You are choosing to be nonconformed to prevailing business practices. You are choosing to curb, to temper, to frustrate the impulse to rule. That is a transformed life—and for that you need faithful company."

The remarkable growth of Good Enterprises, with its unique (for Pennsylvania Mennonites) encouragement of the arts, publishing efforts, and service to tourists, has not happened without strains and some criticism. Not all the Goods' projects have succeeded. Financial problems have sometimes taken a toll. The large volume of quilt and cookery publications turned out by Good Books and marketed with considerable effectiveness has surprised some of the Goods' colleagues in the arts who expected a more idea-centered book list. Some point out that *Festival Quarterly*, in addition to showcasing diverse and innovative writers, appears to have been kept alive partly as an advertising venue for Good Enterprises.

The path is not always clear when one tries to be equally honest and responsive to one's faith, artistic integrity, and marketing impulses. The Goods have consciously chosen to work in this "triangle of tensions," knowing, as Merle has pointed out, that "tensions can destroy or they can refine." At times, they admit, they have been tempted to resolve the tension by jumping to one corner or another. "If you stay in the center of this triangle you can never fully *score*," Merle points out. "We knew years ago that we were choosing to forego respect. We knew we could not be fully respected by the business community because we seem too artsy on the one hand, and too churchly, too charitable on the other.

"We knew we would not be fully respected by the artistic community because we were too interested in connecting creative persons with other persons who would enjoy their creativity. We were too interested in marketing. We couldn't be trusted to have genuinely eccentric artistic integrity. And third, we knew we would not be fully re-

At the event celebrating the publication of *Snake in the Parsonage*—author Julia Kasdorf, poet Jean Janzen, and book editor Phyllis Pellman Good.

spected by the church community. On one hand, we were too businesslike, too self-supporting, too commercial. And on the other hand, some of the things we wrote, produced, or sponsored were too artsy, too maverick, too out-of-control, too outrageous!"

There have been other related tensions as well, including a controversy with a well-known scholar over the question of "marketing" Amish/Mennonites, who should speak for them, and how they should be represented. Should people like the Goods be capitalizing on Amish/Mennonite lifestyles?

Instead of trying to sort out this debate here, it will suffice to say that this kind of conflict points to some of the inherent tensions between Anabaptist-Mennonite religious and communal values, on the one hand, and those of the wider world, including business, on the other. By straddling both worlds, the Goods have had to confront this tension directly and have indeed been criticized for a stance which this chapter has attempted to portray in all its complexity.

So far the Goods have not yielded to the temptation to resolve tensions between worlds by seeking full gratification and respect in any one area. As Merle notes, they relish the freedom "one feels when one's life is not geared to gaining respect—freedom to create, freedom to be honest, freedom to be yourself, freedom to speak the truth."

Some individuals might feel torn between two worlds. The Goods, however, enjoy the sparks that fly from mixing together what are often seen as exclusive areas of experience into an enterprise that is "sort of a business, sort of the church, sort of the arts."

Conclusion

AFTER READING these accounts of Mennonite entrepreneurs, you will likely have developed a number of impressions and reached a variety of conclusions. Among them might be the observation that these people were exceptional in one way or another. On the other hand, the opposite reaction is also likely—namely that they represent the rank and file of humanity, with all of its strengths and weaknesses.

The truth probably lies somewhere in between these two possibilities. What seems to separate these individuals from the rest of us is a combination of individual drive and willingness to take risks, as well as an innovative, creative spirit. The role of serendipity and unusual circumstances in giving rise to entrepreneurial activity and success must also not be overlooked. In most cases, opportunities arose out of our subjects' experiences, which they then pursued with vigor.

A number of the figures would never have become "high-rollers" had there not been a sustained real-estate boom in the North American west during the postwar era into the 1970s. Levi Giesbrecht might be an average building contractor by now had not a friend presented him with an idea, and had not the British Columbia lumber industry been on a long-term upswing. We could list such examples indefinitely. Perhaps what sets these entrepreneurs apart, then, is their desire and ability to seize opportunities as they arise, when others would simply let them pass by.

The reasons for embarking on an entrepreneurial track are complex and partly unique to the individual. We agree with social scientific research that points to entrepreneurship as a social and cultural phenomenon,[1] but our research also supports the notion that some individuals express an unusual and unmistakable "entrepreneurial drive," often at an early age. Bill Dyck, Alta Schrock, and Kurt Janz exemplify this, and others might be nominated as well. Were they merely the products of social and cultural forces, or were they in a certain sense "self-made"? This is an intriguing question, and we hope this collection of profiles begins to provide a nuanced answer.

The focus of the book has been on another question, however—the relationship between religious faith and faith community, on the one hand, and entrepreneurial/business activity, on the other. One might begin to address this topic by asking a few specific questions.

1. Is entrepreneurship a necessary component of human experience, including religious? In what ways?

2. If entrepreneurship is inherent and necessary, how does the Christian faith address the moral and ethical implications?

3. How is entrepreneurship perceived and integrated (or not) in the Anabaptist-Mennonite tradition, and specifically in the local congregational and community setting?

We can only begin to address these questions here, and we invite readers to develop their own interpretations. As to the first, it is safe to say that entrepreneurship is an entrenched feature of modern Western socioeconomic culture—individuals who take on the role of innovator, organizer, and risk-taker emerge in almost every social situation. Human organizations may persist or survive without the presence of entrepreneurs or an "entrepreneurial spirit," but it seems clear that to go beyond mere survival requires just this sort of element.

If entrepreneurs have in a sense become a "necessary" component of Western culture, we suggest that they are necessary in the realm of religious life as well. Why? Because religious institutions tend over time to become traditionalized and sacralized, if not downright stagnant. Some changes and innovations are therefore necessary for the religious institution to flourish and adapt to changing conditions.

The careers of Jacob Shenk, Frieda Kaufman, and Alta Schrock come to mind in this regard, though others in our sample illustrate the principle. For many of the figures profiled in this book, economic and religious entrepreneurship went hand-in-hand. Indeed, it would be difficult to imagine this not being the case in a capitalistic society—economics inevitably pervade and shape all aspects of experience.

The second question goes well beyond the confines of this study but points to the necessity of developing theological responses to an indubitable fact. There have been and will continue to be entrepreneurs who are also Christians. The apostle Paul may be regarded as one of the first entrepreneurial Christians. And Paul taught that there are various "gifts" present among the community of believers, all united in the common purpose of building the church and the kingdom of God (1 Cor. 12:12-31; Eph. 4:7-16). Various branches of the Christian church have taken differing stances on this question, ranging from willful ignorance of the implications of entrepreneurial behavior for religious life to the almost complete submission of such behavior to theological and communal strictures.

Consideration of entrepreneurship from the perspective of the Anabaptist-Mennonite tradition brings us to the third question. How has Anabaptist-Mennonitism understood and involved entrepreneurs in its life? This is not an easy question to answer and is dependent on a number of factors, as the profiles make clear. The church-business relationship has often been tense. Business or entrepreneurial success can pose a challenge to the integrity and self-understanding of the faith community. How can a tradition that takes seriously the Sermon on the Mount reconcile itself to members who, through expression of creative talents and drives, become wealthy and powerful in the "world" as well as in the Mennonite community? Or conversely, how can such individuals accommodate themselves to their faith community? That is the nub of the issue, and it goes to the heart of the Christian attempt to be "in" this world but not "of" it.

The profiles collected in this study provide a broad range of responses to this dilemma. Some individuals, Frieda Kaufman and Alta Schrock, have pursued entrepreneurial activities almost entirely in the context of the church community. One might argue that as women who flourished in the early and middle part of the twentieth century, few other options, save total rejection of their faith community, were available. Jacob Shenk pursued "business" in the wider world, yet his behavior remained attuned to the ideals of his faith and community. He ran his business like a church—a nonprofit organization—and participated in church like it was a business. But if he dedicated his entrepreneurial activities to the church, in private life he expressed impatience with some of the tradition-bound norms of his faith community.

Others, like Abe Kroeker, operated on multiple tracks, becoming leaders in both the world of business and in their church, often finding their niche in the latter by becoming "institution builders." Jacob

Shenk was also this sort of entrepreneur but can perhaps be differentiated from people like Kroeker and Jacob Redekop by the degree of overlap between his entrepreneurial and churchly identities. Redekop's rugged individualism put him farther from the center of church life. As he freely admits, his support of the church has been on his own terms and has resulted in some alienation from church members. Emanuel Mullet had to learn to work in partnership with his co-religionists, shaping his entrepreneurial instincts to achieve a better fit with his wider community as well as the natural environment.

Misunderstandings become possible when entrepreneurs become successful far beyond the levels of other church members. Subsequent bankruptcy, as in the case of Kurt Janz, only compounds the problem. Bill Dyck's choice to pursue a career path in the veiled world of real estate investment resulted in an aura of mystery; others didn't quite know what to make of him. At a point of crisis he renewed his commitment to the church and reintegrated himself into his faith community. As in the case of Levi Giesbrecht and others, a personalized evangelical approach may became an important way religious beliefs are incorporated into everyday business practices. Giesbrecht too experienced something of a personal crisis, and like Dyck, he responded by immersing himself in a broader community—in his case his family, an important component of the traditional Anabaptist-Mennonite community. The faith community may be a source of alienation for some, but it can also serve as refuge from the ups and downs of the business world.

The Pellman Goods are happy existing on the borders between three worlds, that of church, business, and the arts. Their entrepreneurial and artistic drives have led to the creation of an interesting hybrid of these three worlds. This combination requires a good deal of tact and negotiation to keep in balance. All the figures profiled in this study have been involved in some sort of balancing act between ideological commitments and entrepreneurial activity. The difficulty of keeping these elements in balance is often related to the nature and expectations of the local faith community. In some cases entrepreneurial behavior and the accumulation of wealth are not taboo *per se*, although expectations about the use and display of wealth, as well as the expression of personal piety, are clearly present. In others, the nature of the faith community necessitates a greater sensitivity to the impact of aggressive entrepreneurial activity and the rise of wealth.

If the faith community is an important player in determining individual behavior, how can we theorize this relationship? The sociological analysis which seems helpful in proposing a theoretical stance for understanding entrepreneurs belonging to strong religious traditions is "reference group" theory. This theory proposes that social action is determined by membership in groups which have a specific set of values and norms. Robert Merton defines this process as follows.

> Conformist and nonconformist behavior can be adequately described, to say nothing of being adequately analyzed, only if this behavior is related to the membership groups and non-membership groups taken as frames of normative and evaluative reference.[2]

Thus in the case of Mennonites, entrepreneurs' values and behavior can be understood as either conforming to or deviating from the value and normative system of their home group. At the same time, they are understood as exercising their own influence on those norms in the long run. Mennonite entrepreneurs cannot adequately be understood except in reference to their faith community; even if they reject it entirely, their behavior still occurs in reference to it.

In line with reference group theory, and on the basis of the profiles presented in this book, we offer in conclusion some axioms regarding entrepreneurial and economic activity for Mennonites in particular, as well as for members of other broadly similar religious traditions.

1. The more strongly the religious group or congregation (the reference group) emphasizes the community in its ritual and confessional life, the more the potential for rejection and/or alienation will exist for the entrepreneur. Entrepreneurs emerging out of more conservative and traditionalist faith communities will exhibit this characteristic more than others.

2. The stronger and clearer the geographic or ideological boundaries that separate the religious group from the mainline society, the greater individualistic entrepreneurship will be positively skewed toward communally approved economic and business activity. The function of this skewing is to minimize the threat to the values and cohesion of the community.

3. When individuals deviate from religious community or congregational reference group norms, "nothing succeeds like success." As some of the profiles indicate, as long as the entrepreneur is successful, deviance is grudgingly condoned. Failure, however, causes disapproval and rejection. This is likely the result of two factors. First, a successful "deviant" is able to influence the group to become more open. Second, groups almost universally seem to identify with success and disapprove of failure.

4. The faith community's collective negative attitude toward entrepreneurialism may be solid, ambivalent, or almost nonexistent, depending on the inroads the mainstream individualistic ethic has made on the membership. Hence, in a congregation or community where individuals are adopting the individualistic achievement ethic (an assimilationist group), the status of the entrepreneur may be more ambivalent than in a group with low assimilation of this ethic and clear definition of alternate normative rules.

5. The form entrance into entrepreneurship takes is clearly determined by the opportunities present in both the "sacred" community (the immediate reference group) and in the secular world. There is no way of isolating a subsystem totally from the larger one. All the chapters in the book provide illustrations of this principle.

6. The personal development of the entrepreneur and consequent entrepreneurial behavior is to a major extent determined and supported by the family, which is a basic producer of solidarity for reference group membership. This is of course an axiom that has long been known, but it is the impression of many theorists familiar with the Mennonites that the family is unusually strong in this tradition. Most of the chapters bear out this impression.

7. The religious community—the totalistic reference group—provides a significant identity for the entrepreneur, both personally and ethically.[3] All of the profiles show that individual identity exists in relationship with the congregation and faith community. Of great significance is the corollary question: where does identity and ethical commitment and behavior come from when the religious community loses its vitality and no longer determines the individual member? This is one of the most important questions facing an increasingly individualistic Western world, and it confronts Mennonites like everyone else.

8. Individuals emerging out of a strong faith tradition are often

equipped to succeed in the world of business like no one else, a fact which exacerbates the tensions between communal norms and individual desires and behavior. The reference group helps furnish entrepreneurial individuals with a strong moral character and work ethic that takes them far in the world of business, contrary to more cynical views of the requirements for business success. Clean living, fair dealing, and hard work have been the hallmarks of our subjects. They were not sidetracked, by and large, by the kinds of personal problems (marital breakup, substance abuse, business scandal) that often afflict the "movers and shakers" of the world. The dilemma, of course, is that the moral and religious norms that help generate worldly success eventually come into conflict with that success, necessitating some sort of negotiation or behavioral adjustment for the entrepreneur to remain on good terms with his or her religious beliefs and faith community.

Although it has not always received conscious attention, the Anabaptist-Mennonite tradition has generated a strong witness on discipleship in economic affairs. A recent statement by a study committee of General Conference Mennonites points to the need for more reflection on the issue.

> We believe many persons are called to business as a vocation and as such are the servants of God and of the people. Therefore, we urge young people to enter its portals through which they might witness to the Light which was in Christ Jesus our Lord. [However] we are concerned about the fact that the intricate and complex maze of relationships which emerge has often tended to make [persons] neglect [their] Christian faith or dampen [their] witness on ethical issues within the community.[4]

We hope readers have been stimulated to reflect on this topic and to better understand the struggles faced by entrepreneurs with strong Christian beliefs. Perhaps *Entrepreneurs in the Faith Community* will contribute to revision of any simplistic notions about businesspeople who are also Christians. We also hope these stories spur readers to reflect on the creative possibilities open to us all.

Appendix

Questions for Further Discussion

FOR THOSE of you who might be interested in leading a discussion on this book, we include below some possible discussion starters. We also suggest you reread the introduction and conclusion, with the aim of testing the claims made there against the individual profiles. Your questions and/or critiques are likely a good point of departure for further discussion. A general question to consider is the role played by entrepreneurs' wives (as far as can be ascertained) in stories which have featured male entrepreneurs.

Chapter 1. Jacob A. Shenk

1. Shenk's early youth did not seem to predict his later aggressive entrepreneurial life, either in church or in business. Can his life history be explained by his simple commitment to the church, or was he a more complex person than many contemporaries assumed?

2. Was Shenk's unusual attempt to return 90 percent of his business earnings to the church a misguided and misunderstood commitment? Or was it a prophetic act that witnessed to the overlap between religious and secular aspects of life? Do you think such a commitment is feasible for businesses today?

Chapter 2. A. A. Kroeker

1. Education is normally touted as the quickest route to social and economic advancement. What personal and community factors explain Kroeker's early and eager pursuit of education, and his use of learning in both religious and secular entrepreneurship?

2. There seems to have been an ongoing struggle in Kroeker between conservative and more liberal or innovative impulses. What were the contours of this struggle? How was he able to resolve it?

Chapter 3. Alta Schrock

1. How does Schrock's family life and history help explain the emergence of such an unusual (for her time and place) female personality and career?

2. In the face of church and community resistance, what accounts for Schrock's undaunted exuberance in her entrepreneurial adventures and achievements? Why haven't there been more Alta Schrocks in the Mennonite tradition?

Chapter 4. Jacob Redekop

1. What does the Redekop family's typical Russian experience tell us about the so-called "Mennonite work ethic"? Are there special factors which might contribute to this ethic?

2. Redekop's relationship with his brothers and other business partners became strained, finally resulting in separation. What questions does this raise regarding business ethics for church members or ethical behavior between fellow believers?

Chapter 5. Emanuel E. Mullet

1. What peculiarly Amish factors affected the way Mullet pursued his career? Do they make entrepreneurialism in the bosom of the rural Mennonite community more difficult?

2. How does Mullet's story illustrate the particular Amish relationship with the land? How would the story be different if Mullet had been raised in a different sort of community?

Chapter 6. Kurt Janz

1. Janz quickly moved into the construction industry in a strange country even though he came from a remote agrarian way of life and

had a traumatic refugee past. What were the roles played by family and faith community in his career?

2. In what ways is Janz's experience with his congregation helpful in understanding the dynamics of success or failure and entrepreneurialism in a religious setting?

Chapter 7. Sister Frieda Marie Kaufman

1. What are the implications of Kaufman's life story for the nature of men's and women's careers in the church? To what degree have roles changed?

2. Kaufman brought together higher education, health care, and missions in her work; what are the difficulties and challenges of this type of contribution? What kind of entrepreneur was she?

Chapter 8. Bill Dyck

1. By most accounts, Dyck was an unusually intelligent and gifted person, committed to the Christian faith, who moved from a service profession to high level entrepreneurship. What does Dyck's career tell us about gifted people and the challenges they perceive in the church?

2. In what ways does Dyck's entrepreneurial spirit highlight the conflict between commitment to the church and ethics and challenges in the secular world?

Chapter 9. Jay Lehman

1. To what degree was Lehman's entrepreneurial success a product of the low-tech Amish subculture which surrounded him and/or the environmental movement that began in the 1960s?

2. Lehman's career seems to illustrate the possibilities of becoming involved in business as an outgrowth of ideological commitment. Do you think he would have been as wholistically "successful" had he not pursued a service career first? Does his story provide hints about how one might enter business in a satisfying way?

Chapter 10. Levi Giesbrecht

1. What drives Levi Giesbrecht? Is he a naturally entrepreneurial person, or have circumstances conspired to make him who he is today?

2. Does the chapter on Giesbrecht overemphasize the role of family in his life story? Why or why not?

Chapter 11. Merle Good and Phyllis Pellman Good

1. What are the differences between the partnership of the Goods and the traditional husband-wife partnership in Mennonite agricultural communities? How might the concept of entrepreneurship explain the differences?

2. The Goods' entrepreneurial thrusts probably represent the most complex attempt among figures profiled in this book to integrate disparate "worlds" into a satisfying synthesis. What are difficulties and challenges of such an attempt?

Suggested Reading

Berrentine, Pat, ed. *When the Canary Stops Singing: Women's Perspectives on Transforming Business.* San Francisco: Berret-Koehler, 1993. The role of women as the "early warning system" of what is right and wrong with modern business.

Blank, Rebecca. *Do Justice: Linking Christian Faith and Modern Economic Life.* Cleveland: United Church Press, 1992. A fresh look at the gamut of ethical life and modern American economy.

Chewning, Richard C., John W. Eby, and Shirley J. Roels. *Business Through the Eyes of Faith.* San Francisco: Harper & Row, 1990. A good overview of the problems of ethics in business.

Halteman, James. *The Clashing Worlds of Economics and Faith.* Scottdale, Pa.: Herald Press, 1994. The best presentation of an Anabaptist interpretation of economics and faith for lay persons.

Kauffman, J. Howard and Leo Driedger. *The Mennonite Mosaic.* Scottdale, Pa.: Herald Press, 1991. A useful description of Mennonite life, includes some economic activity.

Klassen, Peter James. *The Economics of Anabaptism.* The Hague: Mouton and Co., 1964. A pioneer statement of early Anabaptist/Mennonite teaching on economic life.

Kreider, Carl. *The Christian Entrepreneur.* Scottdale, Pa.: Herald Press, 1989. A path-breaking discussion of Christian faithfulness in entrepreneurship.

Lager, Fred. *Ben's and Jerry's: The Inside Scoop.* New York: Crown, 1994. A refreshing and humorous story of the positive function of candor (honesty) in business.

The Marketplace. Published by Mennonite Economic Development Associates, edited by Wally Kroeker. The best source for analysis of Christian activity in business and economics.

Nash, Laura. *Believers in Business.* New York: Thomas Nelson, 1995. A study of how 65 CEOs integrate faith and business.

Redekop, Calvin, Steven Ainlay, and Robert Siemens. *Mennonite Entrepreneurs.* Baltimore: Johns Hopkins University Press, 1995. A study and analysis of how 100 Mennonite Entrepreneurs integrate faith and business.

Redekop, Calvin and Urie A. Bender. *Who Am I? Searching for Meaning in Your Work.* Grand Rapids: Zondervan, 1988. An Anabaptist interpretation of the meaning of work.

Redekop, Calvin, Victor A. Krahn, and Samuel J. Steiner. *Anabaptist/Mennonite Faith and Economics.* Lanham: University Press of America, 1984. Scholarly analysis of Anabaptist/Mennonite economic practices.

Sine, Tom. *The Mustard Seed Conspiracy.* Waco: Word, 1981. A vital discussion of renewal in the Christian life, including business.

Sutherland, John. *Going Broke.* Scottdale, Pa.: Herald Press, 1991. A careful analysis of bankruptcy including Mennonite experience.

Notes

Introduction

1. In focusing on *entrepreneurship*, rather than business or economics in general, we are singling out those individuals who, by the common definition, "organize, manage, and assume the risk of a business or enterprise" (*Webster's Dictionary*, 1979). This book therefore does not attempt to encompass the entire range of economic activity. However, we feel that analysis of individuals on the "cutting edge" of business or other sorts of enterprises highlights important aspects of the relationship between religious faith and economic activity. For indepth scholarly analysis of this relationship, see Calvin W. Redekop, Stephen Ainley, and Robert Siemens, *Mennonite Entrepreneurs* (Baltimore: John Hopkins University Press, 1995).

2. Three of the chapters in this study profile women entrepreneurs. In the other chapters we have aimed to include and at times highlight the presence of women—normally the wives of entrepreneurs. In most cases they were deeply involved in the entrepreneurial enterprise, and the profiles would have been incomplete without them. Nevertheless we acknowledge that much more work remains to be done in highlighting women's activities and roles in the phenomena under study.

3. Clearly, the many entrepreneurs engaged in small and medium-sized business ventures also deserve more attention; we hope more work will be done in this area in the future.

4. These are the broad trends. Some Mennonites from the Netherlands also migrated to the Eastern Seaboard of the United States in the later 17th century. See Calvin Redekop, *Mennonite Society* (Baltimore: John Hopkins University Press, 1989), pp. 14, 18.

5. Although it is impossible to deal with this variety here, Mennonite identity is being fractured, with theological differences including fundamentalism, liberalism, political divergences from conservative to liberal, social class distinctions from rich to poor with commensurate lifestyles, and a variation on social attitudes such as homosexuality and abortion. These differences have been recently documented in a major survey research project reported in J. Howard Kauffman and Leo Driedger, *The Mennonite Mosaic* (Scottdale, Pa.: Herald Press, 1991). See also Redekop, *Mennonite Society*; Calvin Redekop and Samuel J. Steiner, eds., *Mennonite Identity: Historical and Contemporary Perspectives* (New York: University Press of America, 1988).

6. Robin Williams, *American Society* (New York: Alfred A. Knopf, 1955), p. 391.

7. Max Weber, *The Protestant Ethic and the Spirit of Capitalism* (New York: Scribners, 1958), pp. 156ff.

Chapter 1

1. The vagueness of the report, and the "strangeness" of this type of decision gave Jacob A. Shenk something of a legendary status even while alive.

2. Linden M. Wenger, "The Life of Jacob A. Shenk," *Christian Monitor*, June 1950.

An eyewitness reported, "I saw the plane make many circles over my head, and then I saw the wing explode. Just then the air was filled with papers and many other articles." (Quincey Brown, undated letter). There was a large weather disturbance in the area that day. Dan Hartman, who was flying to Florida, encountered severe weather and heard about his friend Jacob's crash and death upon his arrival at the Jacksonville airport. Dwight Hartman, a veteran pilot, proposes that a consensus has emerged that Shenk hit his head on the framework of the cabin during a serious downdraft, knocking him unconscious and that Weaver, not having any training, was not able to regain control of the plane, which resulted in the wing tearing off.

3. *Ibid.* Local businessman Hartman, operator of the local airport, provided lessons so Shenk could learn to fly. Shenk originally bought a four-seater Fairchild in the mid-1930s but traded it in on a Bonanza in about 1945 since he wanted something faster. The plane cost around $11,000. In 1946 Shenk built a hangar at the Hartman airport, which was less than a mile from his home and hence must have made the logic of flying all the more convincing (Dan Hartman, interview by author).

4. John W. Wayland, *Men of Mark and Representative Citizens of Harrisonburg and Rockingham County, Virginia: Portraits and Biographies of Men and Women.* (Staunton, Va.: The Mclure Co., 1943), p. 317.

5. Information was obtained from interviews the author conducted in 1990 and 1991 with a variety of persons in the Shenandoah Valley and elsewhere who knew Shenk. The names of the interviewees have been withheld to protect their confidentiality, though in the cases of the immediate family, identity is apparent. Interviews are on file with the author; henceforth quotations and remarks with no citation attached are from these interviews.

6. Truman Brunk, quoted in Ellen Shenk, "Jacob Andrew Shenk—A Life Dedicated to God," unpublished paper.

7. John Mumaw, quoted in Ellen Shenk.

8. Lucy Shenk, "Mother Remembers Father," unpublished paper.

9. He did discuss the option extensively with Lucy his wife. Lucy and Jacob had a great amount of respect and love for each other and he valued her opinions. She recalls that though she had great reservations about buying the business and going deeply into debt, she trusted his judgment and agreed to go along with his decision. "This seemed like a big undertaking and we would need to borrow money to make the deal." (Lucy Shenk, interview by the author.)

10. Interview, see above note 5.

11. Lucy Shenk, "Mother Remembers Father."

12. By this statement Lucy meant that Jacob slowly came to realize that his strength was in supporting the work of the church by pursuing other activities with the gifts he had, which included a practical intelligence, understanding of people, organizational, technical, and material skills, along with an unusual degree of order and meticulousness.

13. Paul Shenk, "Recollections of Father Shenk," unpublished paper.

14. *Mennonite Community*, January 1948.

15. This verse was often referred to in the interviews. The fact that it was so well remembered by others tends to indicate that the motto had considerable impact on the public because it corroborated Shenk's integrity—profession and deed should be one.

16. Numerous examples were given by interviewees indicating how Shenk always maintained that each person in business is justified in making a fair profit.

17. This procedure required a meticulous cardkeeping system indicating when the chicks died; the customer would then return the cards to the hatchery for reimbursement. The masses of cards are still extant.

18. Though he advertised generously in the *Virginia Poultryman*, Shenk was given to meticulous modesty and sobriety. Hence he never advertised that his was "the largest" hatchery in Virginia, but knowledgeable people of course knew the rank of a 1.2 million egg capacity—the largest.

19. Dr. Godfrey was the chief disease specialist and geneticist from the United States Department of Agriculture, at Beltsville, Maryland, in which capacity he had consulted with the Shenk Hatchery on numerous occasions. Godfrey had agreed to become an employee of Shenk Hatchery, even though he had national standing. Through his dealings with Shenk, Godfrey had become so impressed with his integrity and advanced program, that he was happy to join the Shenk enterprise. It is not known what financial arrangements Shenk had made with Godfrey. Some interviewees say he would not have come if he had not been offered a share in the company, while others disagreed saying Shenk never offered shares to anyone.

20. When the experimental farm was first introduced, the effects of the program were promising and profitable. Later, however, when Shenk's own breeding flock became infected with pullorum and had to be quarantined, the costs of running the program, including the professional staff and research costs, got so high it was considered by some of his upper management to have sealed the company's fate. Others aver that Shenk was such a good businessman that had he lived, he would have found a way out of the difficult situation.

21. According to interviews with management staff, the personal visits by Shenk to several "hard cases" also communicated to his employees that he was not given to avoid "biting the bullet" by making his employees confront the difficult problem cases.

22. Letter from the Virginia Poultry Federation, May 9, 1950. An illuminating example of his influence within the industry is illustrated by the following story. Shenk felt, like many Christians, that Sunday should not be a day for business or other employments. In an invited address to the Southeastern Poultry Federation at Atlanta, Ga., Shenk mentioned that because of his religious convictions he disapproved of the fact that the convention was meeting on a Sunday. There was no Sunday meeting the following year during the Poultry Federation convention.

23. Julia Gwin, "Jacob A. Shenk: Biography of a Man Who Was a Steward of the Lord," *Virginia and the Virginia County* (March 1952):21.

24. *Virginia Poultryman* (April 1950).

25. The company's net worth was still substantial, but the bank and the management of the company were aware of the financial drain the disease problem and the breeding program were presenting to the company. Another disconcerting factor was that there was no ready buyer at the time the company was facing these problems. In addition, competition in the hatching industry was rapidly coming to a head in the 1950s.

26. Forty years after his death, daughter Ellen wrote "My Search for My Father," *Gospel Herald* (October 30, 1990) in which she states, "I have very few memories of my own. Six years ago I began a search to learn more about my father. . . . As I spent time with my father's memory and with persons who had known and loved him, I began to uncover a deep cache of anger and pain" (p. 774).

27. The advisory committee composed of Alger and Wenger continued to provide general advice to Lucy.

28. Shenk, "Mother Remembers Father." I have heard LeTourneau speak on numerous occasions and recall LeTourneau recounting how he decided to turn his business over to God if he would help him make it successful. LeTourneau also waxed eloquent on flying. "Whenever I had problems I couldn't solve, I would ask my pilot to take me up above the clouds where I could let my imagination loose." It is easy to surmise that this flamboyant stance inspired Shenk, including his use of airplanes.

29. The IRS apparently had a precedent for this type of arrangement which stipulated that after a ten-year trial period, if everything was in order, the company would be given a permanent exempt status allowing it to donate 90 percent of its net profits to charity. The ten-year period was required to see whether the company was using charity as a way of avoiding paying taxes, or deriving some "kickback" or benefit from the practice.

30. Whether the IRS demanded a payment to be kept in escrow pending an audit to make sure Shenk was giving 90 percent as he had indicated, is not clear. No records were found to indicate what happened after 1950.

31. My inquiries about whether the solicitor held to his end of the bargain were met with chuckles.

32. Lucy was later often asked how much they had given, and she replied "I don't know. I can find out, but I won't. The college got a lot of money, but few if any people knew where it came from." Shenk's financial conditions were kept so confidential that even the sales manager, who became the general manager after Shenk's death, said, "I never saw the financial statements of the company."

33. Gwin, "Jacob A. Shenk," p. 52.

34. Shenk's activities on congregational, college, and conference boards were extensive. Ellen Shenk's "Jacob Andrew Shenk," cited above, lists many of them. A. Warkentin and Melvin Gingerich's *Who's Who Among the Mennonites* (North Newton, Kansas: Bethel College, 1943) indicates the following list of boards on which he served before 1942: Zion Church, Building Committee, 1941; E.M.S. North Annex Building Committee, 1941; E.M.S. Auditorium Building Committee, 1941; Supervisory Building Committee, LaJunta Hospital and Nurses Home, LaJunta, Colo., 1942.

35. In several cases, allowing a person to stand as a candidate for these positions was held up until he promised to dispense with the musical instruments in his home.

36. Quoted in Harry S. Brunk, *History of Mennonites in Virginia: 1727-1900* (Staunton, Va.: Mclure Printing Co., 1959), p. 426.

37. This is the way his son Paul defined the attitude his father took on the musical instrument phenomenon.

38. Interview by author. The family remembers that the record player had been loaned to a relative; when the ban was lifted, it was returned.

39. "Insomuch as some of our members are tempted to own, operate, or ride in airplanes for commercial and entertainment purposes, and inasmuch as the present status of the airplane involves an unnecessary risk which is not justifiable for a Christian from a biblical standpoint, and inasmuch as such patronage often involves desecration of the Lord's Day, and disobedience to parental wishes . . . we feel ownership of an airplane involves an expenditure of money that is not consistent with Christian stewardship." One local Mennonite businessman owned and operated an airport and often provided rides on Sunday, which may have figured in the concerns that the conference raised. Jacob Shenk bought his planes from this businessman.

40. Interview by author. This is not to imply that Shenk used his wealth pragmatically. Lucy Shenk maintains, in response to this issue, that "Jacob's motivation in giving

was never to gain recognition by his giving. It was an embarrassment to him to be reminded of his generosity."

41. Interview by author. This same person recalled that "one time I was stranded at a motel since someone had stolen the new Dodge during the night. Rather than telling me I would have to continue my work by bus, Shenk said, 'Sit right there, and I'll send another car.' That is the kind of man he was. His motto was 'Better the Best.' "

42. Shenk further stated that "I have made arrangements and I am not going to pass on the inheritance to my children because it is not mine to pass on." He did not pass significant amounts to his children though they were taken care of.

43. Poultry Federation speech, reprinted in *The Virginia Poultryman* (February 1949).

44. Paul Shenk, "Recollections of Father Shenk."

45. *Ibid.*

46. This response is pregnant with sociological clues to the alienation of successful businesspeople and entrepreneurs from the church. The success of any individual in a close group tends to show relative loss of status for the rest. Further, in a close group, where there is a high degree of consensus on norms of behavior and lifestyle, any deviance is negatively sanctioned, for it threatens the boundaries of the group's existence.

47. There are some qualifications that need to be inserted here. In 1938 the Shenks moved into a new home on College Avenue at the front of the hatchery which, though in good taste, was substantial. This along with the plane which Shenk owned, and a cottage at Sparkling Springs in Virginia, could be considered above-average lifestyle. But the stewardship orientation is reflected in another event Lucy recalls. "One time we had an order in for a new Oldsmobile and before it arrived we changed the order to a cheaper car so we could give the Mission Board $500." Lucy Shenk, "Mother Remembers Father."

48. "Christmas Means Giving," *Missionary Messenger*, December 1947.

Chapter 2

1. Esther Horch in a letter to the *Mennonite Mirror*, Summer 1977, p. 14.

2. Unpublished recollection of Walter Kroeker, Abe's oldest child and one of his students in Bible school.

3. Heather Robertson, *Grass Roots* (Toronto, James Louis and Samuel, 1973), p. 196.

4. *Ibid.*

5. *Ibid.*

6. *Ibid.*, p. 197.

7. W. J. Keith, *Frederick Philip Grove and His Works* (Toronto, ECW Press, n.d.), p. 36.

8. Margaret R. Stobie, *Frederick Philip Grove* (New York, Twayne, 1973), p. 29.

9. Douglas O. Spettigue, *Frederick Philip Grove* (Toronto, Copp Clark, 1969), p. 48.

10. Stobie, p. 32.

11. Robertson, p. 196.

12. *Ibid.*, p. 197.

13. *Ibid.*, p. 198.

14. *Ibid.* As indicated above, Kroeker considered this sort of activity to be "playful," but it may also be viewed in a more disturbing light. Nevertheless, to omit the story would be to gloss over an important dynamic in the local retail trade, as well as aspects of Kroeker's character and approach.

15. *Ibid.*, p. 196.

16. Winkler Bible School Yearbook, 1939-40.

17. "An Evening to Remember Abram and Elizabeth Kroeker." Sponsored by The Mennonite Brethren Historical Society of Canada, Winnipeg, Manitoba, Nov. 20, 1987.

18. Hilda Matsuo, "Taunt Inspired Hard Work," *Mennonite Mirror*, May 1977, p. 13.

19. "An Evening to Remember."

20. P. J. Peters, *A Century of Horticulture in Manitoba: 1880-1980* (Winnipeg, P. J. Peters, 1988), p. 309.

21. Austin Cross, "Corn Belt Extends to Manitoba," *Family Herald and Weekly Star,* Nov. 5, 1941.

22. Peters, p. 309.

23. *Ibid.*

24. "Family Nurtures Business Growth," *Winnipeg Free Press*, May 12, 1991.

25. "Winkler Farm and Business Featured in Manitoba Gov't Bulletin," *Mennonite Observer*, Dec. 7, 1956.

26. Harry Halliwell, "Spuds Incorporated: Way to Beat U.S. Rivals," *The Winnipeg Tribune*, Aug. 25, 1956.

27. William Neufeld, "Mr. Sunday School," *Mennonite Brethren Herald*, Feb. 27, 1981, p. 16.

28. "An Evening to Remember."

29. Esther Horch in letter to *Mennonite Mirror*, Summer 1977, p. 14.

30. "An Evening to Remember."

31. "Successful Blues," *Family Business*, May 1990, p. 10.

32. Peters, p. 308.

33. Walter Kroeker, interview by the author.

34. *Looking Back in Faith: Commemorating the Centennial of Manitoba Mennonite Brethren in Photos and Writing 1888-1988* (Winnipeg, Manitoba Mennonite Brethren Centennial Committee, 1988), p. 56.

35. Winkler Bible School Yearbook, 1939-40.

Chapter 3

1. References will be kept to a minimum. Research notes and transcripts of interviews are in the author's possession and files and in the Penn Alps archives. This chapter represents part of a larger biography in process.

2. In many articles and speeches given by Alta over the years evaluating past projects and promoting new ones, she makes frequent references to God's voice, God's leading, God's control of events. She only followed God's leading and passed through the opening doors. In these cadences the human element and the inordinate entrepreneurial zeal with its huge demands on her time and energy seem nonexistent.

3. In this chapter I use the terms *Amish* and *Mennonite* somewhat interchangeably, to indicate the close historical relationship between the two traditions and the ongoing interaction between the two groups to this day.

4. Today names like Lee (Irish) and Beitzel (German Lutheran) appear in the Amish and Mennonite church registries as an outcome of Benedict's hospitality and Christian caring.

5. This cabin, first built in 1930 on what is now the Yoder farm bordering the Niverton Road, was relocated and restored in 1960 in the Spruce Forest Artisan Village near Penn Alps, Pennsylvania.

6. This magnificent red pine forest can be viewed on a scenic drive northwest of Springs, Pa.

7. Helen Good Brenneman, "Fliederhof—Friendship House," *Youth's Christian Companion*, pp. 530-531, 1951 (April).

8. From a promotional brochure. The firms folded after ten years of operation.

9. As projects developed, and counsel was given contrary to Alta's views, she was frequently able to lobby outside of board meetings to achieve her intent, with the result that people with differing views found themselves outvoted without clear process and were consequently sidelined. This was at times detrimental to the organization. Some of these people today feel that consensus was more a tool and not a fundamental mode of arriving at decisions and guidelines. The "given" in all this is that Alta as founder will always be at the center of board governance. She understandably resists the very idea of rotating terms. She has thus effectively grafted a consensus model onto another kind of power model.

10. Immense credit is due to men like the late Myron Livengood, first chair of the Penn Alps board, and charter members Henry Yoder and Ralph Miller. For over thirty years Miller not only served on various positions on the board but donated thousands of hours on buildings and grounds, special projects, and consultation to a series of administrators in the evolvement of Penn Alps and the Springs Folk Festival.

Chapter 4

1. Information about Redekop used in this article was obtained through eighteen hours of taped interviews with him by the author in his home during the fall of 1990.

2. This information was verified by two telephone interviews with Redekop's bankers, by the author.

3. Interviews by the author with three different individuals involved with the complex confirmed that this was indeed the way in which Redekop managed his business.

Chapter 5

1. Emanuel E. Mullet currently resides in an assisted care apartment in the Walnut Hills Retirement Center, Walnut Creek, Ohio. His wife, Alma, also lives in the Retirement Center. Mullet's health precluded any active involvement in developing this narrative.

2. Ernie S. Infield, a retired professor, interviewed Emanuel Mullet in the early 1980s. The interviews, spread over several days, covered Mullet's background along with a narrative of his business experiences. From those interviews plus earlier contacts, Infield wrote a small book about Emanuel Mullet, *Putting Feet Under Dreams: The Story of Emanuel E. Mullet* (Shreve Printing, 1983). Both Infield and the Emanuel Mullet family consented to my reading the interview transcripts as background for writing this chapter. Much of the discussion concerning Mullet's business experience recorded in this chapter is from these transcripts, though the discussion is supplemented by other interviews with family, work colleagues, and community people, completed during summer 1991, on file with the author. These interviews will be cited only as necessary in the text.

3. From transcript of Calvin Redekop interview with Emanuel Mullet, 1986.

4. The differences between the brothers continued after their decision to split. This affected other areas of their lives as well as the economic area. They were eventually able to reconcile their differences.

5. Joe Yoder, interview by the author.

6. *Daily Record*, December 29, 1979.

7. William Stauffer, interview by the author.

8. *Dayton Daily News,* June 25, 1978.

9. *Dayton Daily News,* June 25, 1978.

10. Levi Beachey, interview by the author.

11. Merle Mullet, interview by the author.

12. A more detailed summary of Emanuel Mullet's business enterprises can be found in Infield's book, *Putting Feet Under Dreams.* At various times in his work life, Mullet was involved in over thirty business ventures. Many of the ventures were similar. The ventures were incorporated separately for several reasons including desire for diversification, structure of ownership with different partners, and economics. Because of mergers, consolidations, and sale of some companies, the number of current existing enterprises is considerably less than thirty.

13. Ervin Hostetler, interview by the author.

14. Wayne Mullet, interview by the author.

15. Ruby Hostetler, interview by the author.

16. Alma Mullet, interview by the author.

17. Lloyd Mischler, interview by the author.

18. *Daily Record,* December 29, 1979.

Chapter 6

1. Kurt Janz and family, interviews by the author. A number of interviews were conducted in 1991 and 1992 in preparation for this chapter. Those interviewed included Kurt and Ruth Janz, Janz family members and friends, former employees and business associates of Kurt Janz, and the pastor of the First Mennonite Church, Calgary. Specific interviews will be cited when pertinent, otherwise it is assumed that data is drawn from these interviews, on file with the author, unless other sources are cited.

2. Much of the foregoing is based on information contained in the unpublished essay by Ted Regehr, "Canadian Mennonite Businessmen and Economic Reconstruction" (1991).

3. Information on the early days of J. A. Builders was obtained in interviews with Rudy Janssen, Gerhard Bartel, and Kurt Janz, by the author.

4. Kurt Janz, interview by the author.

5. Numerous interviewees spoke with fondness of the camaraderie within their social circle during the early years of Scarboro Mennonite Church.

6. Jacob Wiebe, interview by the author.

7. Provincial population increased by over a third, from 1.6 million in 1971 to 2.2 million in 1981. Howard Palmer, *Alberta: A New History* (Edmonton, Hurtig, 1990), p. 328.

8. Calgary had also become an important financial and computer center, attracting investors from around the world. The expanding provincial economy included lumbering and pulp and paper industry, the development of a petrochemical industry, and the extraction of synthetic crude oil from the huge reserves of the Athabasca oil sands. See Palmer, chapter 12.

9. For example, two key persons were given shares in Horton Building Supplies without charge to them.

10. Several examples can be given to demonstrate the dimensions of the oil industry crisis. The Alsands megaproject for retrieving oil from the tar sands at Fort McMurray collapsed. The once high-flying Dome Oil, which had been gobbling up other oil companies, experienced financial difficulties so spectacular that the federal government

and four Canadian chartered banks had to bail the company out. It limped on until it was purchased by the American company Amoco in 1988.

11. Kurt and Alfred's operation was by far the largest of its kind in First Mennonite Church. Although numerous families were severely strained economically as a result of the crisis to the industry, the Janz brothers experienced the only bankruptcies within the church community.

12. Jacob Wiebe, interview by the author.

13. Within the industry and church communities, those most inclined to take a critical stance were often semiretired or inactive building contractors. They tended to regard their own secure economic positions as reflective of acute business acumen and Kurt's problems conversely as indicative of shoddy practices and/or poor judgment. Other critics had long resented the success Kurt had experienced and saw the bankruptcy as a way of "evening out" inequities.

14. Numerous people made reference to the tension between Ingrid and Kurt. The situation is particularly problematic since Ingrid and Ruth (Kurt's wife) are sisters.

15. Four judgments had been placed upon Kurt. These allow the banks and respective mortgage companies to seize any possessions for a period up to ten years. As a result, Kurt still does not have a bank account or any personal estate. Had he gone personally bankrupt these claims would have been nullified.

16. Some subcontractors refused to complete jobs until after having been paid, stating, "I lost money on you last time . . . not again."

17. According to ancient Greek mythology, at the end of its life cycle this fabled bird burned on a funeral pyre only to rise again from its own ashes.

Chapter 7

1. Several biographies of Sister Frieda Kaufman have been written, most of them based on a draft written by herself and then expanded. My sources for this study include Marilyn Bartel, "Sister Frieda Kaufman: Builder of Institutions and Lives." (Unpublished mss., 1966); *Bethel Deaconess Home and Hospital* (Newton, Kan.: Publisher Board of Directors, BDHH Society, 1918); *Mennonite Encylopedia* (Scottdale, Pa.: Herald Press, 1956); Alice Claassen, "Sister Frieda Kaufman," *Pioneers in Profile, Vol. 2* (unpublished mss., 1945); "Deaconess Work and Deaconesses" (Bethel College Historical Library Archives, five boxes); "The Deaconess and Her Ministry," *Mennonite Life* (January 1948); Frieda Kaufman, ed., *In the Service of the King, 1-3* (Bulletin published by Bethel Deaconess Hospital Association, January 1942-December 1944); George E. Kaufman, ed., *General Conference Mennonite Pioneers* (North Newton, Kan.: Bethel College, 1973); Frieda Kaufman, *Inasmuch as I Am a Deaconess* (unpublished mss.); "Frieda Marie Kaufman" (Bethel College Historical Library Archives, four boxes); *Lamps on the Prairie*, vol. 1 (Emporia, Kan.: Emporia Gazette Press, 1942); *Silver Anniversary Memorial 1908-1933* (Newton, Kan.: Bethel Deaconess Home and Hospital, 1933); "Sister Frieda," *The Mennonite* (15 August l944):2-3; Lena Mae Smith, "Life Story of Sister Frieda," *The Mennonite* 49 (15 August 1944):1-2; A Warkentin and Melvin Gingerich, eds., *Who's Who Among the Mennonites* (North Newton, Kan.: Bethel College, 1943).

2. Virginia Liesen Brereton, "Preparing Women for the Lord's Work," in Hilah F. Thomas et al., eds., *Women in New Worlds*, vol. 1 (Nashville, 1981), p. 178ff.

3. James C. Juhnke, *Vision, Doctrine, War: Mennonite Identity and Organization 1890-1930* (Scottdale, Pa.: Herald Press, 1989), p. 162.

4. Juhnke, p. 162ff. Quote from p. 182.

5. For a fuller treatment of the Mennonite deaconess movement, see Lois Barret,

The Vision and the Reality (Newton, Kan.: Faith & Life Press, 1983), pp. 173-78.

6. *Ibid.*, p. 177.

7. Juhnke, p. 182.

8. In 1978 I submitted a questionnaire to all former graduates of the Bethel Deaconess Hospital School of Nursing for their impressions of their years at the school. I received approximately fifty responses of various lengths. I also interviewed many of the nurses who lived in the immediate area. This material was incorporated into my book *Our Lamps Were Lit: An Informal History of the Bethel Deaconess Hospital School of Nursing* (North Newton, Kan.: Bethel Deaconess Hospital School Nursing Alumnae Association, 1978).

9. John Thiesen, "History of First Mennonite Church" (unpublished mss.).

10. Letter, May 4, 1950.

11. Brereton, pp. 192-195.

Chapter 8

1. Bill maintained an ongoing relationship over the next several years with the spokesman for the group, the black man. The families were able to find jobs and get back on their feet. Bill Dyck, interview by the author.

Information for this chapter was obtained from interviews that the author conducted in 1991 with a variety of persons, including Bill Dyck. The names of interviewees are withheld to protect their confidentiality. Interviews are on file with the author.

2. William E. Dyck, the subject of this chapter, will be referred to as Bill, the name he normally used. His father, William W. Dyck, will be referred to as William, and his grandfather, Wilhelm I. Dyck as Wilhelm Dyck.

3. A picture of one of Wilhelm Dyck's factories is one of only a few material possessions that the Dyck family was able to bring out of Russia. Bill Dyck possessed the picture and was well versed in family history. He considered his grandfather a model to emulate. Bill Dyck, interview by the author.

4. Agatha Warkentin, "Wilhelm Dyck Clan" (unpublished family biography, 1990).

5. Wilhelm Dyck liquidated some of his holdings in Russia and tried to transfer over 900,000 Russian rubles to a bank in New York. The transaction apparently never went through. Bill Dyck tried to track down the transaction years later with no success. If it had gone through, Wilhelm Dyck would have had substantial capital with which to operate in Canada. As it was, he was never able to reestablish himself economically in Canada, since he was sixty-six years old when he made the move.

6. Anna Dyck fondly remembers the comfortable life of the landed gentry in Czarist Russia, in *Anna from the Caucasus to Canada* (Hillsboro, Kan.: Mennonite Brethren Publishing House, 1979). Bill Dyck distinguished between the financial success of that side of the family from that of the Dyck side by saying the Dycks were more entrepreneurial—more visionary and open to risk-taking. Bill Dyck, interview by the author.

7. William Dyck was a community leader. He died in 1971, and when the funeral was held all of the town businesses were closed and the flags were flown at half-mast. The new church could not accommodate the crowd. A neighboring church was used for seating to accommodate the overflow who listened in over a public address system. Anna Dyck, p. 212. The Niverville town park is named after him.

8. William Dyck's practice was not to resort to the courts for collection. He operated on the reputation of the customer and took his losses if necessary.

9. William Dyck's sermons are published in William E. Dyck, *Register der Predig-tentwurfe* (Fresno, Calif.: Center for Mennonite Brethren Studies, 1984).

10. Anna Dyck, pp. 178-179.

11. Bill had two older sisters, Emily (6 years older) and Elizabeth (4 years older). His younger siblings are Jake (5 years younger), David (7 years younger), and Elfrieda (12 years younger).

12. The attitude toward work was at least partially out of economic necessity. William Dyck took his work, whether businesses or church, seriously. He rarely took time off to vacation.

13. William Dyck resisted Bill's decision to go to school, though his mother quietly gave her approval. William from time to time would point to the relative prosperity of the children who stayed at home compared to Bill's station in life as a student. Bill Dyck, interview by the author.

14. Much of the accounting requirements were the same as required in the United States. Bill later became a certified public accountant in the United States.

15. Bill Dyck emphasized the need to be prepared in order to capitalize on an opportunity. He usually thoroughly analyzed a community before investing in it.

16. His business card cites Micah 6:8. "He has showed you, O man, what is good. And what does the Lord require of you? To act justly and to love mercy and to walk humbly with your God."

17. In one case Bill was traveling on a Sunday and had a service station attendant do some work on his car. He gave the attendant a copy of the book after engaging him in a dialogue about faith issues.

Chapter 9

1. Judy Rose, "Discoveries," *Pioneer Press*, February 5, 1989. Information for this chapter was obtained from a number of sources, including articles written about the Lehman store, and by interviews with Jay and Ella Mae Lehman and others, by the author, fall 1993.

2. Gene Logsdon, "The Grandaddy of Green Stores," *A Magazine for Environmental Entrepreneuring in Business*, February 1991, p. 24.

3. Jim Corey, "The Ultimate Niche," *Hardware Age*, August 1991, p. 252.

4. Larry Lehman, employee and friend of Jay Lehman, interview by the author. Over one-half of employees are either family members or personal friends of Jay Lehman.

5. Feature articles on the store have appeared in newspapers such as the *Washington Post, Miami Herald, Cincinnati Post & Times*, as well as the Sunday editions of the *Chicago Tribune, San Antonio Express*, and the *Times Reporter* of New York.

6. Galen Lehman, interview by the author.

7. Bill Detweiler, interview by the author.

Chapter 10

1. Frank H. Epp, *Mennonites in Canada, 1786-1920: The History of a Separate People* (Toronto, Macmillan, 1974), p. 195.

2. *Ibid.*, p. 100.

3. *Ibid.*, p. 122; Gerald Friesen, *The Canadian Prairies: A History* (Toronto, University of Toronto Press, 1987), p. 130.

4. Epp, *Mennonites in Canada 1786-1920*, p. 225.

5. J. Winfield Fretz, *Pilgrims in Paraguay: The Story of Mennonite Colonization in South*

America (Scottdale, Pa.: Herald Press, 1953), pp. 9-18; Fritz Kliewer, "The Mennonites of Paraguay," *Mennonite Quarterly Review* 11 (January 1937):93-95.

6. Kliewer, "The Mennonites of Paraguay," p. 94.

7. Levi Giesbrecht, interviews by the author, tape recordings, 1990-91, Surrey, British Columbia. All quotes by Levi are from these interviews. Other interviews cited in this chapter were also conducted by the author in 1990-91.

8. David Herlihy, "Family," *The American Historical Review* 96 (February 1991):1-16.

9. This has become clear through interviews with family members and others, such as the pastor of the Giesbrecht's Vancouver church. Henry Kliewer, interview by the author.

10. Levi's brother Vic corroborates this in his own experience. Victor Giesbrecht, interviewed by the author.

11. J. Winfield Fretz found that during the early 1950s the average Paraguayan Mennonite farmer could expect to gross $450.00 in a good year, and much less in a poor or mediocre one. During their first twenty-five years in Paraguay, farming had remained essentially at the subsistence level for most Mennonites. Fretz, *Pilgrims in Paraguay,* pp. 145-149.

12. Frances Redekop, interviewed by the author.

13. M. B. Percy, *Forest Management and Economic Growth in British Columbia* (Ottawa: Minister of Supply and Services, 1986), p. 1; *Review of the Canadian Forest Products Industry* (Ottawa, Minister of Supply and Services, 1979), p. 19.

14. Free trade came to an end in 1987 with the imposition of a fifteen percent export tax on softwood lumber by the Canadian government. There has since then been an ongoing dispute with the United States over the status of Canadian lumber, with the U.S. imposing countervailing duties of its own. In early 1994 a free-trade panel ruled in favor of the Canadian side in the dispute. The final outcome of the new North American Free Trade agreement vis-à-vis softwood lumber remains to be seen, but one would expect free trade to be the result here as in other areas.

15. Percy, *Forest Management,* p. 5.

16. *Review of the Canadian Forest Products Industry,* pp. 29-35. This study points out that although the trend has generally been toward consolidation, "The softwood lumber industry in Canada is still characterized by a high degree of fragmentation, particularly in comparison to other industrialized sectors" (p. 32).

17. *Review,* pp. 31-32; Percy, p. 6.

18. Percy, pp. 5-7.

19. *Ibid.,* 1990, pp. 4-5; Statistics Canada, "Production, Shipments and Stocks on Hand of British Columbia Sawmills," (Ottawa, Minister of Supply and Services, 1984), pp. 4-5.

20. Frieda Giesbrecht, interviewed by the author.

21. This is corroborated by the other partners and the secretary, Frieda Giesbrecht, as well as by a night-shift foreman. Chris Paetkau, interviewed by the author.

22. Chris Paetkau interview; Slawomir Grzemik, interviewed by the author. Al Wedel, interviewed by the author. Frieda Giesbrecht interview.

23. Henry Kliewer interview.

24. Scot Robinson, interviewed by the author.

25. Cliff Miske, interviewed by the author.

26. Marty Schuetz, interviewed by the author.

27. Erwin Cornelsen, interviewed by the author.

Chapter 11

1. The author has drawn heavily on three sources for this profile: a taped interview with the Goods conducted by Calvin Redekop in 1985; notes from a speech presented by the Goods at a Mennonite Economic Development Associates (MEDA) meeting in the fall of 1991; and an interview with the Goods conducted by the author, December 15, 1993.

2. From an editorial in *Festival Quarterly*, 16, no. 4 (1990), p. 5.

3. From an editorial in *Festival Quarterly*, 17, no. 3 (1990), p. 5.

Conclusion

1. For more see Calvin W. Redekop, Stephen Ainley, and Robert Siemens, *Mennonite Entrepreneurs* (Baltimore: Johns Hopkins University Press, 1995).

2. Robert Merton, *Social Theory and Social Structure* (Glencoe, The Free Press, 1957), p. 357.

3. "Totalistic reference groups" refers to the degree to which the religious community is a reference group that goes beyond the more sectoral concept of reference group espoused by earlier theorists. In the case of the Mennonites, the congregation and larger faith community are the summary reference groups for Mennonite membership.

4. Cited in Calvin W. Redekop, Victor A. Krahn, and Samuel J. Steiner, eds., *Anabaptist/Mennonite Faith and Economics* (Lanham, Md.: University Press of America, 1994), p. 400.

Entrepreneurs in the Faith Community:
Profiles of Mennonites in Business

JOANNA BUHR teaches in the Faculty of General Studies at the University of Calgary, Calgary, Alberta, where she earned her graduate degree in the field of Canadian ethnic studies. Her primary area of research has focused on research and writing on the Canadian ethnic experience. She is currently working with a six-person legal team representing Bosnia/Herzegovina in the International Court of Justice in their action against the former Yugoslavia (Serbia and Montenegro) for massive and repeated acts of genocide against Bosnian citizens, especially Muslim women and girls.

JACK DUECK grew up in Coaldale, Alberta, and received musical and theological training at Mennonite Brethren Bible College in Winnipeg, Manitoba; an M.A. in literature from the University of Western Washington; and a Ph.D. from Notre Dame University, Notre Dame, Indiana. He taught at Goshen College for eleven years and has been an entrepreneur and business consultant for a number of years. At present he is president of People Management Associates and director of development at Penn Alps, Grantsville, Maryland.

VICTOR A. KRAHN was a self-employed carpenter before establishing a wood-finishing factory and later a furniture factory in Abbotsford, British Columbia. He later earned a B.A. from the University of Waterloo, Ontario, Canada, and has subsequently founded Krahn and Associates, specializing in business plan development. He is also director of business development at Community Opportunities Development Association in Cambridge, Ontario. He is co-editor of *Anabaptist/Mennonite Faith and Economics* (University Press of America, 1994).

266

WALLY KROEKER earned a B.A. at Tabor College, Hillsboro, Kansas, and an M.A. in theology from Mennonite Brethren Seminary, Fresno, California. He has worked in journalism since 1967, primarily in the areas of business and religion. Previously, he worked for the *Regina Leader-Post, Winnipeg Tribune, Saskatchewan Business Journal, Moody Monthly,* and edited the *Christian Leader.* He currently edits *The Marketplace,* a magazine for Christians in business published by Mennonite Economic Development Associates. He is a grandson of Abe Kroeker.

CELIA LEHMAN has written three books—*Nzuzi and the Spell,* (privately published, 1992), *My Best Friend Is God,* (Standard Publishing Co., 1973), *Come Walk with Me Thru Needle's Eye* (privately published, 1991)—has been a correspondent for two newspapers, and writes feature articles for a tristate magazine. She received a B.A. from Goshen College and an M.A. from Kent State University and taught in Zaire, Africa, for two years. Lehman has been active in community affairs including the promoting of a new heritage center, serving on a state-level stewardship commission, and participating in the Kidron Mennonite Church.

THEODORE W. LOEWEN received a B.A. from Bethel College, North Newton, Kansas, and a J.D. from the University of California, Hastings College of the Law in San Francisco. A licensed California attorney, he also teaches part-time in the Business Department of California State University, Fresno. He is active in the family fruit tree business in Reedley, California. He has served on the boards of Bethel College and Kings View and is active at First Mennonite Church in Reedley.

BEN REDEKOP is a Ph.D. in history at the University of British Columbia. He has published articles on Mennonite and European intellectual history. He operated a bicycle business in Hillsboro, Kansas, for several years before he studied for his B.A. at Fresno Pacific College, Fresno, California. He resides in Vancouver, British Columbia.

CALVIN REDEKOP is professor emeritus, Conrad Grebel College, Waterloo, Ontario, Canada, and has taught at several Mennonite colleges. He received a B.A. at Goshen College, an M.A. at the University of Minnesota, and a Ph.D. in history at the University of Chicago.

Redekop served in MCC in Akron, Europe, and South America. He has studied Mennonite communities and institutions in North America, Mexico, and Paraguay. He has been involved in business and is active in MEDA.

PHIL JOHNSON RUTH lives in the southeastern Pennsylvania township of Lower Salford. He is the author of a number of books of regional history and the editor of several others. His most recent book is *Sowing Seeds of Faith: The Founding and First Fifty Years of Penn View Christian School, 1945-1995* (Editorial and Photographic Services, 1995) Ruth's writings and photographs have appeared in a variety of publications, including *Festival Quarterly*. Among the venues to have exhibited his photography is People's Place Art Gallery, Lancaster, Pennsylvania. Ruth is a graduate of Goshen College and the University of New Hampshire.

WILLIS SOMMER is associate professor of business and holds appointment as the Howard Raid Chair in Business at Bluffton College. He is a certified public accountant. He is a board member of several institutions and organizations where the interaction of ethics, theology, and economics occur, including a major study of Mennonite Mutual Aid entitled "Mennonite Institutions and Mennonite Capital" in Redekop, Krahn, and Steiner, eds. *Anabaptist/Mennonite Faith and Economics* (University Press of America, 1994).

KATIE FUNK WIEBE is a professor emeritus at Tabor College, Hillsboro, Kansas, having taught English there for twenty-four years. Her education includes a B.A. (Tabor College) and M.A. (Wichita State University). She has written extensively in many church periodicals and has published numerous books, including *Alone: A Search for Joy;* (Tyndale, 1976), *Bless Me Too, My Father* (Herald Press, 1988), *Prayers of an Omega;* (Herald Press, 1994), and *Border Crossings* (Herald Press, 1995). Of particular interest to her and often a subject of her writing has been the role and history of women in the church, particularly the Mennonite church.